The Himalayan Garden

The Himalayan Garden

Growing Plants from the Roof of the World

JIM JERMYN

TIMBER PRESS
Portland, Oregon

Pages 2–3: Everest and Lhotse, eastern Nepal GEORGE SMITH
Pages 4–5: Meadow scene with foliage of *Meconopsis napaulensis,* Lamjung, central Nepal DIETER SCHACHT
Title pages: *Meconopsis napaulensis,* Langtang, central Nepal DIETER SCHACHT

Published in 2001 by Timber Press, Inc.
The Haseltine Building
133 S.W. Second Avenue, Suite 450
Portland, Oregon 97204, U.S.A.

Designed by Susan Applegate
Printed in China

Library of Congress Cataloging in Publication Data

Jermyn, Jim.
    The Himalayan garden: growing plants from the roof of the world / Jim Jermyn.
      p. cm.
    Includes bibliographical references (p.).
    ISBN 0-88192-500-4
    1. Alpine gardens. 2. Alpine garden plants. 3. Alpine gardens—Himalaya
Mountains. 4. Alpine garden plants—Himalaya Mountains. 5. Native plants for
cultivation—Himalaya Mountains. I. Title.

SB459 .J47 2001
635.9'528'095496—dc21   00-064830

To Alison,
not only for her patience with the word-processing
but also for her enthusiasm and encouragement

Contents

Foreword

THAT MIGHTY range of mountains, the Himalaya, is a treasure house of plants that has long held a magical attraction for botanists, plant hunters and garden lovers. To seek its plants in their natural surroundings is an unforgettable adventure. The serious traveller will also study climatic and soil conditions so as to find clues to their needs in cultivation, and may, if permissible, collect living material and seeds. There have been many explorers who have spared no effort, braved every hardship and risked their health to find new plants for our gardens. Some of them, notably Kingdon Ward and Ludlow and Sherriff, have left vivid narratives of their collecting journeys.

In the 1970s I was privileged to take part in several treks in the Himalaya. Having worked in the Munich Botanic Garden for thirty-three years, I saw the plants in a new light through these expeditions. One April in Langtang, Nepal, we saw the superb leaf rosettes of *Meconopsis napaulensis* growing in dry powdery soil, and a year later the very same plants were opening their delicate yellow flowers in their full glory. It was then July, in the monsoon season; everything was dripping with moisture and all the vegetation was erupting into growth.

For thirty-two seasons I have worked in the Schachen Alpine Garden at 6100 ft. (1860 m) in the Bavarian Alps, and these treks gave me the opportunity to apply what I had learned in the Himalaya to the day-today tasks of alpine gardening. I enjoyed a quiet sense of happiness whenever some tricky plant, perhaps one that I had brought back, opened its flowers. Amongst these in the summer of 1977 were *Primula wigramiana* from Lamjung and *Androsace mucronifolia* from Kashmir; both were confirmed to be the true species by the late George Smith, a *Primula* connoisseur of our generation.

Every gardener who cares for plants in a favoured spot outdoors or in a trough on the patio can share this quiet happiness, and such triumphs need not be confined to rarities. What would our gardens be without Himalayan plants—the swarms of splendid primulas, the hundreds of rhododendrons, the delicate pleiones, and the brilliant blue meconopses?

My father Wilhelm Schacht and his immense knowledge of plants and joy in their beauty stimulated me to spend my life in the world of gardening. I owe him a great debt of gratitude.

In 1974 I first met Jim Jermyn and in the ensuing decades I got to know him well. Jim's experience as a nurseryman and as the discoverer of so many plants in the wild gives him impeccable credentials to write on the Himalayan flora as seen in our gardens. He is no mere copier of other men's writings; his book is based on his experience as a practical gardener, as witnessed by his achievements as owner of Edrom Nurseries. His book will certainly give immense pleasure to gardeners and plant lovers and will encourage them to persevere in what is perhaps the most enthralling of all hobbies. In a world blighted by futile overactivity and the unceasing pursuit of money, gardening can be the best of all counterbalances.

DIETER SCHACHT
Munich
translated by D. Winstanley

Dieter Schacht (right) with his father Wilhelm in the Schachen Garden, southern Germany DIETER SCHACHT

Preface and
Acknowledgements

OVER THE last twenty years I have gained immense pleasure as a lecturer visiting horticultural societies great and small. The main theme of my talks has encompassed the subject of alpine plants, but I have often focused on the cultivation of genera endemic to the Himalaya, in its widest definition, which forms an arc of about 1500 miles (2410 km) ranging from northern Pakistan eastward across Kashmir in northern India, taking in part of southern Tibet, most of Nepal, the Indian state of Sikkim, the independent kingdom of Bhutan and finally south-western China. This region is sometimes called the Sino-Himalaya. At the conclusion of my lectures many individuals have asked if I would consider writing down my experiences in the form of a book—so here is the result of those requests! To provide a broad view of the most popular Himalayan subjects, I have included, where appropriate, information about related species from south-western China while aiming to preserve the overall theme of the book.

Readers should be aware that I have never travelled to the Himalaya. This book, however, covers the cultivation of plants—it is not an appraisal of the various species in their native habitat. A deep understanding of their endemic growing conditions has been essential for me to grow these plants successfully, and this understanding has been achieved in no small way as a result of enjoying hours of private slide viewings, an intimate venue which has enabled me to feel almost that I have been to Nepal and the Sino-Himalaya.

I wish to assure the reader that this is a horticultural publication containing material as scientifically correct as it is balanced between science and horticulture. This book is based on my opinion and experience of growing Himalayan plants and listening to other experienced growers the length and breadth of Britain as well as in the United States, Canada, Europe and Japan. Throughout the book, I refer to times of the year as they are experienced in my south-eastern Scotland garden. Gardeners in the southern hemisphere and in different climatic zones are likely to know, or will learn through experience, how to adjust their gardening practices accordingly.

Many gardeners are captivated by these plants but are put off by negative comments regarding their culture. Amongst exciting plants from anywhere in the world, particularly from the realm of alpine species, many *are* quite simply impossible to grow successfully, or at least only with the most extreme care. But I will not be focusing on these overly specialised plants, as they are best viewed in botanic gardens on refrigerated benches and the like. Instead, I will introduce a vast paradise of plants—from woody subjects, climbing plants, bulbous species and of course a wealth of alpines—all relatively available and growable within the scope of most able gardeners. I will endeavour to give practical advice on these Himalayan plants, including where to plant them and naturally how to set about propagating them.

Before becoming proprietor of Edrom Nurseries, my apprenticeship started at Ingwersen's Nursery in Sussex, England; then through a number of year-long assignments, first at the Munich Botanic Garden under the tutelage of Dieter Schacht, then at Jack Drake's Nursery in Aviemore, Scotland; and finally setting up a new nursery in northern Italy on the side of Lake Garda. I have been privileged to meet many horticulturists who have shared their experiences with me. This accumulated knowledge is very much responsible for my having been able to grow these wonderful and diverse Himalayan species, and for enabling me to pen my own experiences.

It remains for me now to offer my sincere thanks to all the many individuals who have helped me map out my career in horticulture. It is to my parents that I am most greatly indebted, for all their support and encouragement in the formative stages of my education and for enabling me to move north to Scotland and advance my career as owner of Edrom Nurseries. The close proximity of the Royal Botanic Garden in Edinburgh to our home has been instrumental in providing inspiration, and I am very thankful for all the help that the many staff members have given me over the years. I wish to thank John and Marissa Main for giving me access to the Herbarium at the Royal Botanic Garden in Edinburgh during the writing of this book.

Finally I am indebted to those who have contributed the photographs that bring this book to life. I thank Robert Smith for lending me slides from the collection of his late brother George Smith. A very special mention must be made of Dieter Schacht. His contribution of slide material made the writing of this book possible.

CHAPTER ONE

Ecological Divisions of the Himalaya

O VER THE last twenty-five years of growing plants from the Himalaya, I have come to realise that the one greatest benefit towards growing them successfully is understanding the conditions of their native habitat. I first gardened in the south-east of England and since 1980 have been growing Himalayan plants in the south-eastern borders of Scotland where the conditions are markedly better for plants enjoying a cooler habitat. Yet whilst in business and exhibiting in London I frequently have met up with enquiries such as: "Here I am living in the south-east of England with this driving urge to grow the Himalayan blue poppy. I know it prefers an acid soil and requires a cooler growing season, plenty of summer moisture and a relatively dry winter dormant period. It seems as if all the blue poppy's requirements are the very antithesis of my conditions here in England. What will I do? I can't move house. How do I know how to doctor the prevailing habitat?" Thus, we need to understand the basic habitat in which the favourite plant grows back in the Himalaya. Of course we cannot re-enact these conditions in our own suburban gardens, but we can modify the given conditions, supplementing the situation to suit the plant. I like the word *improvise*—it is positive and suggests getting on with the situation in which we find ourselves, though it sometimes implies a lack of planning. I therefore prescribe a measure of planned improvisation.

The term "Himalaya" as we popularly call this mountain range means in the ancient Sanscrit language of India "Abode of Snow." What a fine description of this vast stretch of peaks. Forming an arc of about 1500 miles (2410 km) in length, the Himalaya ranges from the river Indus in northern Pakistan and eastward across Kashmir in northern India, taking in part of southern Tibet (Xizang), most of Nepal, the Indian state of Sikkim and independent Bhutan. This Himalayan arc includes the Tibetan Plateau, the highest and largest plateau in the world, which incorporates the world's highest peak, Mt. Everest at 29,000 ft. (8850 m). Situated between the tropical and temperate zones of the earth, the plateau has an elevation of 13,100 to 16,400 ft. (4000–5000 m) and is often referred to as the "Roof of the World." Many of its alpine plants are to be found at altitudes in excess of 19,700 ft. (6000 m). A stretch of the imagination is required to grasp the diversity of flora that this vast Himalayan system incorporates and the many species still to be discovered and understood.

The Himalaya encompasses a pronounced variation in natural habitat. Clearly therefore I must explain a little about these marked divisions—the temperate, subalpine and alpine zones—ecological divisions from which we will choose our favourite species. With an understanding of these varying conditions we must then assess our own situation, wherever we are gardening.

A bird's-eye view of the Himalaya gives a clear sight of the snow-covered peaks, an indication of the inevitable climate prevailing there. Nevertheless generalising too much about the climate can be misleading as each well-known range within the massif of the Himalaya has its own defined climatic variation. Nepal in particular is home to many plants favoured in gardens around the world. In Nepal the hot, humid summer winds blow in from a southerly aspect, and as they strike the southern flanks of the mountains they are forced to rise. The winds cool and then deposit vast amounts of rain, characterised by the monsoon which drops up to 100 in. (250 cm) annually, not surprisingly encouraging the forests of *Rhododendron* for which the Himalaya is so famous. In these conditions many plants thrive, including many members of the Ericaceae, the heather family. The west coast of Scotland, which is subject to higher-

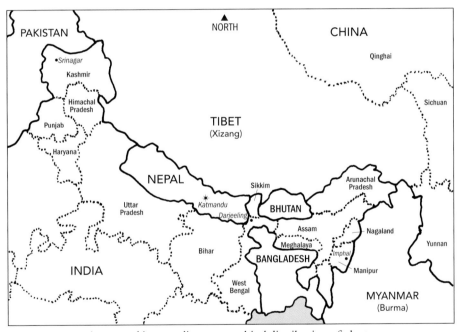

Areas used in recording geographical distribution of plants.

than-average rainfall than that expected in the British Isles as a whole, makes a comfortable home for plants endemic to the cool, damp habitats in the Himalaya. Scotland is not alone, as other parts of the world also enjoy higher-than-average summer rainfall and cool temperatures.

Once the southerly winds have passed over the tops of the southern flanks of the Himalaya, the excess water has been shed and little in the way of rain will fall during the summer in the high inner valleys. With as little as 25 in. (64 cm) of annual moisture, some of which is winter snow, the inner valleys present ecological subdivisions important for gardeners to grasp. The map of the Nepal Himalaya highlights some of the most popular areas for plant hunters, including many locations mentioned in this book. The simple diagram of the vegetation zones in the Himalaya roughly shows the altitudes distiguishing the ecological subdivisions.

The climatic variation between the ecological subdivisions throughout the vast range is significant and is relevant when considering the challenges of cultivation at home. Three seasons are generally recognizable in the Himalaya: a cold period from October to February, a hot period from March to June and the monsoon season with heavy rains, particularly in

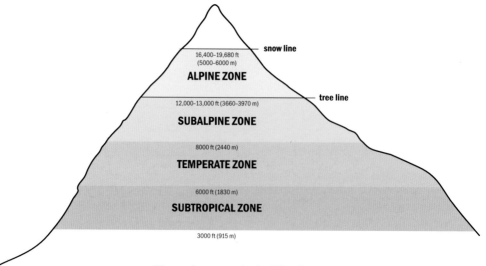

Vegetation zones in the Himalaya

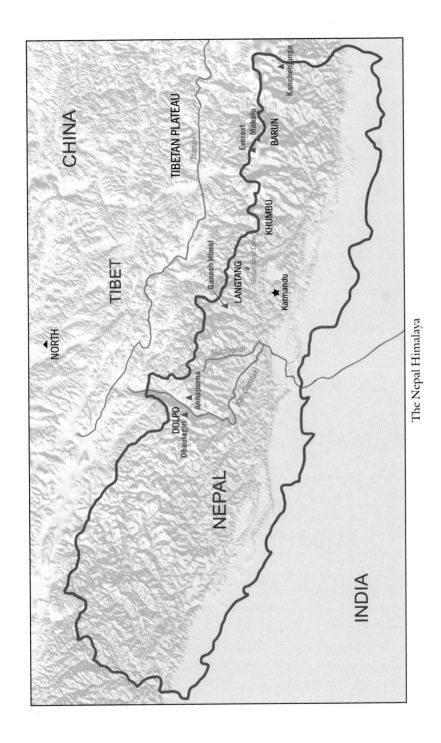

The Nepal Himalaya

the east, from June to September. The monsoon begins to affect eastern Nepal in early June and spreads westward to the rest of Nepal in early July.

Within the great range are countless inner valleys, most of which are cradled within the massif. These broad, glacier-worn valleys, which are prominent for example in the Everest, Langtang and upper Kali Gandaki areas, are little affected by the strong winds that often desiccate the main valley floors. The partial rain screen of these high inner valleys creates still different ecosystems. To the north of the main Himalayan range is a high desert region similar to the Tibetan Plateau. Though hardly a desert as we normally picture, this area is called the Trans-Himalaya and encompasses the arid valleys of Mustang, Manang and Dolpo. This habitat is in the main a rain shadow area and receives significantly less precipitation than the southern slopes. It presents a notable variation that must be taken into account as we consider species from this general area, such as the very choice *Androsace tapete,* found commonly in west-central Nepal in these drier conditions.

Generalising on the rock formation and soil types throughout the regions is fairly safe, which helps greatly when choosing a satisfactory position in the garden. On the whole the Himalaya consists primarily of metamorphic rocks with extensive areas of igneous rocks in the south. Limestone mountains are an exception, and we have to move well across to the east into Yunnan to meet up with the Jade Dragon Mountains in the Lichiang Range, forming an impressive chain of craggy limestone peaks. The Lichiang Range is somewhat detached from the real Himalaya, but it does exemplify the need for caution when it comes to basic geology and choosing the correct soil type for our favourite Sino-Himalayan species. The plants discussed in this book will grow more successfully if the natural pH of the soil is neutral to acid, measuring 6.5 or less.

Let us get a taste of the ecological divisions within the Himalaya by following the typical trek of the plant hunters as they enter the popular Marsyandi Valley in central Nepal. Until 1977 these headwaters were practically closed to Western travellers, but in this year the Nepalese government opened up a great part of this region to trekkers. Along the walk into the valley, note the change in vegetation with the effect of altitude.

Khung Valley, Dolpo—part of the Trans-Himalaya, central Nepal GEORGE SMITH

After five hours by bus from Katmandu, the plant hunters set out from the small village of Dumre at 1500 ft. (460 m) on a long walk in a northerly direction in relentless sunshine. The ideal time for flowers is the last two weeks in July and the first two weeks in August. The first few days of the trek bring limited altitude gain until they reach the village of Bahundanda at around 4250 ft. (1300 m), which gives splendid views both up and down the Marsyandi. Reaching this still lush and subtropical altitude, the trekkers are led into patches of woodland full of ferns and orchid-encrusted trees. The climate here is hot enough for bananas and mangoes. The village of Syange leads into a deep gorge presenting a transition from the subtropical to the temperate, exemplified initially by fine stands of *Lilium nepalense* on grassy banks from 4900 ft. (1490 m) upwards. Within the gorge, conifers gradually dominate the vegetation, typified by *Pinus wallichiana, Picea smithiana, Tsuga dumosa* and *Taxus wallichiana*. At about 6000 ft. (1830 m) familiar herbaceous plants appear such as *Anemone rivularis, A. vitifolium, Bergenia ciliata, Potentilla, Geranium, Euphorbia* and *Thalictrum*. This transition continues up to 9500 ft. (2900 m) where the plant hunters break free from predominant forest and into open countryside after seven days into the trek. At this altitude all tender plants are left behind. Remember that this is central Nepal—the same altitudinal differences and ecological divisions are not necessarily true in north-western Nepal where the coniferous forest gives way to meadows at 13,900 ft. (4240 m). The little state of Sikkim in India, just east of Nepal, presents a picture similar to that of central Nepal, as do parts of Bhutan and Tibet.

Breaking into the open meadows of the Marsyandi Valley at 9500 ft. (2900 m), the plant hunters can see that agriculture still thrives in the wide valley floor below, provided irrigation can be arranged by diverting streams to flood the fields during the growing season. These high damp meadows provide an abundance of *Primula* species so familiar in our gardens such as *P. sikkimensis*. Hardened enthusiasts of alpine plants for which the Himalaya already provides a rich provision of garden species should brace themselves! The most abundant diversity inhabits a broad band along the upper edge of the alpine meadows and at the base of the extensive unstable screes, which stretch from 12,950 to 14,000 ft.

View of a Nepalese valley showing each of the ecological zones DIETER SCHACHT

Meadow scene with yaks, before the monsoon, Langtang, central Nepal
DIETER SCHACHT

(3950–4270 m). Higher still into the stable screes, specialised alpine plants are found such as *Cremanthodium purpureifolium, Delphinium nepalense* and *Saussurea gossypiphora*. These plants present gardeners everywhere with a genuine challenge.

This spotlight on central Nepal and the rich valley of Marsyandi is just a tiny glimpse of what the Himalaya has to offer and of the challenges we face growing many of these sensational plants in the garden. Generalising is never sufficient, but this example of the Marsyandi Valley sets a useful guide, which can act as a benchmark.

To highlight how easy it is to misunderstand the conditions in nature I want to mention a group of Himalayan *Primula* that has always fascinated me. It is the section *Petiolares*, the petiolarid primulas, of which quite a number of species are popularly grown throughout the world. Their needs are often misjudged partly due to the varying conditions in which they grow in nature. While *P. calderiana* and *P. pulchra* could loosely be described as snow-melt plants—those that emerge from a dry winter rest under a blanket of snow to a brief period of flowering and vegetative growth—many other species such as *P. boothii, P. irregularis* and *P. whitei* are primrose-like in habit. Occurring in temperate forests quite often at moderate altitudes, they very often remain active during the dry winter season from October to May. As the monsoon rains end in late September the herbage of most herbaceous plants withers as they enter a period of dormancy until the return of the rains in early June. At this time many of the leafy petiolarid primulas, typically *P. boothii* and *P. irregularis,* lose their large summer leaves and replace them with smaller, tighter rosettes of leaves covered in a farina, or mealy coating, that presumably helps to prevent desiccation. These tighter rosettes will anchor and support the plant until the flowering season, which is generally around April. The condition of the forests where they grow provides little in the way of competition at flowering time, when they can monopolise the attention of passing insects for pollination. By the time the rains come, the seeds will have ripened and sprouted, and the seedlings have a full season of growing ahead of them, hence the brief viability of the seeds of many of these petiolarid primulas. I wanted to highlight this glimpse at the behaviour of one group within one section of *Primula* in the Himalaya, because so often we read or are told that all petiolarids require a particular situation in the garden, but on the contrary, a variety of habitats prevail within the Himalaya, calling for discernment on our part as gardeners.

Those of us who treasure our new plants, whether they be purchases, gifts or personally propagated from seed, will want to make some preliminary research to find out their true origin. Armed with some basic knowledge of the region of the Himalaya from which the species were collected we will stand a far better chance of succeeding where many have failed. I will concentrate my writing in the following chapters on the well-trodden valleys of Nepal, also covering other regions and countries where significant collections have led to introductions that have become both popular and amenable to our gardens.

CHAPTER TWO

Plant Hunting, Conservation and the Future

FOR ME the Himalaya is a constant lure, an intractable, forbidding place that hides treasures we might never quite grasp. When our eyes rest on a favourite plant in the garden, ponder for a moment what was involved in its original introduction to horticulture. When was it first found? And in what pocket of the earth? Who collected it? How did it reach our gardens? I have always yearned to have free movement in countries such as Bhutan and Tibet, but I suppose that would be naïve considering the current political climate.

Entire books have been written on the subject of plant hunters, with the Himalayan region featuring prominently amongst them. We can correctly apportion lavish praise and recognition on the intrepid pioneers of several generations of plant exploration. I am bound to have my own favourite plant introductions, and often my thoughts return to that great partnership of Frank Ludlow and George Sherriff. From time to time in this book I have been moved to make reference to and even quote these celebrated plant collectors. The late Sir George Taylor, former director of Kew, said of them: "The combined results of the Ludlow-Sherriff expeditions—botanical, horticultural, ornithological and entomological—are a magnificent contribution to our knowledge of the natural history of a region of breath-taking grandeur still greatly unexplored" (Fletcher 1975).

Frank Ludlow and George Sherriff came from very different backgrounds. Ludlow graduated from Cambridge in 1908 with a bachelor of arts degree in natural science. During the course he read botany under Professor Marshal Ward, the father of Frank Kingdon Ward. Ludlow became vice-principal of Sind College in Karachi, where he was also professor of biology and a lecturer in English. After the First World War, when he was commissioned into the Ninety-seventh Indian Infantry, he went into the Indian Education Service. In 1927 Ludlow retired to Srinagar, Kashmir, intending to travel extensively in the Himalaya, collecting specimens particularly of birds and only incidentally of plants for the British Museum of Natural History. He stayed at the consulate in Kashgar with the consul general, Williamson, and there in 1929 met George Sherriff, a friend of Williamson's. They discussed plans to explore Bhutan and Tibet in the years ahead.

The meeting of Ludlow and Sherriff in Kashgar was the beginning of a long friendship. They were two very independent individuals. Ludlow, the older of the two by fifteen years, was made very much in a scholarly academic mould. To him anything mechanical was a closed book. Sherriff, the precise, efficient soldier, was an expert mechanic and electrician, equally talented in his chosen line. Sherriff excelled at games at Sedbergh and upon leaving was determined on a career as a professional soldier. He went on to the Royal Military Academy at Woolwich in London, where he was commissioned into the Royal Garrison Artillery early in 1918. Soon after going to France he was gassed and spent the rest of the war in a hospital. He entered the consular service in 1928 when he was appointed British vice-consul in Kashgar, eventually becoming consul before leaving in 1932.

The outbreak of the Second World War put a temporary end to the Ludlow and Sherriff expeditions. They were both accepted for military service in India. The war over, Ludlow met Sherriff in Kashmir in 1945 to discuss further expeditions. They both kept a daily diary of all their travels and endeavoured to ensure the comfort of the entire party in their company. Each evening they were suitably fortified with the "Treasure Whisky" from the Sherriff family distillery at Bowmore, Islay.

In 1950 Sherriff retired to Scotland where at Ascreavie, Kirriemuir, he and his wife created a garden strongly reminiscent of the Himalayan scene. He died on 19 September 1967. On returning to the United Kingdom Ludlow took up a position at the British Museum where he worked on the Ludlow-Sherriff collections. He lived on to the age of eighty-six, dying on 27 March 1972. Theirs proved to be a truly great partnership. Despite the great mutual respect they had for each other and their selflessness and harmony of views, they always referred to each other by their surnames, Ludlow and Sherriff, as was the practice in those days.

Inevitably an end had to come to these rewarding expeditions, but Ludlow and Sherriff were unable to put a seal on exploratory work in the Tsangpo area of south-eastern Tibet. This vast and topographically difficult country is surely the greatest existing sanctuary of horticultural and botanical riches still untapped, and without doubt there remain to be discovered many first-class plants of garden value. Ludlow wrote in a letter dated 17 June 1949, "It would be grand if I could conclude my research with an investigation of the Tsangpo Gorge, wouldn't it? Just think of the plants there, there were twenty different Rhododendrons at Pemakochung in four days and we didn't go more than a couple of miles from the monastery or ascend higher that 10,000 ft. (3050 m). Nature has run riot there. New species by the dozen flaunting their blooms asking for discovery and demanding a name" (Fletcher 1975). Has the situation changed since then? No expeditions have returned to this area in Tibet to resume collecting where Ludlow and Sherriff were forced to cease as a result of the political climate. However, an ongoing field study is being carried out by Chinese botanists, and the magnificent *Flora of China* (Science Press 1995) is a testimony to much of their work.

Without question the golden years of exploration in the Himalaya were between 1920 and 1950. It was Frank Kingdon Ward and Lord Cawdor who led the way in 1924–25 when they entered Tibet via the Chumbi Valley. Botanically and horticulturally this was one of the most fruitful of all Kingdon Ward's expeditions. Our gardens are the richer for three notable species from the expedition: *Meconopsis betonicifolia*, *Primula florindae* and *P. alpicola*. This success set the scene for subsequent collecting trips to south-eastern Tibet. Kingdon Ward was with the further expeditions which led to his sensational introduction, *Lilium mack-*

liniae—surely it is the queen of lilies—that he discovered in 1946 in Manipur on the borders of Burma, now Myanmar, and Assam near Imphal. South-eastern Tibet indeed showed itself to be equal in horticultural wealth to the "Eldorado" discovered by George Forrest in north-western Yunnan. Forrest's massive input as a collector is a little removed from the core of the Himalaya that this book focuses on, but I must mention his 1904–32 contributions, which resulted in wonderful introductions of such genera as *Rhododendron, Primula, Omphalogramma, Meconopsis, Lilium, Nomocharis, Pleione* and *Gentiana. Gentiana sino-ornata* is perhaps one of his most significant introductions, still not surpassed in form by the many reintroductions made from 1991 onwards from this rich and much-visited province of China.

The golden years of exploration were continued by Ludlow and Sherriff, who made such valuable introductions to our gardens from 1934 through to their last expedition in Bhutan and south-eastern Tibet in 1949. It was in July 1934 on the Nyuksang La near Sakden in Bhutan that Sherriff found a plant which he said surpassed in beauty all the primulas and every other plant on the pass—a most magnificent form of *Meconopsis grandis* (L.S. 600), which he and Ludlow had first recorded from Bhutan in 1933. It was occupying open stony ground beside the lovely burgundy *Primula waltonii*—what a sight! This could well be ranked as Sherriff's finest introduction, from a horticultural perspective, and is now appropriately known in gardens as *M.* George Sherriff Group. Each time I reread the following passage from Ludlow's diary on his finds in the Lo La Chu Valley in Tibet, dated 29 June 1936, I wonder how these men coped when they finally left this paradise of flowers: "It gave me one of the greatest thrills of my life. On its northern slopes, in a region of incessant rainfall, grew the most amazing variety of plants I had ever seen. Day after day we scoured the hillsides, and always we returned with a bulging press [herbarium specimens] and floral treasures new to our collection" (Fletcher 1975). These plants were not only new to their collection but new to science as well. One such plant was the most lovely primula Ludlow had ever seen and which he had the honour of naming after his mother. It was the superb but rather tricky *Primula elizabethae*. Ludlow and Sherriff also made an expedition to Kashmir, introducing such fine plants as *P. reptans* and *Aquilegia nivalis*. Yet it was their many years in Bhutan and Tibet which featured so strongly amidst a significant contribution to horticulture.

Further expeditions have been made since 1949, but not on the scale of Forrest's collections in Yunnan or Kingdon Ward's and Ludlow and Sherriff's in Bhutan and south-eastern Tibet. Nepal occupies the largest part of the Himalaya, and sadly it was little explored botanically until

Meconopsis George Sherriff Group, Schachen Garden, southern Germany
DIETER SCHACHT

1960, yet a few significant collections were made from 1950 onward. In 1950 Lowndes visited the Marsyandi Valley in central Nepal and introduced *Rhododendron lowndesii,* not only an attractive subject for a peat bed but also parent to some fine hybrids of horticultural merit. The first expedition to western Nepal, carried out by Polunin, Sykes and Williams, brought in some fine garden plants. One of the most important of the early Nepalese introductions came in 1954 from an expedition by Stainton, Sykes and Williams. It was a primula of the section *Soldanelloides,* named after the leader of the expedition, *Primula reidii* var. *williamsii* (S.S.W. 1770). Stainton, Sykes and Williams also made significant collections of *Meconopsis* from the Lamjung Himal in central Nepal at around 14,000 ft. (4270 m). The Herbarium at the Royal Botanic Garden in Ed-

Foliage of *Meconopsis regia* in October, Lamjung, central Nepal
DIETER SCHACHT

inburgh holds collections of *M. regia* carefully preserved in the form of pressed herbarium specimens. How sad that this stately giant amongst *Meconopsis* species, a monocarp that dies after flowering, has now long been lost to cultivation and has never been reintroduced. How many other valuable garden introductions have been lost and now deserve a reappearance?

The geography of eastern Nepal means that it presents a challenge to collectors, but a successful trip was organised in 1971 by Beer along with Lancaster and Morris to the Jaljale Himal, taking in the rich . They made fine collections of seed including *Sorbus microphylla, Lilium nepalense* and *Primula obliqua*. Their collections are numbered with the prefix "B.L.M." The Royal Botanic Garden sponsored a highly successful seed-collecting trip to the same region in 1991 — the collection numbers hold the prefix "E.M.A.K." At the west end of the Himalaya, a Swedish botanical expedition in 1983 concentrated on northern Pakistan and the Karakoram. Their finest introductions included *Delphinium brunonianum* (S.E.P. 53); *Androsace mucronifolia* (S.E.P. 134); *Potentilla nepalensis* (S.E.P. 259), a personal favourite of mine; the rare *Primula duthieana* (S.E.P. 296); and good collections of *Paraquilegia grandiflora*. Also at this west end of the Himalaya, seed collections have been made by Chadwell in Kashmir, leading to valuable introductions of *Primula elliptica* and *P. macrophylla* along with the lovely *Aquilegia fragrans*.

Through the following chapters, I mention individuals from the amateur gardening sphere with a sharp eye for a good garden plant, who have made important introductions to horticulture. But does the plant hunter still have a future, and if so is it morally sound to participate in such a practice in the light of a genuine concern to preserve the world's flora in the name of conservation? My feeling is that the answer is a qualified yes. Who of us has the right to say we should not enjoy nature to the full and, where there is a genuine need, introduce to our gardens in a controlled manner new material or superior forms of a species known to be free from the endangered list? Quite naturally, care should be taken to collect only when there is a genuine horticultural need. What can the point be in countless collections being made, as they surely are, of species so well known in gardens and widely available within the trade such as *Meconopsis napaulensis*, *Primula sikkimensis* and *Paraquilegia grandiflora*? Of much greater concern is the wholesale collecting of bulbous material, particularly *Cypripedium* and *Pleione* from China along with *Lilium* and *Arisaema*. Reports suggest that whole populations of some species have been collected, making a mockery of conservation and showing that many of us as gardeners have an unashamed appetite for plants at any price that in many cases we have little hope of growing.

I would very much like to see botanic gardens continue to develop fruitful liaisons with their counterparts and colleagues in Beijing and Darjeeling, for example, lending weight by supporting expeditions to desirable areas to reintroduce material of horticultural importance. We should remember that fresh genetic material will from time to time strengthen existing gene pools, hopefully therefore retaining vigour amongst plants that may well be struggling in our changing climate at home. If future expeditions are planned to collect plants or seeds from the Himalaya, is the rate of surviving material sufficient to qualify the sponsorship of such trips? Again, yes is the answer. Times have changed, though, with economic strains felt amongst many botanic gardens, some having to finance themselves privately. Most well-known bona fide nurseries no longer have the time or finances to dabble in the cultivation of some of the more demanding species. Care therefore must be taken to identify the recipients of newly collected material to provide an above-average chance of survival regardless of unforeseen circumstances. Selected amateurs may well be the best recipients now, those enjoying growing conditions which favour the cultivation of the particular plants and who can raise limited stocks, disseminating them at the appropriate time.

I make no apology for belabouring this section, as it seems so timely with many garden centres and do-it-yourself stores enjoying a boom in their industry. So often the unwitting purchaser of plants is quite oblivious to the origin of the material on offer. Blame is not always easily apportioned.

While writing this piece in late February, I cast my eyes with excitement at a breathtaking clump of *Primula whitei* with its delft-blue flowers nestling in a posy amongst silvery, meal-covered foliage. This is a sterile Bhutanese clone collected by Ludlow and Sherriff in 1949, possibly *P.*

whitei (L.S. 20619), representing part of their, then, unique introductions sent home as living material by jet air. Let me illustrate what was involved after their careful collection in the field. Sherriff and Hicks, a colleague who joined Ludlow and Sherriff on a few expeditions, left Bumthang, in Bhutan, on 13 October 1949 and reached Ha on 24 October, there to find Ludlow awaiting them. During the course of seven months the three of them amassed beautiful material for 5000 gatherings for the herbarium, as well as some 600 collections of seeds, bulbs and tubers, the largest collection ever made from Bhutan. In addition ninety-three lots of living plants which Sherriff proposed to fly to London were now packed in three loosely woven bamboo hampers. Three tiers of plants filled each hamper, the individual plants wrapped in moss so that once in Britain they could be forwarded to specified gardens. The plants left Calcutta by British Overseas Airways Corporation on 11 November, and Taylor, later Sir George, was at the London airport when the plane touched down next day. On the whole the plants travelled well, but some losses were inevitable, considering the length of journey and the change from their cool, wet alpine haunts of Bhutan through the

Primula whitei, Edrom Nurseries, Berwickshire JIM JERMYN

high temperatures in the lower part of the country to Kalimpong and on to Calcutta where temperatures would no doubt have been close to 100°F (38°C). At that time this effort of Ludlow and Sherriff to introduce living plants, by air, into cultivation in Britain was the greatest one of its kind and proved a fitting climax to their years of collecting.

I am sure that lovers of Himalayan plants would heartily agree that these men added greatly to our knowledge of the flora within this region of the eastern Himalaya and south-eastern Tibet, and their strenuous efforts on hazardous expeditions have enriched our gardens and enhanced our horticultural expertise. So, it is almost exactly fifty years later that I feel suitably humble as I look down at the perfect beauty of *Primula whitei*. The species has not been officially reintroduced in this form and great care has to be taken to maintain its tenuous hold in cultivation. I therefore fully support legal and well-meaning collecting trips to the Himalaya and at the same time welcome greater responsibility towards conservation. Positive expressions have been made about the preservation of the giant panda in Sichuan, as with a more responsible approach to woodland conservation throughout the Himalaya, so let us be upbeat about the future and remember the part we play as the consumer. Should we, however unwittingly, continue to purchase any sort of plant material, bulbous or fibrous rooted, that has been dug up illegally for commercial purposes, then we are adding fuel to the glowing blaze of plunder that will continue until the demand ceases. At the same time, the continuation of such illegal practices further fuels the lobby who feel that all plant collecting should be curtailed.

It may be good to reflect as we walk amongst our favourite plants, to appreciate the efforts of the aforementioned collectors and the countless individuals I have not referred to by name. Our gardens are the richer for their endeavours, and as new introductions filter into horticulture both now and in the future, let us be enthusiastic with a balanced and reasonable approach to the whole subject.

CHAPTER THREE

Temperate Zone

T HE TEMPERATE zone occupies a belt loosely from 6000 to 8000 ft. (1830–2440 m), where typically in Nepal the evergreen oak (*Quercus* spp.) and *Rhododendron arboreum* predominate as forest cover. The subalpine zone, controlling an altitude roughly from 8000 to 12,000 ft. (2440–3660 m), offers a change in woody species, with coniferous subjects such as *Abies* and *Tsuga* more commonly in evidence, along with some deciduous birch (*Betula* spp.), right up to the tree line. The flora thriving in these forest conditions is both limited and rather specialised, typified by such plants as the semi-epiphytic orchids of the genus *Pleione*. This genus has been making a great impact in horticulture in the late decades of the twentieth century, and later in this chapter I recommend the Himalayan species for the woodland garden and give some thoughts on cultivation.

A number of plants from the temperate zone of the Himalaya have become very popular. Keen plantsfolk have sought to find the ideal landscape for plants growing naturally in the deciduous forest zone as well as those enjoying cooler conditions despite being found in the full sun of higher elevations. Therefore both woodland and peat gardens can be appropriate garden habitats for these plants from the temperate zone.

The Woodland Garden

Several reasons prompt gardeners to plant up an existing woodland. An existing deciduous canopy may well have provided years of accumulated leaf litter, boosting the soil's humus level and offering a perfect, acid soil type for many favoured Himalayan species. I cannot overemphasise the need for a deciduous woodland, avoiding at all cost a solid coniferous cover. An occasional evergreen specimen such as Douglas fir (*Pseudotsuga menziesii*) or pine (*Pinus* spp.), however, could be beneficial for some specialised subjects whether they be of Himalayan origin or otherwise. In many areas, serious gardening can be limited due to a lack of shelter, so I can also heartily recommend a woodland to combat the ravages of severe winds. On many occasions when gales have been thrashing our east coast of Scotland I have retreated to the woodland and suddenly found myself in an eerie calm of unbelievable relief. The woodland is a unique sheltered habitat which nurtures species that otherwise would have stood no chance.

This is all very well if we already have the provision of an established deciduous tree canopy—let us thin out and start planting. But what about those of us who have smaller gardens with a few woody specimens providing only dappled shade? The later section dealing with the peat garden and its plants may provide an appealing course of action. And for those who have unoccupied land presenting the possibility of planting a woodland, or "spinney," then please do not give up due to the time it takes to establish trees. In exposed sites a belt of trees should be planted to give the leeward planting a better chance of establishment. Do not be afraid to plant a thick belt of intermixed seedlings to kickstart establishment. Try *Larix* and *Tsuga,* together with *Cupressus* to fill out the gaps. The woodland itself can be planted with a variety of favourite species of trees from a whole host of deciduous genera including birch (*Betula*), oak (*Quercus*) or rowan (*Sorbus*). Try to give each specimen tree ample space, up to 20 ft. (6 m).

TREES & SHRUBS

Once the canopy trees are established, beds can be formed and midsized trees and shrubs can be planted. Dig the soil well, and if it is extremely heavy in nature, work in acid leaf mould or coarse sphagnum peat along with coarse sand to help loosen it. At the other extreme, if the soil is light with a lack of body, then add lots of leaf mould and continue to do so until the natural cover provides its annual leaf drop.

If shelter is already in place, consider planting a representation of the larger-leafed *Rhododendron* species along with some of the finest magnolias. These plants will require patience, but just imagine the joy in seeing a young rhododendron first produce flower buds instead of vegetative, or growth, buds. Thus armed with such a positive attitude let us plant a

Forest zone, Langtang, central Nepal DIETER SCHACHT

few specimens of the stunning, taller-growing rhododendrons such as *R. lacteum* or *R. fictolacteum* with huge lemon-yellow or cream-coloured trusses of flowers with lovely inner markings. *Rhododendron fortunei* has bell-shaped, lilac-pink, fragrant flowers in loose trusses. The sensational *R. cinnabarinum* from eastern Nepal has waxy, tubular flowers with varying shades from apricot to the red of *R. cinnabarinum* var. *roylei*. A smaller-leafed species that loves the woodland conditions and brightens up a corner in May is *R. augustinii* with blue flowers in amazing profusion. In the hunt for specimen rhododendrons the choice is great and, not surprisingly, fraught only with knowing where to stop. Self-control may be enforced at some stage due to available space and the bank balance.

Having chosen specimen rhododendrons, I would next consider autumn-colour subjects prior to the main body of planting. I could not cope without a selection of some of the best rowans we know and love, or more exactly, the pinnate-leafed section *Aucuparia* of the genus *Sorbus*. How can we choose from so many lovely species and cultivars? Part of

Rhododendron cinnabarinum, eastern Nepal GEORGE SMITH

the fun is the fact that so many are apomicts, meaning they breed true by producing seed without fertilisation taking place. The seed is genetically identical to the seed-bearing parent, so when friends come round and covetously admire the specimen of *Sorbus cashmiriana* with its stunning, fat, white fruits held in ample clusters, pluck off fruits and pass them on and calmly relate how their progeny will be just as they see them there. Another form of *S. cashmiriana* is a must have. Like the type species, *S. cashmiriana* (S.E.P. 492) forms a small tree, but it displays wonderful pink berries in autumn. We owe this introduction to the Swedish Gothenburg expedition to Pakistan. Swedish collector Harry Smith made a valuable collection of a fabulous clone possibly belonging to *S. koehneana*. Known horticulturally as *S.* 'Harry Smith 12799', this apomict from Sichuan forms a small tree with lovely reddish autumn colour and masses of white fruits. Another renowned collector, Joseph Rock, introduced an absolute winner from north-western Yunnan in 1932. No woodland garden could possibly be complete without *S.* 'Joseph Rock', as it simply holds the stage with its glorious scarlet autumn foliage together with deep, golden yellow fruits. On the east coast here in Scotland, our fruit-laden clone of this tree is stripped in the autumn as flocks of the thrush-like fieldfare and redwing find a welcome break and first meal after their crossing of the North Sea along their westward migration. This satisfying sight is surely another fine reason for planting members of fruiting *Sorbus* in the woodland garden.

In 1969 the Royal Horticultural Society gave the Award of Garden Merit to *Sorbus sargentiana,* which was introduced by Ernest Wilson from Sichuan in 1908. This allrounder, slow-growing in habit, produces enormous trusses of smallish red fruits accompanied by large leaves of a fine dark red colour. As though these traits did not suffice, watch out for the fat, sticky, horse-chestnut-like buds in winter. Finally I would like to sing the praises of *S. monbeigii.* This white-fruiting species was introduced in 1991 after being collected on a trip to Yunnan sponsored by the Royal Botanic Garden in Edinburgh. The collection numbers from this trip carry the prefix "C.L.D." Upon seeing young seed-raised saplings of this collection, I was particularly drawn to the stunning scarlet autumn foliage colour. Certainly it is one small tree to look out for.

With rhododendrons and rowans in place, the woodland garden is developing a backbone, leaving a little space for some smaller shrubs and perhaps a few more specimen conifers. The available area obviously will dictate when to curtail this planting of tall and midsized woody subjects so as to leave room for planting the beds of herbaceous material. I love to create "vistas," or beds specifically designed to give an opportunity to view plants. Of course a sloping garden creates this facility more readily, allowing us to look down on specimens such as *Magnolia campbellii* or deciduous conifers coming into their own in the autumn such as the dawn redwood (*Metasequoia glyptostroboides*), a fast-growing yet graceful tree with lovely golden brown autumn colour. If a treat is allowed then find space for the much-sought-after golden larch (*Pseudolarix amabilis*), introduced from China by Robert Fortune in 1852. Its foliage turns bright yellow in the autumn. If these conifers make an impression in the vista then magnolias can do the same. I recommend *Magnolia campbellii*, the Himalayan pink tulip tree. It loves warmer climates but is well worth planting, provided future protection is assured.

I rate highly the species *Magnolia globosa* from the eastern Himalaya. It is easily raised from seed and soon attains the size of a large shrub to small tree. What I love about this plant is its ability to please at a level where we can all reach to enjoy its sumptuous, nodding, creamy white, rather globular flowers in June, but it is the fragrance reminiscent of citrus and pineapples that stops people in their tracks.

I would certainly plant a few maples (*Acer* spp.) and at least one of the superb snake-bark species such as *Acer davidii* or *A. hersii*, both having the added joy of producing rich autumn colour. One final specimen is a small deciduous shrub from China, *Lindera obtusiloba*, which is so rewarding in the late autumn when many other plants have dropped their leaves and it still offers a show of butter-yellow. The rather large ovate leaves, three lobed at the tip, are so attractive as they change colour that it is no surprise it received an Award of Merit in 1952 from the Royal Horticultural Society. Now let us pause and take stock.

PREPARATION FOR UNDERPLANTING

Next, it is time to prepare beds for planting herbaceous material. As I have said, most Himalayan and Sino-Himalayan subjects prefer an acid soil. A neutral-to-acid soil is ideal. Purchasing a soil pH test kit is easy and will give a quick answer as to whether the soil is suitable, thus enabling the project to continue. If the pH is too high, do not proceed. No expense should be spared to improve the soil humus. Barrow loads of acid leaf mould, along with highest quality sphagnum peat will repay the efforts greatly in years to come. The soil should be open and friable, lumpy, yet loose, retaining moisture but not wet. During planting, I always have a few buckets handy with a further provision of sphagnum peat mixed with leaf mould and a supply of coarse sand.

What about supplementary fertilisers—are they necessary and which should we use? Sometimes they should be utilised, notably with woody subjects requiring a help along to establishment. I recommend a balanced granular fertiliser containing the three primary requirements for growth: nitrogen (N), phosphorus (P) and potassium (K), together with magnesium and minor trace elements. Nitrogen encourages plant growth, notably in the foliage and stems, and promotes a good colour in the leaves. Phosphorus, or phosphate, especially is required for good root growth, particularly at the seedling stage. It also promotes seed and fruit development in later stages of growth. Potassium, or potash, is important for building up plant starches, sugars and fibrous tissues. It promotes sturdy growth and improves quality of fruit. None of these primary requirements should be high in percentage but rather a balanced low percentage. Each country has its own fertiliser manufacturers, usually offering an organic or inorganic choice. I find myself trying to utilise organic fertiliser when food crops are involved and inorganic when planting ornamentals, but in many cases relative to the woodland, little or no added fertiliser is necessary. So, rather than continually mentioning the addition of fertiliser through the rest of the book, I will presume that the gardener has it available in a bucket and when it is needed will apply a light dusting of it in the preparatory hole and thoroughly mix it into the soil prior to planting. Also I will presume that all plants are watered in after planting on all occasions.

Consider how to irrigate the garden, if it is indeed feasible and legal to do so. A by-product of rubber tyres called "leaky pipe" is now available on the market, providing an ideal means of watering at low cost with minimal disturbance to the garden and user. Now is the time to lay out this porous piping around each bed a few inches below the surface, remembering to situate it at the top side of a slope to encourage seepage. As the garden is establishing, the plants best appreciate when the water is applied in the evening or early morning. I strongly discourage the use of overhead sprinklers or misting systems as they can give plants a false sense of security, fooling them into thinking they are obtaining water when they are only receiving surface moisture. A hot, dry spell can spell death for plants used to overhead watering, even for mature specimens, as no moisture has reached the root where the plants need it. In my experience overhead irrigation also poses a danger through splash that can spread disease. For these reasons I recommend either watering by hand, for small plots, or using a porous-pipe method of irrigation.

Once the soil is ready, plan what to plant and where to locate the plants in the beds. Consider all-year-round colour and plants that will tolerate positions closer to the trees where the root interference will be subsantial and drying out inevitable. The position of the paths should be incorporated now, too. Perhaps a path can lead to some surprises, such as trees and shrubs with overhanging fragrance. Try and avoid positioning a favourite specimen with fragrant or sumptuous flowers in the middle of a bed away from a path, thus risking all and sundry stamping across plants to admire it. Edging the paths with cut birch timbers is both sensible and attractive, and a path topped with coniferous leaf mould and bracken is pleasing to walk on.

Personal taste is always the prime criterion when planning any aspect in the garden, just as is true inside the home. Will the garden take on a natural look or a rather formal, even manicured approach? Along with the concept of personal choice comes the will of nature. But the natural woodland garden is not an excuse to plant out the subjects and leave the rest to nature. If that were the case, in five years' time the whole site may well be an entangled mass of bramble, lesser celandine or a whole host of endemic woodland perennial weeds that have spoiled the garden. Rather, the natural approach is to control most aspects of the feature by weeding, pruning, thinning, dividing, and mulching without disturbing the relationships that have formed between the various types of species planted. Planting a woodland garden forms a whole new ecology, with food chains, for example, between birds and insects, which depend on our careful management, including responsible use of certain insecticides and herbicides.

BULBS

I must emphasise that while the subject of this book puts the spotlight on the Himalaya I would not prescribe tunnel vision to the degree that excludes plants from other regions. It may well be appropriate to incorporate stands of winter- and spring-flowering bulbous subjects such as snowdrops (*Galanthus*), *Erythronium* and *Trillium*, for example. To this end my objective wherever possible would be to bring about all-year-round colour and effect in the woodland. Plant association is very significant, making advanced planning beneficial, without the need necessarily for elaborate plans and a landscape architect. Plant association should not just enhance the overall aesthetic effect but also bring about a natural blending of species in the garden. For example the many cobra lilies (*Arisaema* spp.) make spectacular plantings; planting them adjacent to a sprawling evergreen such as a species of *Gaultheria* or *Vaccinium* would provide protection for both the underground bulbs and the emerging shoots. If finances allow, why not be a little extravagant and purchase a range of exciting nursery-grown bulbous species and a few orchids? A special site needs to be found for the orchids and choice bulbous species to afford maximum protection and a reasonable depth of soil to help control the moisture content, for extremes of wet and dry are potentially disastrous.

Along with a severely dented bank balance, our bulb tray holds some plants of the lady's slipper orchid (*Cypripedium tibeticum*) along with another orchid species, *Calanthe tricarinata,* some lily species including *Lilium mackliniae* and *L. nepalense* and some large bulbs, resembling scaly tennis balls, of the sensational giant lily (*Cardiocrinum giganteum*). It is early spring and the subjects are still dormant, an ideal time to plant them. The soil is beginning to warm up and the risk of severe frost is diminishing but should a sudden drop in temperature threaten, be prepared to cover the site with layers of pegged-down fleece for extra protection. If plants have been purchased by mail order, I recommend hardening them off by placing them in a tray of slightly moist peat in a cool, frost-free shed for several days prior to planting, thus lessening the shock.

Each plant or group of plants should be clearly labelled in the bed both to identify the subject and to make clear its juxtaposition in the scheme. My wife considers the beds I plant to bear close resemblance to a cemetery with rows of headstones above smoothly manicured grounds. Of course she is right, yet if only she would reserve judgement until the next stage when I will either prepare a written plan of the area with the plants carefully mapped for my record or transfer the labelling system onto a less eye-catching one made of neutral-coloured fencing wire cut into short 1-to 2-ft. (30- to 60-cm) lengths to which aluminium labels are attached.

For the cypripediums and calanthes, work into the soil several handfuls of coarse sand and a good portion of well-rotted pine needles. No added fertiliser should be incorporated at all. The cypripediums will have one or more growth buds resting amongst a mat of fibrous root. Plant these so that the buds are situated just beneath the surface of the soil.

Cypripedium tibeticum is often confused with other members of this much-sought-after genus, providing a challenge for taxonomists. This species has a broad range from eastern Himalaya to Tibet and western China. In the wild the plants generally grow in clusters up to 9 in. (23 cm) tall with generally large, solitary, pouched flowers of deep purple with attractive veining and flushing. A choice and indeed similar species is *C. himalaicum* found growing from western Nepal through to southeastern Tibet. Both are fully hardy to 10.4°F (−12°C) as long as the newly produced shoots are protected from late frost. Flowers can be expected during the late spring to early summer. The Himalayan *Calanthe tricarinata* is later flowering but prefers the same cool situation and a comparable planting technique. In the summer, flowering stems rise some 12 in. (30 cm) carrying a lax spike of glowing greenish yellow flowers with a reddish brown lip.

A similar bed will suit the lilies. The giant lily (*Cardiocrinum giganteum*) flowers in early summer to midsummer with 6-ft. (2-m), stately spikes carrying a number of large funnel-shaped flowers on terminal stems, each flower white with a red-marked throat and a powerful fragrance sure to filter through the whole woodland on a summer evening. It is found growing in dense forest throughout the Himalaya, but the form found in Yunnan is also well worth looking out for, with its distinct green flushing to the flowers. These bulbs can be purchased in sizes from ping-pong ball to tennis ball depending on their age; prices differ accordingly. They take more than five years to flower from seed.

I would buy three to five bulbs and plant them in a group. Many authorities recommend shallow planting very near the surface. I would not disagree with this, although I have experienced no ill effects when planting as deep as 6 in. (15 cm). Eventually the bulbs seem to work their way

Cypripedium himalaicum, Langtang, central Nepal DIETER SCHACHT

towards the surface, presumably projected by the force of their very substantial root system. As with all lilies, I recommend preparing holes with plenty of added gritty sand worked together with the endemic soil to prevent rotting during wet spells.

After the stately spikes of *Cardiocrinum giganteum* have ceased flowering they may be left for the seed to ripen, which may take well into the autumn. Eventually, in December in climates like mine, cut the spikes down near the ground and bring them under cover for further ripening of the seeds. As the seed capsules begin to brown and dry out they can be cut off the spikes and hung up in paper bags to dry, prior to cleaning and subsequent sowing. Chapter 6 offers more detail on this process.

In winter whilst the stumps of old giant lily stems remain we can return and lift the decaying bulb along with two or three young bulbs which have formed alongside it. The soil should be dug over and rejuvenated with fresh leaf-mould, and the young lily bulbils should be replanted a few inches deep, ready for the whole process to repeat, with projected flowering two or three years hence. Due to inevitable "soil tiredness" I would not recommend continual planting of similar species in the same soil over many generations. Move them about and we are thus obeying one of the most fundamental rules of horticulture and can save ourselves much unnecessary worry from unwanted pests and diseases. Perish the thought of monoculture in a woodland garden, home to a single genetic collection of one genus. To allow this would be inviting an inevitable attack of a deadly virus and the introduction, in the case of a lily monoculture, of the ravages of lily beetle. Any emphasis placed on one type of plant is danger lurking around the corner. To promote variety in our woodland planting I suggest two Himalayan *Lilium* species, *L. nepalense* and *L. mackliniae,* meriting pride of place close to the edge of a path, nestling amongst a few of the dwarfer *Rhododendron* species such as *R. chamae-thomsonii,* *R. tsariense* or the ever popular *R. sanguineum,* all suitable in dappled shade.

Lilium nepalense is an extraordinary species endemic to the Nepalese Himalaya, often growing in grassy banks in the wooded zone. It is exotic as its arching 2- to 3-ft. (60- to 90-cm) stems sway with the weight of large greenish trumpets opening out with reddish purple centres. One

Cardiocrinum giganteum, Edrom Nurseries, Berwickshire JIM JERMYN

merit of this plant horticulturally is its stoloniferous, spreading habit. It even has the ability to send a stolon travelling under a path to reappear a distance from its mother plant, without ever becoming a nuisance. Propagation is therefore simple, involving the lifting and transplanting of bulbs during the dormant season. I have never been too keen on staking or supporting plants in an informal setting, yet some of the more robust lilies carry such weighty blossoms that some support may be judicious. My preference is to procure short lengths of leafless branches and place them carefully amongst the emerging lilies to lend a little tasteful support.

The second species is rather special and, along with *Lilium nepalense,* often is available from specialist nurseries; it is *L. mackliniae,* flowering in June. This was one of Frank Kingdon Ward's finest introductions from Manipur, Burma (now Myanmar). He named it after his wife, Jean Macklin, who is justly proud of such a fine garden plant. Every year on 5 June Jean gets out her diary and reads the twelve-page entry for that day in 1946. The day was one of celebration, not only because they were on their honeymoon but because on this day she and Frank first saw the pink *L. mackliniae* on the upper slopes of the mountain Sirhoi Kashong in what was then India's Manipur state: "There were thousands in flower. It was the happiest day of my life and we were in ecstasy, absolute ecstasy" (personal communication).

I would certainly plant the bulbs of *Lilium mackliniae* in front of a low-growing evergreen rhododendron to allow the stately 18-in. (46-cm) stems carrying several large soft-pink, pendent, bell-like flowers to provide a satisfying background. Once planted, this lily, as with most of the true species, should be left alone. The bulbs of the non-stoloniferous subjects do not enjoy handling but can be easily raised from seed, which is exactly what to offer to friends when they ask for some of this exquisite species. The seed capsules will turn yellow as they ripen in the late summer and then a brownish colour prior to opening and dispersing the seed. As with all lilies — and the cardiocrinums though they take longer to ripen — just as the capsules begin to crack open, carefully cut the flower stalks down to the ground and place the capsules into a paper bag marked clearly with the name of the plant. The bags are best hung on a line with clothes pegs in a light, open, airy shed to ripen fully. In late autumn the

capsules can be safely opened and the seed cleaned prior to winter sowing, which I explain further in Chapter 6. The seedlings will germinate
through the following year, whereupon I recommend repotting the
whole mass of seedlings in a loam-based compost and leaving for a full
year. The bulbils can be pricked out then and held over in deep boxes of
a leafy soil to wait for planting out in the garden in another two years.
Yes, this is a patient five-to-six-year project, surely part of the fun of gar-

Lilium nepalense, Munich Botanic Garden, southern Germany
DIETER SCHACHT

Lilium mackliniae, Edrom Nurseries, Berwickshire JIM JERMYN

dening, but the glorious flowers of *L. mackliniae* make all this process so rewarding.

HERBACEOUS PLANTS

It may bring some light relief to highlight a group of straightforward plants that merit a place in any woodland garden. Hardy spurges (*Euphorbia*) are guaranteed to brighten up any dull corner with a bold splash of colour, which will be useful, particularly as we develop vistas for late-spring to early-summer colour. *Euphorbia* is a genus of plants native to various parts of the world including the Himalaya. I recommend the species *E. griffithii* because it is easy to obtain and grows well in challenging sites where protection is not yet established.

When discussing the hardy spurges, we should know the definitions of some botanical terminology. As gardeners we love flowers and foliage and lavish praise on their particular features, but is it not true that as we look down at a bold stand of *Euphorbia griffithii* we may hesitate for a moment to ponder over what to call the various parts we want to describe? The typical hardy spurge has three kinds of leaf. The stem leaves I will loosely describe as traditional leaves; the floral leaves look much like flower petals with lovely shades of yellow, orange or lime-green; and located between these two are the whorl leaves which occur at the base of the umbel of true flowers which are miniscule and need not concern us as gardeners. The brightly coloured floral leaves attract insects and play a significant role in the reproductive process for this important genus. As we admire these showy plants we probably will be singing the praises of these three types of foliage rather than the flowers. Two other important facts about hardy spurges are that the seed is always borne in threes and their white juice is poisonous and may give uncomfortable side effects, as I once experienced when taking cuttings of *E. myrsinites.* Try to avoid getting the juice on the skin or in the eyes, but if you do, wash it off promptly. Not surprisingly some species, notably *E. wulfenii,* have been recommended to be planted as a deterrent to that adorable yet mischievous pest, the mole.

In the woodland garden I suggest planting bold patches of *Euphorbia griffithii* and *E. wallichii. Euphorbia griffithii* (L.S.H. 18685) is of profound importance horticulturally, owing its introduction to Ludlow, Sherriff and Hicks from Bhutan in 1949. Found growing in damp, grassy scrub in the eastern Himalaya, it has fine strong stems carrying stunning red-coloured floral leaves and spreads generously by underground stolons. Stolons are slender stems usually creeping on the soil surface. The species is a classic amongst herbaceous plants and has some splendid cultivars worth seeking out, including *E. griffithii* 'Fireglow', 'Dixter' and 'Fern Cottage'. These selections have floral leaves of burnt orange and autumn foliage of yellow to flame-red.

My favourite is the cultivar *Euphorbia griffithii* 'Robert Poland', commemorating one of the great characters of the late twentieth century, now long retired from his nursery trade. He was instrumental in providing me with some of my fondest memories and most-valued training as a student. I particularly remember planting rows of perfectly grown herbaceous liners, or young plants, in "whalehide pots," traditional paper-like pots that rot in the soil, ready for marketing to the top parks departments around London. Working alongside seasoned horticulturists such as Poland was an unforgettable experience, trying to soak up the common-sense approach that only comes from decades of genuine hands-on experience with a wide range of garden plants. This euphorbia originated in his nursery in Ardingly, West Sussex, and enjoys floral leaves of a brighter and richer red than those of 'Fireglow' on a more robust plant.

The Himalayan *Euphorbia wallichii* from Nepal, my second recommended species for the woodland garden, is somewhat dwarfer in stature, growing up to 2 ft. (60 cm) in height. Its fine clumps show off floral leaves of a lovely, glowing golden yellow over a long period in late spring. They prove valuable as contrast to blue-flowering plants nearby.

A number of popular herbaceous plants lend themselves to woodland conditions, especially *Thalictrum*, *Bergenia*, *Podophyllum,* and *Rodgersia*. One of the most attractive of the meadow rues is *T. chelidonii*. It is frequently encountered in deciduous woodland from Kashmir eastward to southern Tibet at altitudes of 8860 to 11,800 ft. (2700–3600 m). This tall perennial often exceeds 6 ft. (2 m) high in nature, with attractive lilac-pink flowers in clusters above the typically toothed foliage on branched stems. Many of the Himalayan bergenias grow in open, sunny aspects in

nature and would therefore be out of place in this section, but one I remember growing very happily in woodland conditions in the Munich
Botanic Garden was *Bergenia ligulata* var. *ciliata*, simply *B. ciliata* as some
botanists prefer. A drift of this variety around the base of a tree should
provide a fine show in the spring. Short stems carry dense clusters of
flowers varying from white through to pink. The foliage turns bright red
in the autumn. Be sure to add humus to the soil before planting. The
spring-flowering *Podophyllum hexandrum* (synonym *P. emodi*), belonging to the Berberidaceae, the berberis family, is a freely available plant de-

Bergenia ciliata, Kashmir DIETER SCHACHT

serving wider praise. As the spring season develops, the plant unfurls mottled foliage in pairs, each pair later subtending a large pink flower. This is a pleasing combination, but the latter part of the season brings the bonus of hanging red fruit containing several seeds to facilitate propagation.

Rodgersia offers many species of popular bog plants that respond well in a woodland, too. A 1992 introduction of *R. nepalensis* caught my attention in the Royal Botanic Garden in Edinburgh. It would lend valuable architectural form to a mixed planting including *Meconopsis* and *Primula* species. The greenish white flowers are attractively held in a one-sided, curved cluster on noble 2-to 3-ft. (60- to 90-cm) stems.

If we are not careful it is possible to have a rather unbalanced flowering emphasis in the springtime. Summer colour is naturally less prolific due to the seasonal effects on flowering in nature, yet a number of *Gera-*

Podophyllum hexandrum, Kashmir DIETER SCHACHT

nium species will lend themselves to giving late colour in the woodland. Deserving the spotlight is *G. wallichianum,* fairly widespread throughout the Himalaya. Although this species needs space, as it spreads in a scrambling fashion with branched stems, it dies back completely in the winter. This valuable species is easily propagated from seed, resulting in some lovely colour forms. My favourite is *G. wallichianum* 'Buxton's Variety' with white-centred, clean blue flowers held in pairs over beautifully lobed foliage which assumes a reddish autumn colour. Pink to reddish-purple flowers occur in the wild and often are available in the trade—all adding to the beauty of this late-flowering species.

Daphne bholua, central Nepal DIETER SCHACHT

For the same end of the season *Crawfurdia speciosa* is worth seeking out as a climbing member of the gentian family, Gentianaceae, found in eastern Nepal scrambling over *Viburnum*. The effect of the crawfurdia is a cascading series of stems with brilliant blue, gentian-like flowers followed by reddish-purple, fruiting capsules. If this exciting plant is chosen, a suitable compatriot would be the winter-flowering *Daphne bholua*, as both require a sheltered position away from the most severe ravages of frost. The daphne is now available in many forms, some more deciduous than others. *Daphne bholua* 'Jacqueline Postill' is a firm favourite with an abundance of purplish pink flowers emitting a powerful fragrance.

PRIMULA & MECONOPSIS

The woodland canopy should not be so dense as to prevent some effective light transmission, and where more than the average light filters through, beds may be prepared for two highlights of this book, primulas and blue poppies (*Meconopsis* spp.). Neither the larger *Primula* nor *Meconopsis* species grow in woodland conditions in nature, but my experience has found that many species grow well in dappled shade and most require shelter from the strongest winds and excessive summer heat that seem to accompany our changing climate, shelter that the woodland garden can give. The combination afforded by the taller primulas and blue poppies is a sight to behold in June and July. (The primulas that enjoy boggy conditions are discussed in the section on bog gardens in Chapter 4.)

These beds need space and a depth of soil away from the close proximity of tree roots. The lime-free soil needs to be well prepared with added humus. Well-rotted manure is beneficial for the primulas but it is not a favourite of *Meconopsis*, so incorporate it sparingly throughout the bed. Bold drifts of these plants is the finest way of showing them off, and should a naturally occurring stream be running through the wood, possibilities abound for both these and the bog-liking primulas.

Meconopsis species fall conveniently into two groups, the perennial species and the monocarpic species, those flowering once and then dying. The latter group is valuable despite their short-lived nature because they produce copious amounts of seed to ensure a means of propagation. Often the stout rosettes of the monocarpic species' foliage produced over a period of some four to five years prior to flowering provide the most decorative appeal. The most freely available species is *M. napaulensis,* established in gardens in the 1960s following the successful introduction from Nepal by Stainton, Sykes and Williams. Many meconopses grown today are of hybrid origin, as *M. napaulensis* has been crossed successfully with *M. regia* and *M. paniculata. Meconopsis regia* is now no longer in cultivation and awaits reintroduction. The foliage of all these species is variable and its size depends greatly on the fertility of the soil in which it is growing. The leaf colour varies from a lovely silver to shades of yellow, but all leaf shapes are much dissected. At flowering the stem may assume a height from 3 to 6 ft. (0.9–2 m), with a stately spike or cyme of yellow, pink or ruby-red flowers, often up to ten, in the shape of cups or goblets,

Open valley with *Betula utilis* var. *jacquemontii*, Kashmir DIETER SCHACHT

a magnificent sight indeed. The variety *M. napaulensis* var. *wallichii* produces blue or more rarely white flowers on a splendid spike and generally in just two or three years from seed.

Meconopsis paniculata is similar to *M. napaulensis* and is generally separable only to the trained botanical eye. The most noticeable difference is that the stigma of *M. paniculata* is reliably soft purple in colour and the stigma of *M. napaulensis* is green. A wonderful form of this species was collected in the Ghunza region in eastern Nepal by Mike Hirst. It consistently produces foliage of a sensational ginger-orange colour along with yellow flowers. In time no doubt, if the two species are planted in

Meconopsis napaulensis, Langtang, central Nepal   DIETER SCHACHT

the same bed, *M. paniculata* will hybridise with *M. napaulensis* and this distinctive leaf colour will be lost. Planting it well away from potential mates could ensure its purity.

Meconopsis superba must reign supreme amongst the monocarpic group of Himalayan poppies. Its ample silver-haired rosettes produce flowering spikes up to 5 ft. (1.5 m) in height carrying flowers that appear from the leaf axils on the stem. Each flower is of the purest white, four-petalled, sometimes more than 3 in. (8 cm) across, with the noted feature of a striking, deep purple-black stigma. Propagation is, as with all these monocarpic species, by means of seed best sown at the end of the year in an acid-loam compost. Sow thinly, otherwise rotting will cause heavy losses. This lovely species generally takes at least three to four years to flower from seed.

A distinct and fine plant I heartily recommend primarily for its foliage

Meconopsis napaulensis, rosette, Langtang, central Nepal
DIETER SCHACHT

is the Nepalese species *Meconopsis dhwojii*, introduced by Stainton, Sykes and Williams. It is ideal in the woodland setting where its rosettes of highly dissected leaves are a showy purple-bronze shade. The lemon-yellow flowers are held in graceful panicles.

As indispensable as the monocarpic meconopses are, the perennial blue poppies take centre stage in June and July when their glorious flowers draw every eye. Though I am recommending these plants for the woodland, they will thrive equally well in an open, sunny aspect, provided sufficient shelter can prevent the flowering stems from wind damage. In fact I must emphasise that a densely shaded woodland garden may be unsuitable for the perennial species of *Meconopsis*. A sunny glade is the premium position in the woodland to create a large bed with soil that is several feet deep and naturally fertile.

I will endeavour to focus on some of the finest, both in flower and constitution, from the wide choice of both species and hybrids available. The species most easily raised from seed and most widely available is *Meconopsis betonicifolia*, Kingdon Ward's introduction from Tumbatse in south-eastern Tibet in 1924. He said of his first sighting of the plant, "Among a paradise of primulas the flowers flutter out from amongst the sea-green leaves like blue and golden butterflies" (Fletcher 1975). What a horticultural achievement his introduction proved to be. Variable in both flower colour and stature, it is a very special herbaceous plant. It is strongly perennial yet benefits from regular division of the clumps every three years in March or early April just as the new foliage begins to appear, thus making it easier to discern where to part the clumps. As with all the perennial species and hybrids, never allow it to flower in the first season. Yes, it is hard to remove that first flower bud, but doing so will assure annual production of blossom forever. At flowering *M. betonicifolia* will attain 2- to 3-ft. (60- to 90-cm) stems carrying many flowers varying from sky-blue through to palest blue. It also produces a fine white form, *M. betonicifolia* 'Alba'. Where an alkaline or limy soil is prevalent, flower colour may be purple, causing disappointment for some.

The highly variable *Meconopsis grandis*, closely related to *M. betonicifolia*, is to be found in Nepal, Sikkim, Bhutan and south-eastern Tibet. Such a wide distribution indicates not surprisingly considerable variation in form. Personal taste may dictate whether to choose a more lance-olate-leafed form from Nepal or the lobed variety from Tibet. Without doubt the clone previously known in horticulture as *M. grandis* 'George Sherriff 600' is one of the easiest to grow and finest in flower. The confusion surrounding this name and the various plants offered in the trade has always been a puzzle to me. When Ludlow and Sherriff sent seed home under this collection number various packets would have been sent to gardens and nurseries alike. Plants would have been raised and, as in the case of those grown in a nursery such as Jack Drake's of Aviemore,

Meconopsis betonicifolia, Schachen Garden, southern Germany DIETER SCHACHT

Scotland, they would have been subsequently offered to the public. Some variation is inevitable together with obvious similarities. For this reason we should expect considerable variation in form when purchasing or viewing plants under this name. The selections named *M. grandis* 'Branklyn' and 'Jimmy Bayne' are both from this introduction and merit a place in the woodland garden. Each of these form healthy clumps in three years, after which they need division. In moist, rich soil stems can reach 3–4 ft. (90–120 cm) with plentiful, dark blue flowers hanging down with their orange-yellow anthers in June and July.

The Meconopsis Group was formed in Scotland in 1998 to try to clarify the identity and nomenclature of the perennial blue meconopsis currently being grown in gardens. At a meeting held on 10 June 2000, the group unanimously decided to adopt a new name for *Meconopsis grandis* 'George Sherriff 600'. Since clearly several different plants were in commerce under this name, they agreed to adopt the name *M.* George Sherriff Group in accord with the *Intertantional Code of Botanical Nomenclature*.

The natural hybrid between the two species *Meconopsis betonicifolia* and

Meconopsis betonicifolia 'Alba', Schachen Garden, southern Germany
DIETER SCHACHT

M. grandis is *M. ×sheldonii,* easily the finest for the garden of all blue poppies and a prime choice for the woodland garden. *Meconopsis ×sheldonii* was raised by W. G. Sheldon in 1934 at Oxted in Surrey, England. It fully deserves its 1937 Award of Merit from the Royal Horticultural Society. This hybrid is widely offered in the trade, raising some confusion as to the validity of the name. The Meconopsis Group concluded that the name *M. ×sheldonii* should be given only to the clone that won the Award of Merit. At this time, a new name has not been chosen for this group of hybrid forms, but I am comfortable that the plant pictured in this book is the Award of Merit plant with the correct and valid name. In the garden, this hybrid is hard to surpass, as it produces 4-ft. (1-m) stems with many nodding turquoise-blue flowers blooming over a long period in the summer. This vigorous grower is best planted in the spring. Division, as mentioned earlier, should be carried out in the spring every three years. After some six years, or after two divisions, I recommend moving the planting of *Meconopsis* to a new bed of "virgin soil" or at least to a bed which has been utilised for a different type of plant. Soil sickness is a logical result of monoculture and one which can only be overcome by good husbandry.

A pollen-fertile strain of this hybrid, named *Meconopsis ×sheldonii* 'Lingholm', has been developed and disseminated by Mike Swift, head gardener at Torosay Castle, Isle of Mull, Scotland. Now widely available, this is a fine and beautiful blue poppy with the added virtue of copious seed production.

No bed of blue poppies would be satisfactory without some companion to enhance and share the beauty. I suggest interplanting stands of the taller primulas which can be lifted and divided along with the poppies as they break into growth in spring. I cannot overemphasise here that such a bed will require an abundance of moisture during the growing season through the leaky pipe or similar means of ground irrigation. Suitable *Primula* species to join this bed would be those from the section *Sikkimensis* as classified by Wright Smith and Fletcher (1948), together with some from the section *Candelabra*. The candelabra primulas are often recommended for a bog garden, too. From the richly fragrant choices in the section *Sikkimensis* come the finest forms of *P. sikkimensis* found growing throughout the Himalaya. It is a true classic from the region, like the blue poppy, with rich umbels of up to twenty pendent, yellow flowers on 3-ft. (90-cm) stems. Closely related is the burgundy-coloured species *P. waltonii* encountered amongst *Meconopsis grandis* in Bhutan. A variable species found growing abundantly in the Tsari region of south-eastern Tibet is *P. alpicola,* also closely related to *P. sikkimensis* and reportedly crossing freely with it in that region. In its true form, the species is quite distinct with its leaves narrowly oval and rounded at the base. The flowers again held in umbels are fragrant and found typically in shades of lemon-yellow, white and purplish blue.

Fine drifts of the candelabra primulas are highly recommended for the woodland with their variety of colours. The only true woodland species is the Japanese endemic *Primula japonica,* but those from the Himalaya will grow admirably in a man-made woodland setting. The golden yellow flowers of *P. helodoxa* offer a glowing contrast to the blue poppies. This species is so closely related to *P. prolifera* that any confusion of nomenclature should not concern us as gardeners. Rather let it be known that these two species are evergreen members of the section *Candelabra.* *Primula helodoxa* was first introduced from Yunnan by Forrest. It has flowering stems often in excess of 3 ft. (90 cm) bearing up to seven whorls of wonderful golden yellow flowers. A mixed planting of *P. bulleyana* or *P. chungensis,* both orange flowered, with the purple-red *P. pulverulenta* make for a fine show. Hybrids are produced freely, including pleasant pastel shades. Once this marriage of *Primula* and *Meconopsis* has become established it is hard to imagine a finer sight in the woodland glade than this summer's day view.

PETIOLARID PRIMULAS

To conclude this discussion of the woodland garden I would like to devote some time to the *Primula* species of the section *Petiolares,* a group quite variable in their natural habitat. A very successful way of growing these popular primulas was pioneered by horticulturist-plantsman Alex Duguid, who ran Edrom Nurseries in south-eastern Scotland for many years with The Misses Logan Home. He utilised a natural birch (*Betula pendula*) woodland in which he had planted a number of the larger-growing *Rhododendron* species introduced by Kingdon Ward and Ludlow and Sherriff. Always taking great pains to try and re-enact the conditions a plant enjoys in its native habitat, Duguid reproduced almost the exact home conditions for the lovely *Primula whitei* (synonym *P. bhutanica*), found growing in Bhutan. Here is Sherriff's description of the natural habitat he and Ludlow saw in 1937: "We crossed the Lamse La [12,400 ft., 3780 m] where, in the thick *Rhododendron* and *Abies* forest, a rich reddish-pink form of *R. hodgsonii* was very abundant along with the pale lemon-yellow *R. campylocarpum,* the bright red *R. smithii* and the salmon-pink form of *R. cinnabarinum.* This was the Phobsikha district and *Primula whitei* was in such profusion as to colour large areas of the steep damp slope of the *Rhododendron* forest with delft-blue or pale blue-violet. Every time I see that primula I think it is the prettiest one I have ever seen and always I feel elated however many times I see it" (Fletcher 1975).

Although I have never seen *Primula whitei* in the wild, I can echo Sherriff's conclusion from my own horticultural experience of the species. The secret of success with this plant and all the petiolarid primulas found in the temperate zone is to find a cool, slightly sloping site in dappled shade, with an acid soil at least 1 ft. (30 cm) deep. Plant them in the spring in groups of five to seven to provide a fine show of spring colour. The first to flower, as early as February, is *P. whitei.* Overwintering, resting buds resemble mealy hen's eggs and gradually unfurl with a rosette of farinose, or mealy-textured, leaves and a beautiful posy of china-blue flowers. To protect both the flowers and the farina it may be beneficial to cover the plants with a well-secured pane of glass. After flowering, during a damp spell in May, divide congested clumps and keep them moist during their period of transition and re-establishment.

Some clones of *Primula whitei* are sterile, but others are fertile. When seed is set the capsules will swell to the point at which the seeds become clearly visible through a thin layer of tissue, in late spring to early summer, prior to the fruit opening and dispersing the contents. At this moment before the capsules open, collect the capsules, open them and carefully lay the seeds onto a piece of card. Sow the seeds immediately in a soil-based seed compost, covering them with a thin layer of sharp sand. Germination sometimes takes place in the autumn but more frequently the following spring. This method of seed harvesting and immediate sowing is most prominently necessary amongst the petiolarid primulas.

Other species I would suggest for this woodland bed, to accompany *Primula whitei,* would be the easily grown and most widely available pink-flowered *P. gracilipes* found widespread in the Himalaya. *Primula edgeworthii* (synonym *P. nana*) from the western Himalaya is variable in colour from lavender-blue to pink and pure white. A splendid hybrid between *P. whitei* and *P. edgeworthii,* raised by the sharp-eyed Margaret and Henry Taylor of Invergowrie, Dundee, is *P.* 'Tantallon' with heavily farinose foliage and glowing, dark blue flowers in February and March. The sterile hybrids such as this one may need more regular division. A personal favourite of mine is the late-flowering effarinose introduction of Ludlow and Sherriff found close to the Bhutan-Sikkim border, *P. petio-*

Primula gracilipes flowering in October, Lamjung, central Nepal
DIETER SCHACHT

laris (L.S.19856). I named a selection *P. petiolaris* 'Redpoll' due to the nomenclatural confusion surrounding this species and the number of wrongly named plants masquerading under the name *P. petiolaris.* 'Redpoll' forms a tight, green rosette with a disc of purple buds nestling through the winter until April when they open out to the most vivid plum-red flowers. It is a remarkably robust plant for a 1949 collection, remaining highly resilient against attack from virus. It is not known to produce seed yet benefits from being divided up and replanted.

Finally for the petiolarids, I suggest seeking out good forms of the variable *Primula boothii,* seemingly widespread in the Himalaya although often collected at lower elevations. The late George Smith once collected a fine form of this species in Nepal with typically purplish, effarinose foliage and a beautifully fringed flower of a pinkish purple shade. A later in-

Primula edgeworthii, Edrom Nurseries, Berwickshire JIM JERMYN

troduction was made by Tony Schilling, *P. boothii* (S.2634), from the Annapurna district of central Nepal, and his white form, *P. boothii* var. *alba,* has maintained good constitution. This species is easily grown and even more easily propagated, making it meritorious in horticultural terms.

During a cooler, damp spell in August the clumps of *Primula boothii* can be lifted and divided to good effect, but during the process the leaves practically fall away from the rosette. With a little care, glean leaf cuttings by severing the best quality mature leaves that have a little axillary bud already formed at the base of the leaf blade. Prepare a seed tray with an open compost of equal parts sphagnum peat and leaf mould or perlite. The leaf cuttings, each with an axillary bud, can now be placed into the compost at an angle. Make sure the leaf blade is well anchored down, but overly firming the soil is not advisable. Water in well and cover the tray with a thin film of polythene. Within a few months little plantlets will form from each of the leaf axillary buds. Keep them protected through winter and they will be ready for potting up in the spring or planting back into a suitable bed. Other petiolarid primulas can be propagated this way successfully, including *P. petiolaris, P. gracilipes* and *P. irregularis.*

These are my personal choices for planting in the woodland garden. They represent just a few species of those found in the vast Himalayan range. Before moving into the peat garden, which is in many ways a refinement of the woodland landscape, I want to focus on the increasingly popular genus mentioned in the first paragraph of this chapter.

PLEIONE

It always fascinates me how it is that first impressions can either make or break an experience, depending on how the image was presented. Serving my apprenticeship at both W. E. Th. Ingwersen's in Sussex and in the Botanic Garden in Munich, I encountered beautifully grown pleiones, and they made a great and favourable impression on me. Since those early days, I have never given them the attention I desired, due to my specialising in hardy alpine plants. Pleiones should be regarded as subjects for pot culture, not for the open garden.

In Germany, pleiones have been called windowsill orchids, appropriately so, for indeed they may be given a cool but frost-free environment during their winter dormancy. This member of the orchid family, Orchidaceae, has been accorded the much needed scrutiny of botanists and taxonomists with the results being published in the form of an up-to-date monograph by Cribb and Butterfield (1999). A number of species have recently been rediscovered in the wild and introduced into cultivation, bringing their total number to about fifteen. They are not truly terrestrial or epiphytic species but tend to grow mainly on the deep litter in forest glades and on moss-covered rocks, old tree stumps and commonly

Habitat for pleiones, Lamjung, central Nepal DIETER SCHACHT

on the lower branches of trees. They are generally found at cooler altitudes ranging from 3300 ft. (1000 m), in the case of *Pleione formosana* in Taiwan, to 13,100 ft. (4000 m). Although technically considered to be semi-epiphytic pseudobulbs, they may be regarded as easily grown. Their main requirements are a cool rest or dormancy in winter, a humus-rich compost which will hold air as well as moisture and a regime of feeding during the summer growing season in order to build up the next-season's pseudobulbs. As well as feeding, maintaining humidity around the plants is very beneficial, as is protecting them from direct sunlight at the hottest part of the day. If species such as the deep yellow *P. forrestii* are the most exciting and sought after, being from Yunnan, the ones found in the "true" Himalaya are still highly desirable.

The species that may be encountered fairly readily in the Himalaya, most notably in central Nepal, are *Pleione praecox, P. humilis* and *P. hookeriana*. In 1992, the species *P. coronaria* was rediscovered by a team of Oxford University botanists in the Ganesh Himal, first having been discovered by Adam Stainton in 1962. I will concentrate on the first three species and add a few notes on this last one.

Pleione praecox is an extremely variable species widely distributed from the Uttar Pradesh to south-eastern China growing on the moss-covered trunks of trees such as *Rhododendron arboreum* or steep mossy banks. It is generally found at altitudes between 5900 and 8200 ft. (1800–2500 m). The pseudobulbs are barrel-shaped with a short conical beak, showing a characteristic green and maroon mottling. The flowers are borne on a short stalk, rose-pink in colour, white within with yellow markings on the teeth. In nature it generally flowers in October and November but in cultivation more usually in September and October. Despite flowering in the autumn, this species still requires a winter rest as with the spring-flowering types.

The long-term survival of these Nepalese species of *Pleione* is under threat. Although great efforts are being made both in the Himalaya and in China to control deforestation, there are areas such as in central Nepal where late-1990s observations would suggest the contrary. The main reason for felling these old endemic trees, such as the great firs (*Abies spectabilis*) and hemlock (*Tsuga dumosa*), is to open up grazing pastures. The trees are ring-barked, or girdled, and left to die. This is sad, and it is hoped that help will be given to the local people to encourage less destructive practices in the pursuit of land for grazing.

For lovers of these orchids a visit to central Nepal would be well rewarded in May or June when the thrill of scrambling up through forests of *Abies* and *Rhododendron arboreum* culminates in masses of *Pleione hookeriana*. Some have observed "an individual fir tree supporting colonies [of pleiones] in 'successive pillows' of moss well over 65 feet [20 m] up into the crown of the tree" (Kretz 1987). The habit of this species is unique in that it has the ability to reproduce by means of stolons. The

Pleione praecox, flowering in October, Lamjung, central Nepal DIETER SCHACHT

flower colour varies widely from pure white to shell-pink with the lip-markings often lightly tinged with yellow. It will rank as one of the most beautiful of all pleiones but is a little more challenging to grow, no doubt due to the cooler conditions in which it is growing and the often densely shaded sites.

Observations in the field, most notably amidst the ancient Dharchy forest, lying at 9800 ft. (2990 m) in central Nepal, suggest that another species, *Pleione humilis,* often grows with *P. hookeriana*. It is rather unlikely that they will hybridise as their flowering periods do not overlap. *Pleione humilis* generally commences flowering in late January whereas *P.*

Pleione hookeriana in cultivation DIETER SCHACHT

hookeriana flowers in May or June. *Pleione humilis* is an outstanding species easily recognised in flower with its lips heavily marked and spotted with dark red, contrasting with the white to rose-pink petals. Rather typically it is found growing in thick moss on the branches and trunks of rhododendrons. The forest in central Nepal consists of gnarled, old specimens of *Rhododendron arboreum* up to 50 ft. (15 m) in height with an understorey containing *Daphne bholua*, *Sarcococca* and *Pieris*.

The pseudobulbs of *Pleione humilis* vary greatly in shape and colour, but they are generally flask-shaped with a long neck and olive-green in colour. In cultivation this species is often the first to flower in February, after which it has a short rest and then produces new roots at the end of March. By contrast *P. hookeriana* is latest of the spring-flowering species, blooming in April or May. Curiously, *P. humilis,* while slow to increase, often produces up to fifty tiny bulbils from the top of the old pseudobulbs.

Rhododendron arboreum, Langtang, central Nepal
DIETER SCHACHT

The final Himalayan species and the last one recorded is *Pleione coronaria,* confined to a restricted area in the Ganesh Himal. Often encountered on a blanket of moss, it may choose a variety of woody hosts, most commonly *Tsuga dumosa* but also *Rhododendron barbatum.* It occupies habitats between 8500 and 9200 ft. (2590–2810 m) in altitude, possibly flowering in April and May. When it was first found by Stainton, it was regarded as a pink-flowered variant of *P. humilis,* but distinctions separate the two species. In the case of *P. coronaria,* the flower is made up of the characteristic petals and sepals together with the most prominent lip, or labellum. With most pleiones, and markedly so in *P. humilis,* the margin of the lip is crinkled and fringed, but in *P. coronaria* the margin is made up of a row of entire lamellae, or ridges of callus. *Pleione coronaria* may be found growing with *P. humilis* but this latter species can be spotted easily when in growth by its characteristic medusa-like heads of young bulbils sprouting from the crowns of the previous year's pseudobulbs.

Pleione humilis in cultivation WILHELM SCHACHT

I hope that the restricted locality of this unique species will be protected from the ravages of deforestation, but another danger threatens. From time to time, these pleiones are offered by wholesale nurseries in Nepal to European customers. On one occasion 5000 pseudobulbs of *Pleione coronaria* were offered in the trade after being collected in the Ganesh Himal. This species is ranked as vulnerable by the International Union for the Conservation of Nature, which should encourage us as gardeners to be sure to purchase nursery-grown material and not wild-collected plants.

For those just starting out with these lovely orchids, a few tips on cultivation may be beneficial. The best containers for growing pleiones are clay pans up to 6 in. (15 cm) in depth. Normal pans are 3 in. (8 cm) in depth, but however deep, they must have plenty of drainage holes. The compost may be quite simple or more complicated in formation—a popular and simple formula is one part coarse grade perlite, one part composted bark, and one part chopped sphagnum moss for retaining moisture. It is this last ingredient which is most important for the Himalayan species, as the habitat has indicated.

After the summer growing season, pleiones will go dormant during the autumn, with the exception of the Himalayan *Pleione praecox,* which flowers late and rests during the winter. By late November the leaves of all pleiones will have dropped and they will have no living roots. All pleiones are best grown in a greenhouse during the winter resting period. From resting until the flowering buds can be seen, the night temperature should be between 32 and 40°F (0–4°C). A greenhouse will need the provision of a supplementary heater to lift the temperature at night as an air frost will damage the pseudobulbs. The pans may alternatively be kept in a well-aired, cool but frost-free room in the home. All pleiones, whether they be autumn- or spring-flowering should be repotted during this rest period in late November or early December.

Having prepared our chosen compost with the suggested ingredients we will now take the cleaned pans and place a piece of 1/16-in. (1–2 mm) stainless steel mesh over the drainage holes to prevent the entry of pests. The slightly moist compost may now be placed in the pan nearly to the top. It should not be firmed in any way. The pseudobulbs are now carefully positioned about 1 in. (2.5 cm) apart and compost placed around them at about half their height. The compost at this stage, should be moist, but only just, as the young shoots are susceptible to rotting if it is too wet. As the flower buds begin to show, the night temperature should be held at about 42°F (5°C) with a corresponding rise of up to 42°F (5°C) in the day temperature due to the sun's heat. The first signs of aphids may appear now, and a thorough spray of a systemic insecticide will prevent damage from this pest to the emerging flowers. A little water may be given at this stage. At flowering time transfer the plants from the greenhouse where they were held over winter into a glasshouse or cold frame. Many people will keep them under glass all year round.

When the leaves start to form from late April onwards, take care to provide shading from direct sunlight. Once the flowers have gone over by late May, the leaves will be growing vigorously. At this stage give the plants a foliar feed with a nitrogen-phosphorous-potassium, or NPK, ratio of 2:1:1 (such as Chempak no. 2 in the United Kingdom) at one-third the recommended strength. Water this into the compost at weekly intervals.

At the end of May the pans may be removed from the glasshouse and transferred into a cold frame or a bench where they will receive light but be protected from the sun when it is at its maximum elevation in mid-June. During hot and dry spells take care to water the plants while ensuring that the compost never becomes soggy. It is best to allow the pans almost to dry out between waterings. The most beneficial action during such spells is to frequently dampen down the foliage with a fine rose attached to the watering can. In the evening after a hot day they appreciate an overhead spray.

Continue feeding until the leaves have reached full size in about early June. Then change the formula to reduce the nitrogen and increase the potash, or potassium, as this will help to ripen the pseudobulbs and produce flower buds. A recommended feed would be an NPK ratio of 1:2:2 (such as Chempak no. 8 in the United Kingdom). By the end of September the leaves will start to turn yellow, eventually turn brown and then fall off. Watering can be reduced and then ceased when the leaves have all gone.

Once the night temperatures begin to fall it is appropriate to bring the pans under cover again, either into a greenhouse or the house, where their moisture supply can be controlled. Whilst plants are still out in the open they may need some supplementary covering during long wet spells.

Pests and diseases are minimal with the exception of one very serious scourge. It is a minucx te, false spider mite by the name of *Brevipalpus,* which can just be seen with the naked eye as a tiny spot on the undersides of the pseudobulbs. It is the saliva that these mites secrete that is so harmful, causing the growth of leaves and roots to cease in severe cases or become stunted in slight attacks.

Commercial growers can utilise a chemical by the name of Childion which, when diluted to the recommended dose, is applied as a soak for the dormant pseudobulbs. Badly affected plants may have to be destroyed by the amateur grower until an effective control is supplied to the general public. Care must also be taken when purchasing new stock, to ensure it is free of *Brevipalpus.* It appears that both ivy and some ferns act as hosts for the pest so these should not be grown beside pleiones. Care must also be taken to control mice during the winter, as they will eat the pseudobulbs.

Propagation is quite simple. Lift the dormant pseudobulbs each year in early December and cut away all the dead roots. *Pleione* pseudobulbs are of annual duration only, so throw away the old shrivelled bulbs at this stage. With some species, each large pseudobulb should produce two or perhaps three flowering-sized pseudobulbs each year. These are about the size of a rosebud. The Himalayan species are slow to increase, but as mentioned before, *P. humilis* produces a mass of tiny bulbils which may be dibbled in to the same compost as that for the flowering-sized pseudobulbs. In the case of all these little bulbils it is best to cover them completely and exercise patience, as they will take two to three years to reach flowering size.

Each grower will no doubt experiment with a choice of compost formula according to the local prevailing growing conditions, but few rewards are greater than a crowded pan of pleiones in full flower. While the four Himalayan species may prove more challenging of culture than the countless hybrids raised from Chinese parents, they are a valuable part of the Himalayan flora and of immense importance in horticulture.

The Peat Garden

Many keen plantsfolk have found that employing a peat garden has served them well, providing an ideal home for a variety of plants, including many Himalayan species. Yet, some people will ask, will this type of landscape put further pressure on a commodity which is already under threat? I feel it wise to look at the use of peat from as wide a perspective as possible. Exercising conservation in the peat industry is undoubtedly important. At the same time we might look to countries like Russia, Finland and Latvia, just three lands in possession of vast reserves of peat which could be exported, providing welcome income to them without damaging the more fragile peatlands in other parts of the world.

One reason that this is a type of gardening that will have broad appeal is that it can be as large or small as desired. For example, the much-visited peat garden laid out in the Royal Botanic Garden in Edinburgh covers a large area, while I have just constructed one that fits into a shady corner, 10 by 6 ft. (3 by 2 m), and contains more than fifty plants. This type of feature is such a useful component in the Himalayan garden because (1) it is relatively cheap to construct, (2) it requires only a small area of land and (3) certain plant species thrive in this situation as in no other artificial setting. Dedicated gardeners will experience a greater measure of success with certain plants in a peat garden because of the environment's moisture retention, its extra coolness and its provision of unimpeded root run, the last of which is essential for many Himalayan subjects.

An early reference to peat walls appeared in the journal of the Royal Horticultural Society in 1927 in an article on Logan Gardens in the south-west of Scotland. At that time the owners constructed the peat walls to support terraces of soil in which were planted dwarf rhododendrons along with lilies, primulas and meconopses, many of which were new introductions that George Forrest and Reginald Farrer had collected in China. Later in the century, a number of famous gardens in the United Kingdom included peat gardens such as the Royal Botanic Garden in Edinburgh, the Savill Garden at Windsor Great Park and the Royal Horticultural Society's Garden at Wisley. These constructions have been in the main on a large scale.

Let me suggest a landscape on a smaller scale. Where space is restricted, a peat garden will open opportunities that simply do not exist with other types of gardening, provided that the peat blocks used in the construction are of good quality and are not allowed to dry out. The species I suggest, when planted between the blocks of peat, will send out runners helping to bind the blocks together and to break up a potential sterile look.

WHAT IS PEAT?

Peat is formed in several stages and develops in a variety of forms. The sequence of its development begins when water flows into a basin or hollow and the ground becomes sodden. The endemic flora in such a habitat is typically made up of sedges, cotton grass and various mosses, most notably sphagnum. These plants grow and die, and their residue falls to the bottom of the hollow, building up so that the water becomes shallower. As the dead plant material falls below the water level its decomposition continues in the absence of air, thus forming peat. This is known as basin peat.

This gradual development takes a very long period of time and at this stage the surface vegetation, predominantly sphagnum moss, begins to form the next type of peat known as raised bog or raised moss. Raised bog peat is the youngest peat, though still many thousands of years old, and typically in central Ireland it can be 30 ft. (9 m) deep. This young sphagnum peat can hold up to twenty times its own weight of water. This moisture retention is a great asset for growing some of the more challenging Himalayan species.

LOCATION & CONSTRUCTION

A peat garden can be constructed in a small space within a garden. Ideal sites for the peat garden are the north side of a building, perhaps a difficult north-facing slope, or the shady side of small trees and shrubs, yet not directly under their canopy. The small peat garden is essentially an attractive part contributing to the garden as a whole, yet it is very personal, perhaps the home for a collection of special plants and individual favourites that can only be grown successfully in such a dedicated habitat. I must emphasise that this is a home for lime-hating plants. Readers may think that because this is a specialised unit of peat blocks with an artificial acid soil infill, it can be constructed over an alkaline substrate. Sadly this will result in much extra work combating the effects of alkaline water leaching into the area from higher ground.

A good site is on a naturally sheltered gentle slope, yet not at the lowest point. Many of the plants for the peat garden are early flowering. Although the lowest point will attract beneficial moisture, notably on a light soil, it may also be a frost hollow. My experience shows that in April here on the east coast of Scotland we are almost always subjected to late, rolling radiation frosts that play havoc with early bloom and fresh growth. It would be grand not to need protective fleece spread all over the garden. Dwarf rhododendrons, cassiopes and even the new growth on some petiolarid primulas have been badly damaged, sometimes fatally, by late frosts. Do have this keenly in mind when choosing a site.

In consideration of where to locate the peat garden, I must relate an alarming experience with drips from an overhead deciduous tree canopy. I have never noticed any detrimental effects of planting any subjects directly in a natural woodland. That said, I once chose to site "in my nursery area" a collection of containerised stock plants, consisting mainly of hardy orchids and liliaceous species (*Lilium*, *Nomocharis* and *Cardiocrinum*), which meant putting them under a canopy of deciduous trees including hornbeam (*Carpinus*) and hazel (*Corylus*). During a wet spell in the summer months I noticed a sudden scorching effect on the lush foliage of the stock plants, which led to dire consequences. We all know the effect of industrially induced acid rain. Further study may reveal acids and other toxins that are released from the foliage of certain deciduous trees and the type of effects likely to be realised on susceptible plants. In the meantime I suggest caution.

An open, exposed site with a southerly aspect will almost assuredly cause a severe drying out of the project and a complete desiccation of the peat blocks. In dry areas supplementary irrigation will be necessary. Porous piping will prove beneficial for the plants while the peat blocks will need a gentle hosing down with an appropriate rose, or hose-end sprayer, in April, May and June.

Before constructing the peat garden the site needs to be cleared of any perennial weeds that could establish in the garden and prove almost impossible to eradicate. Obtaining the right peat blocks may prove to be a challenge. Look for a prime cut, a block of finest quality sphagnum peat, solid yet fibrous, in a block about 18 by 12 by 9 in. (46 by 30 by 23 cm). It sounds like being sent to the butcher for a prime cut of beef, and indeed so, we are just as concerned about the quality of peat blocks. Most suppliers are concerned with peat for fuel, but peat for burning is of no use in the garden. Be specific and ask for decent-sized blocks of the finest quality.

If the blocks are weathered and dry when delivered place them all in a tank of water, and weight them down until they have absorbed sufficient water to be useful for the construction.

To construct the peat bed, place the peat blocks as for bricks (see figure). The wall should always lean backwards, keeping the rear of the blocks in contact with the soil. Low walls of about 2 ft. (60 cm) high are easy to both construct and maintain. Position the blocks to give the impression, once the plants grow in, that they are bound together with plants, rather than being too much of a feature themselves, as are the rocks in a rock garden. One's artistic flair can come to the fore—the blocks can be cut with a sharp bread knife to any desired size. The whole look can be quite informal according to one's desire.

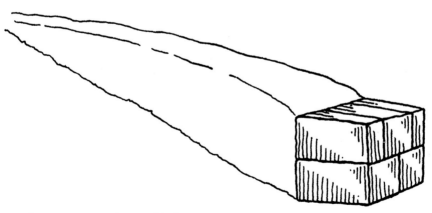

The correct way to lay peat blocks

Once the blocks have been positioned it is important that no air gaps remain either behind or between them. I recommend back filling with equal parts soil and granular peat, allowing for inevitable sinkage. Though peat is an inert substance that does not supply nutrient to the plants, no fertilisers should be applied prior to planting, as some of the chosen plants will want little or no added feeding. The only addition that I would consider at this stage, and certainly an integral part of this type of garden, is some stepping stones. Do not consider walking on the peat blocks. They would be severely damaged, and the very nature of the peaty soil that we have back filled with will not withstand footprints either at planting or for general maintenance. The stepping stones should not be overly intrusive but rather simply large enough for any work to be carried out without stepping on the soil.

Prior to positioning any plants it is important to be comfortable about the condition of the soil, allowing plenty of time for settlement. It would be beneficial to lightly tread the whole area then rake it over when it is not too moist and if necessary add further back-fill prior to commencing with planting.

SHRUBS & DWARF WOODY SPECIES

As with most types of gardening choose the larger plants first as a backbone for the intended landscape. A few shrubs may be selected for this purpose, one or two deciduous species with added autumn colour and some evergreens such as the dwarf rhododendrons. At this stage I must issue a mild word of warning about some wonderful shrubby species, particularly amongst the dwarf *Vaccinium* and *Gaultheria* species, that have the capacity to travel a little farther than is usually anticipated. Be cautious. For a modest construction, perhaps about 25 ft. (8 m) in length with a two-tier terrace and a total width of 9 ft. (2.7 m), let me recommend some fine Himalayan species to plant in both the walls and the bed area.

So wide is the choice of species and hybrids from the wonderful genus *Rhododendron* that restricted space will determine the range to plant in the peat garden. It may be that one or two species may be chosen primarily for their form and foliage colour rather than for their outright blossom. Here is a selection to choose from.

A relatively dwarf species of great note is *Rhododendron anthopogon,* widespread in the Himalaya and not surprisingly variable in habit and flower colour with forms as dwarf as 1 ft. (30 cm) and others up to 3 ft. (90 cm). A lovely cultivar to look out for is *R. anthopogon* 'Betty Graham' (L.S. 1091) with deep pink flowers. It earned an Award of Merit from the Royal Horticultural Society in 1969. Another fine one is *R. anthopogon* 'Annapurna' (S.S.W. 9090) with lemon-yellow flowers. *Rhododendron anthopogon* is certainly a first-class species with fine forms to choose from. In this type of garden I could not be without a few selections of the variable species *R. calostrotum,* with a wide distribution from northeastern Burma, now Myanmar, south-eastern Tibet and into Sichuan.

I wish I could understand the botanists' revisions of the genus *Rhododendron,* particularly regarding this species. As is so often the case, a gulf of difference resides between the view a scientist perceives through the microscope and the view a horticulturist develops through years of handling these plants—oh, for a sensible marriage between the two. I always refer to the common-sense view of *Rhododendron* as seen by Cox who often merges the classifications of both Cullen and Chamberlain with Davidian. The superb species *R. calostrotum* comes into this category of confused nomenclature. Look out for *R. calostrotum* subsp. *calostrotum* 'Gigha', awarded a First Class Certificate in 1971. It offers a lovely combination of masses of rose-crimson flowers over compact, glaucous foliage. *Rhododendron calostrotum* subsp. *keleticum* is a prostrate or mound-forming plant with neat foliage and large purplish crimson, widely funnel-shaped flowers. From a horticultural point of view this form should enjoy specific ranking rather than being sunk into the realms of *R. calostrotum.*

When choosing dwarf rhododendrons it may be a good idea to visit a garden collection of both species and hybrids to help make a personal choice from the vast array in the horticultural trade. A useful but variable species for the peat garden is *Rhododendron fastigiatum,* a native of Yunnan with a more compact, mound-forming habit than its name would suggest. Fine glaucous foliage and masses of light purple to blue-purple spring flowers adorn these low, up to 2-ft. (60-cm) bushes. When choosing a good blue-flowering species I could not go beyond *R. idoneum* from Yunnan and Sichuan, which I always felt gave the best true-blue-coloured flowers. But when checking out availability of this species I found confusion surrounding its name. In the reclassification of the genus *Rhododendron* by James Cullen and David Chamberlain in 1973, the name *R. idoneum* was lost, being sunk into the species *R. telmateium*, a quite different plant with lavender to rose-pink flowers. From a horticultural point of view *R. idoneum* would have been better retained as a separate taxon. Suffice it to say that this is a species well worth seeking from a specialist nursery. The modern hybrids, on the other hand, have made a great impact in horticulture the world over and have come into their own in this type of garden project. *Rhododendron* 'St. Merryn' is genuinely compact and a wonderful blue-flowered hybrid having *R. impeditum* and *R.* 'St. Tudy' as parents.

Moving on to some of the finest dwarf rhododendrons with yellow flowers, I have found *Rhododendron lepidostylum* to be reasonably hardy on the east coast of Scotland. It has a compact habit with wonderful silvery, glaucous foliage and large, pale yellow flowers in May. As far as award-winning hybrids are concerned, there are many to choose from. My preference would be the hardy range of hybrids raised by Peter and Kenneth Cox of Glendoick, Perthshire, in Scotland. Surely the reason for producing a hybrid is to enhance the vigour of a plant and reproduce a superior progeny. In the case of this genus the results can be very pronounced, as with the superb *R.* 'Chikor', proving to be one of the most popular of all dwarf hybrid rhododendrons, compact in habit with masses of pendulous, yellow flowers. It is a hybrid between *R. rupicola* var. *chryseum* and *R. ludlowii*. Another outstanding yellow-flowering hybrid with a spreading nature is *R.* 'Curlew', a sight to behold when in full flower in May. I love the unusually coloured hybrid raised by Ticknor in the United States, *R.* 'Shamrock', a cross between *R. keiskei* and *R. hanceanum* 'Nanum', forming a compact bush with chartreuse-yellow flowers.

To introduce some variation in height, I suggest *Rhododendron racemosum*, a species with a more erect habit widespread in the province of Yunnan. A variety of forms are available. *Rhododendron racemosum* 'Rock Rose' produces lovely clear pink flowers in profusion during April and May on erect bushes attaining 4–5 ft. (1.2–1.5 m). A plant showing a

Rhododendron rupicola var. *chryseum* with *Corydalis cashmeriana*, Schachen Garden, southern Germany DIETER SCHACHT

similar habit but dwarfer in stature is the hybrid *R.* 'Anna Baldsiefen', raised in the U.S., with clusters of vibrant, star-shaped pink flowers in April. A compact species widely available in the trade yet restricted in its distribution in nature is *R. sargentianum,* found in only a few localities in Sichuan. Forming dense mounds, this species generally displays flowers of a delicate cream to pale yellow. The hybrid *R.* 'Sarled' is the progeny of *R. sargentianum* crossed with *R. trichostomum*. It is similar to *R. sargentianum* with flowers opening pink and turning to white. Two of the showiest white-flowering hybrids making a significant contribution in gardens are the American *R.* 'Dora Amateis', proving a wonderful hardy addition with large white blooms lightly tinged pink and growing up to 2 ft. (60 cm), and Cox's *R.* 'Ptarmigan', which remains compact with a profusion of purest white flowers in late spring.

Meriting pride of place in the peat garden, yet at no time tolerating dry conditions, is *Rhododendron campylogynum,* widespread in the Himalaya from south-eastern Tibet to Yunnan. Over compact little bushes always are the joy of nodding, thimble-shaped flowers from May through to June, somewhat extending the season of rhododendron bloom. There are a number of clones and my experience is that once one meets the fascination of this species, the search is always on for better forms. *Rhododendron campylogynum* var. *myrtilloides* has mauve-pink thimbles, while *R. campylogynum* 'Bodnant Red' grows a little more erect and produces lovely crimson-red flowers.

I cannot conclude my list of recommendations from the seemingly endless supply of rhododendrons on offer without describing two rather rare and exciting species commemorating celebrated plant hunters. *Rhododendron lowndesii* was first introduced by Lowndes from the Marsyandi Valley of central Nepal in 1950. This little treasure demands a sheltered position tucked between peat blocks where the deciduous shrublet will form a neat mat studded with numerous flat, yellow blooms on erect pedicels. The second is Kingdon Ward's *R. pumilum* (K.W. 6961), known popularly as Kingdon Ward's Pink Baby, quite simply one of the most charming and pleasing of the dwarf forms amongst this significant genus. He would have been justly proud of his introduction, which gained an Award of Merit in 1935. It is distributed widely from eastern Nepal through Sikkim into south-eastern Tibet, where it is plentiful. Ludlow and Sherriff reported a local colony in the latter region displaying pure white flowers, what a fine introduction this would have been. The type species grows typically in a bun up to 9–12 in. (23–30 cm) with trusses of up to three pink, thimble-like flowers. Although the plant is fully hardy to 14°F (–10°C) and an evergreen, in harsher areas a cloche cover would be prudent.

I can tolerate panes of glass or cloches in the garden on few occasions, but I make exception for these two rhododendrons. They are distinguished plants requiring special position and glass cover during the coldest periods. Whilst training at the Munich Botanic Garden I was most impressed by the practical, yet labour-intensive method of contending with the hard winters by covering many parts of the rock garden and the more tender plants with branches from evergreen conifers. With specialised subjects such as these two rhododendrons, a few handfuls of loose, dry larch (*Larix*) needles collected from the current autumnal leaf drop can be tucked around the plant as extra protection in addition to the more substantial cover provided by the branches. By employing practical methods such as these it is possible to grow a wider range of plants, including some of the more tender subjects, with no fear of the ravaging effects of winter.

Moving away from rhododendrons but remaining within the Ericaceae, the heather family, I would like to introduce a few members that will form the backbone of the peat bed. The genus *Cassiope* includes a number of Himalayan species and garden hybrids which have made a massive impact both in gardens and horticulture. In my nursery business, I have found the greatest sales in general usually come between the months of April and June, which coincides with popular flower shows where exhibits of spring-flowering plants have included bold shrublets of *Cassiope* hybrids hidden with a snow-like cover of white bells. A more eye-catching sight is hard to create.

I cannot overlook another abiding memory of the spring shows of the Scottish Rock Garden Club, really amateur classes held around the major towns and cities in Scotland. I recall the sight of the late Harold Esslemont and Jack Crossland carrying huge pots of *Cassiope wardii* bulging with hairy, whipcord-like foliage clothed with myriads of wholesome, hanging creamy-white bells. Long before the judges carried out their duties, I would cast a mere glance at such a beautifully grown specimen and promptly reach the personal decision that, yes, another Forrest Medal

Cassiope wardii, Inshriach Alpine Nursery, Aviemore JIM JERMYN

for the most meritorious plant in the show would go to the now-celebrated growers. One day it was my pleasure to welcome Crossland and his wife at our nursery, and prior to their tour around the garden Crossland opened up the boot of his car to reveal a huge pot with a specimen of *C. wardii* growing in a mass of live sphagnum moss. He could no longer manage the growing and showing of such plants and wanted to pass on this multi-medal-winning specimen. I felt a great weight of responsibility as he added wistfully, "You'll have cuttings rooted in no time and offer it in your catalogue!" Here is a subject almost impossible to strike from cuttings, yet it is easily propagated by layering or by disentangling the underground stems with their tiny root hairs and bringing them on in a pack of sphagnum moss. Crossland's generosity is a feature of a generation now passing away, but hopefully those of us now shouldering the charge of growing such choice plants will emulate our predecessors in encouraging youngsters into the wonderful pastimes of horticulture and gardening.

Cassiope wardii (L.S.T. 4734) was first collected by the late Sir George Taylor in south-eastern Tibet by the Tsangpo Gorge, and must surely be one of the most striking and beautiful of all the Himalayan species. He found it growing amongst rhododendrons on open moorland as well as in large colonies on exposed gravel banks where it must have been a sight to behold with its fastigiate branches of tightly ranked leaves covered with silvery, silky hairs and huge white bells. In the peat garden, it is crucial that the site for these splendid cassiopes when flowering in April and May will be protected from the first sunlight following a late frost which will most assuredly spoil the blooms. A plant association including this *Cassiope* noted by Ludlow and Sherriff in south-eastern Tibet would be well worth re-enacting in our gardens; it includes *Omphalogramma vincaeflorum* and nivalid *Primula calliantha* along with *Lilium souliei* and *L. nanum*. This combination uses the very nature of these spreading evergreen cassiopes to provide just the protection the other subjects are looking for. I will turn again to omphalogrammas near the close of this chapter.

A second species of *Cassiope* is the exquisite *C. selaginoides,* available in the trade under its superlative form *C. selaginoides* (L.S.13284), which gained an Award of Merit in 1954. It is akin to *C. wardii* yet exhibits narrower, erect whipcord growth while still showing off its immense white globular flowers held well clear of the foliage. A number of easily grown hybrids of great horticultural merit were raised by the late R.B. Cooke of Corbridge, Northumberland. Two such hybrids are both readily available in the trade. *Cassiope* 'Muirhead' is the finest of all hybrids, claiming its parents as *C. wardii* and the Japanese native *C. lycopodioides* and forming strong, compact shrublets with downy foliage and the characteristic white, bell-shaped flowers. *Cassiope* 'Randle Cooke' is parented by another fine Himalayan species, *C. fastigiata,* less often seen in nurseries, together with the prostrate *C. lycopodioides.* Although distinct, they bear a resemblance and are easily grown. *Cassiope* 'Randle Cooke' is generally more vigorous in habit and shows a less downy growth. It is a wonderful free-flowering subject for the peat bed.

Cassiope fastigiata DIETER SCHACHT

Both the genera *Gaultheria* and *Vaccinium* play an important role as valuable dwarf evergreen shrubs that serve to bind the peat blocks together, at the same time providing superb cover for some bulbous subjects. *Gaultheria cuneata* was introduced by Ernest Wilson from the Chinese province of Sichuan and forms wide, shrubby mats of wedge-shaped glossy foliage that assumes attractive reddish tints at the close of the season. In August, showy white fruits, or "orbs," are a highlight until visiting birds recognise their attraction. *Gaultheria nummularioides* is one of my favourite species ever since first enjoying its scrambling habit on the peat walls at Jack Drake's wonderful nursery near Aviemore, under the Cairngorm Mountains. It is found widespread in the Himalaya and was introduced on several occasions, including the expedition of Len Beer in eastern Nepal. The species is a superb prostrate subject with wiry shoots carrying its leaves in pairs with attractive pinkish flowers and purplish-black fruits. A few species with startling blue fruits are deserving of a position in the peat garden, including the much sought-after *G. sinensis,* introduced from Burma by Kingdon Ward. Foliage that produces attractive autumnal tints of reddish orange is perfect company for the large blue fruits. The two species *G. thymifolia* and *G. trichophylla* are similar, the latter being the stronger grower but both binding the peat blocks together in a most attractive way with neat foliage and greenish blue fruits in the autumn. All these gaultherias can be easily propagated from ripened cuttings—those from the new season's growth, also called soft wood cuttings—in the late summer or from seed. Carefully extract the seed from the fruits after they have been allowed to partially dry out, which will ease removal of the seeds from the pith.

Vaccinium serves a purpose similar to that of *Gaultheria*. The most popular species play host to the favourite berries collected on acid moorland and bogs and turned into tasty tarts, pies and sauces to accompany fine main courses such as venison. But instead of getting carried away with the culinary delights of this genus, let me return to the peat garden where a selection of these shrubs will provide fine background for some special *Nomocharis* species or liliaceous plants. If the garden can allow several feet of space a good choice would be the vigorous, large-leafed *Vaccinium glauco-album* (B.L.M. 251), found in eastern Nepal and reintro-

Fruits of *Gaultheria trichophylla*, Langtang, central Nepal
DIETER SCHACHT

duced by Beer in 1972. Its oval leathery leaves are outstandingly glaucous on the upper surface, and large blue-black fruits appear in the autumn. At the other extreme is the neatly growing *V. moupinense*, which is somewhat similar to *V. delavayi*. My experience has been that the attractive evergreen foliage reliably colours to a lovely orange in the autumn, giving the peat garden valuable late colour. Another distinct dwarf species is the Himalayan *V. nummularia* noted for its bristly, arching shoots with double rows of small attractive leaves. The rose-red flowers are held in dense clusters and followed by edible black berries.

BULBS & CORMS
The following subjects may not immediately seem to conform to the category of bulbs and corms, but a rather thin line differentiates a tuber-

ous root and a non-tuberous root or a bulb and a plant with a persistent leaf base. A bulb can be formed in several different ways. Think of an onion as a classic bulb; it consists of swollen fleshy bases of leaves. A corm such as typified by the crocus is a swollen stem base often surrounded by the dry bases of old leaves. A potato, then, is a fine example of a swollen underground stem, often called a stem tuber or rhizome. A root tuber is a fleshy root which may be single or branched as in *Roscoea*. Armed with these basic botanical explanations I would like to highlight a few genera that simply thrive in the peat garden situation and provide much of the "cream," as it were, for this mini landscape.

Many of the Himalayan species of *Lilium* have been considered difficult, possibly as many gardeners have attempted to grow them either in pots or in too dry a situation. If there is a group that we in the trade will sometimes refer to as being a challenge—in other words nearing the impossible but not so as to detract from sales—it is the alpine species from the Sino-Himalaya that require cool, moist conditions yet never can be waterlogged. This challenging group, including *L. souliei* and *L. lophophorum*, should thrive in the peat wall when the specimens are planted directly between the blocks where they can be kept permanently cool. Two closely related species that require room to travel about as they spread by underground lateral stolons are *L. lankongense* and *L. duchartrei*. The former is found growing widespread in scrub and shrubberies in Yunnan and lends itself admirably to scrambling in amongst dwarf *Rhododendron* or *Vaccinium* where the 3-ft. (90-cm) flower stems can be held amongst the shrubs to show off the fine turk's-cap flowers, often up to six in number, of a pale rose-pink spotted with purple and beautifully fragrant. *Lilium duchartrei*, growing from Gansu to Yunnan in China, is of the same habit and stature but displays superb heavily spotted, white flowers. Both are easily propagated by lifting the bulbils during the dormant season.

A species that seems to have taken an unusually long period to enter the realms of horticulture, given its original introduction by George Forrest in 1919, is *Lilium henrici*. He found it in the Kong-Salween divide on the margin of thickets, and it is distributed locally in Yunnan. Growing up to 3 ft. (90 cm) typically, the plant has open hood-like flowers of pure white with a deep reddish purple blotch at the base of each petal, always much admired at flowering time in late June. It has a clear link with *Nomocharis* with which it could well be confused. Once obtained and established it presents no more of a challenge than *Nomocharis*. Another species closely related to *Nomocharis* is *Lilium oxypetalum* and its variety *L. oxypetalum* var. *insigne*. Both are easily grown and fit perfectly into the peat garden amongst dwarf rhododendrons. The type species from the western Himalaya grows to about 1 ft. (30 cm), carrying a single yellow nodding flower. The variety *L. oxypetalum* var. *insigne* grows a little taller and has somewhat fuller flowers more akin to *L. mackliniae* in a lovely dusky pink colour. The dwarfest of the Himalayan species is *Lilium nanum* found fairly widespread throughout the region, growing easily and producing 3- to 4-in. (8- to 10-cm) stems, each with generally a solitary, drooping, bell-shaped flower of purplish pink.

Two challenging plants should be given pride of place and sanctuary by planting their bulbs between the peat blocks to ensure fewer extremes of temperature and moisture content. The first is *Lilium lophophorum*, rather special but by no means difficult in this situation, found fairly commonly in open woodland and in alpine meadows with dwarf *Rhododendron* in Yunnan and Sichuan. Short stems of 6 to 9 in. (15–23 cm) carry a solitary pendent flower, rarely two or three flowers, akin to a lemon-yellow lantern. A wonderful species indeed is its neighbour *L. souliei*, found in the same area but often preferring humus-rich soils. Almost resembling flowers of *Fritillaria*, these once again solitary pendent bells are deep maroon in stark contrast to their yellow relatives.

Closely related to the lilies is the distinct *Notholirion* which produces a smaller bulb with a brown outer tunic. The most widely distributed of the species is *N. macrophyllum* found from western Nepal through to south-eastern Tibet at altitudes ranging from 9000 to 13,000 ft. (2750–3970 m). This easily grown plant is most suitable in the peat garden where it may be planted to good effect amongst dwarf rhododendrons. The height of the flowering stems may be as short as 9–12 in. (23–30 cm) in nature, but in the garden they may reach up to 2 ft. (60 cm) with up to five purple funnel-shaped flowers. As with other members of the lily family, Liliaceae, this species easily may be raised from seed with flowering expected some three years thereafter.

Another close relative is the liliaceous genus *Nomocharis,* often thought of as Himalayan plants for the aristocrat. The price of bulbs can indeed be prohibitive, but this simply reflects the number of years that nurseries patiently have taken to bulk up the bulbs to a saleable age from seed, generally around five or six years without unnatural forcing or overfeeding which can reduce the time period but also the quality. The peat garden is as fine a home as can be given to this outstanding genus. The cool conditions will certainly suit the bulbs. They are best left well alone once established, meaning that seed must be relied upon as the means of propagation. The nomenclature of this genus has received the attention of botanists since I commenced my apprenticeship, and I wonder what the late

Lilium nanum, Langtang, central Nepal DIETER SCHACHT

Mary Knox-Finlay of Keillour Castle would have had to say. She, along with her husband, grew these species together with many lilies to perfection. The specific names are of greatest importance when identifying material in the wild, in this case notably in the Sino-Himalaya. Once we have planted the bulbs of several species together in the peat garden and have begun saving the seed to propagate material, the resulting progeny will invariably share characteristics of each of the parents, revealing hybrids that will fit names such as the popular hybrids called *N. ×finlayorum*.

The name *Nomocharis* translated means "grace of the pasture," and appropriately so, for they are all truly outstanding plants whatever the name given to bulbs we purchase from the nursery. Two of the best-known spe-

Notholirion macrophyllum, Langtang, central Nepal DIETER SCHACHT

cies, *N. aperta* and *N. pardanthina,* have been reintroduced in the 1990s by the excellent expeditions organised by the Royal Botanic Garden in Edinburgh to that rich haven for plants, the province of Yunnan. These species were originally introduced into gardens by Forrest around 1914. They are so closely allied to lilies—the main difference is that the flowers of these *Nomocharis* species are much flatter and semi-nodding when fully open. *Nomocharis pardanthina* now incorporates the very popular *N. mairei,* which certainly does closely resemble it, and will grow up to 3 ft. (90 cm) in height with up to five flowers arising from the axils of the upper leaves. The flowers are ample in size, often up to 3 in. (8 cm) across, pale pink, blotched with purple, with the inner three tepals much broader than the outer and characteristically fringed along the margin. *Nomocharis aperta* is similarly distributed in Yunnan and Sichuan and is often found growing in moist soils amongst rhododendrons and the ground cover *Sorbus reducta.* Both these species are widely available in the nursery trade. Generally more slight of growth than *N. pardanthina, N. aperta* produces one to three terminal flowers often a deep pink with numerous small dots

Nomocharis pardanthina, Schachen Garden, southern Germany DIETER SCHACHT

and tepals without fringe. The final species available and easily grown in these conditions is *N. saluenensis,* similar to *N. aperta* but with broader foliage and dwarfer in stature. The large, open flowers are generally unspotted with a marked white throat. All *Nomocharis* species generally flower during June and July in northern Britain.

Take care when preparing a position for and planting any of these species or hybrids of *Nomocharis* and *Lilium.* Select a sheltered site where a dark evergreen background will set off the delicate pink flowers. The planting is best carried out in the spring with flowering-sized bulbs, about the size of a shallot, before they come into growth. Prepare a hole some 6 in. (15 cm) deep and incorporate a few handfuls of clean, gritty sand together with the peaty soil, and then plant the bulbs a good 3–4 in. (8–10 cm) below the surface. Gently firm the soil and carefully mark the site, adding a good watering to complete the job.

Closely related to both the genera *Lilium* and *Nomocharis* is *Fritillaria cirrhosa,* found in many parts of the Himalaya, Tibet and western China. Although variable, most forms are very beautiful and will grow satisfactorily in exactly the same position as the lilies, where they gain support amongst the branches of dwarf rhododendrons. The flowering stem will grow typically up to about 1 ft. (30 cm) with a solitary flower, broadly bell-shaped, green in colour with varying amounts of purple-brown and lovely tessellations, or chequers. *Fritillaria cirrhosa* may be raised from seed but takes up to five years to flower, as do the lilies.

Also in the lily family is a popular woodland plant performing admirably in the peat garden. *Paris polyphylla* is distributed throughout the Himalaya from Kashmir through to China. It is a rather curious creeping rhizomatous plant with leaves in a whorl and erect stems up to 12 in. (30 cm). The flowers are solitary surrounded by leaf-like perianth segments. The showy white-flowered form of *P. polyphylla* var. *yunnanensis,* is stunningly beautiful with lime-green to yellow perianth segments and a white ovary. This plant was introduced by the successful Sino-British Cangshan Expedition in 1981, giving it the collection number S.B.E. 1031. Once the fruit is ripe it may be opened to reveal attractive orange-red seeds. Along with simple division of the dormant clumps, propagate by sowing the seeds as soon as they have been collected.

A fascinating group of Himalayan plants deserving some prominent coverage for the peat garden is the genus *Roscoea*, a member of the ginger family, Zingiberaceae. Few of the sixteen species found in the Sino-Himalaya present any difficulty or prove tender when planted at least 6 in. (15 cm) deep in the peat garden. They all have curious fleshy roots of a rubbery texture which prove brittle when handled, but once established in the peat garden the plants will spread about, both underground and by seed. They are amongst the last of all deciduous subjects to re-emerge from the soil in May. The flowers are wonderfully exotic, reminiscent of terrestrial orchids with a large lower lip. To bring out their best I recommend a position that is not too shady. When planting, incorporate a generous amount of gritty sand to improve the immediate drainage around the roots. Because of their late-spring to early-summer emergence, take care with weeding to avoid damaging the dormant shoots. Most of the species flower throughout the summer months, giving colour to the garden at a most valuable time.

Fruit of *Paris polyphylla* in October, Lamjung, central Nepal
DIETER SCHACHT

Now to highlight some popular species and personal favourites that have made a notable impact in horticulture. The best known of all the species is *Roscoea cautleoides,* found growing abundantly in Yunnan. It varies in colour from its characteristic lemon-yellow, through white and pink to fine shades of purple. Growing typically to 12 in. (30 cm), the flowering stems carry several flowers in succession. Those who have seen them in the wild become ecstatic when encountering them growing en masse with their stemmed inflorescence held high, in clearings between rhododendrons and pine thickets. Indeed it is a privilege to witness a forest floor dotted with flashes of lemon-yellow. I am sure the few who really appreciate what they have seen must hold to these abiding memories for the rest of their days, just as the rest of us go back each year to our own favourite bluebell wood or orchid meadow, satisfied that such an

Paris polyphylla var. *yunnanensis* f. *alba,* Royal Botanic Garden, Edinburgh
JIM JERMYN

experience will keep us going until the following year. Surely that is just what gardening is all about—taking a relatively small area of ground and re-creating a patch of nature's unsurpassable beauty.

A later introduction is the easily grown *Roscoea tibetica* from western China, south-eastern Tibet and Bhutan. Once again this plant can be seen at its best in the Cangshan Mountains near Dali, Yunnan, carpeting the pine-needle-covered floor of the forest. It is, though, equally at home in lush meadows where it is seen growing up to 12 in. (30 cm) in height, looking somewhat similar to its western cousin *R. alpina* which has flowers varying in colour from deep purple to pinkish purple.

Some readers may be looking for the lovely species *Roscoea humeana*, occasionally found in cultivation. It, too, is common in Yunnan in all its mid-purple, white and rare yellow forms. I have experienced some difficulty growing this species in company with its cousins in a cool peat bed. This may be due to the fact that in nature it frequently grows in a limestone area with its root system firmly embedded in the limestone rocks,

Roscoea alpina, Langtang, central Nepal DIETER SCHACHT

quite the opposite conditions to those of the peat garden. *Roscoea purpurea* is amongst the easiest species to cultivate but requires more space due to its inherent vigour. It is very similar to *R. auriculata,* and the botanical differences between them I am bound to say are too minor to worry the gardener. *Roscoea purpurea* is fairly widespread in the Himalaya, with showy flowers generally pale lilac to mauve. A stunning variant found in the Ganesh Himal, Nepal, displays a remarkable burgundy-red flower. Thus far it is named *R. purpurea* 'Red Gurkha', but is not yet available in the trade. Though horticulture sometimes laments a major revision of a genus with its resulting name changes, the wonderful revision of *Roscoea* carried out by Jill Cowley and published in the *Kew Bulletin* in 1982 was much needed and widely accepted. I am a little baffled though by the name *R. scillifolia* given to two very distinct plants that are highly suitable for and worthy of a place in the peat garden. The first is a miniature form with soft pink flowers appearing in August and September only a few inches high and spreading happily by means of seed. The second is a plant I once grew under the name *R. yunnanensis.* Now considered a form of *R. scillifolia,* this plant is taller, growing up to 9 in. (23 cm), with distinct plum-black flowers. The propagation of roscoeas is quite simple, with the congested clumps easily but carefully divided during the growing season, which is short. Perhaps divide just after flowering. The root system, like a mass of elongated jelly babies, or jelly beans, is brittle and should be handled carefully. Tease apart the shoots and replant them deeply and firmly. As autumn progresses the leaves of roscoeas will elongate and the decaying flower-head will be well encapsulated in the sheath of upper leaves. A notable swelling will indicate the location of the seed capsules, which should be carefully removed and placed in a marked paper bag and hung to ripen in a shed with a few windows to let in natural light. The seeds can be sown around the turn of the year, and following germination they will often reach flowering size in two years.

A popular genus belonging to the campanula family, Campanulaceae, is *Codonopsis.* A number of its species will perform well in the peat garden provided a spot is found that is not too shaded. The genus falls into two groups, the first with carrot-like roots and the second with tuberous roots like potatoes. The foliage has a characteristic pungent smell when touched resembling that of a fox. Those with the odd-shaped potato-like tubers tend to be of a twining nature. Of two good twining species, *C. convolvulacea* is a fairly well-known species from the Himalaya through to western China. The tubers should be planted at least 6 in. (15 cm) deep at the base of a dwarf evergreen shrub such as a rhododendron or *Daphne retusa*. The fragile shoots will emerge in early summer and need a little help to reach into the branches of the neighbouring shrub. Wiry stems will intertwine with the shrub's branches and produce broadly bell-shaped, blue flowers with a marked reddish ring on the inside. *Codonopsis convolvulacea* 'Forrest's Form' has always been popular and has a larger flower and more pronounced inner ring. At one time a stunning white form was available in the trade as *C. convolvulacea* 'Alba', but it is now called *C. nepalensis* 'Himal Snow', a name which certainly conveys a little more than the old one. It is simply a very fine pure white form that is well worth looking out for. A second species I recommend was newly discovered in the late 1990s in the Langtang region of Nepal. Named *C. greywilsonii* it has broader flowers than *C. convolvulacea* that are pure white in colour—an exciting introduction.

Of the non-twining types surely the queen of the genus is *Codonopsis dicentrifolia* from Nepal. It has large, deep blue, scentless flowers chequered white within. It grows on ledges and in crevices on steep cliffs, and I strongly recommend positioning the carrot-like roots between the peat blocks and allowing a place for the attractive flowering stems to tumble down. A species widely grown but often mistaken for its close relative *C. clematidea* from Afghanistan, *C. ovata* is found in Kashmir. This easily grown species produces attractive downy foliage and erect flowering stems with solitary, pale blue, nodding bells beautifully marked within. This genus is important for the peat garden as it flowers late in the season, and with the exception of *C. dicentrifolia,* its species are not overly demanding of culture. All species are easily raised from seed.

To conclude the bulbs and corms I would like to highlight one of the great joys of the peat garden, *Corydalis,* plants that enjoy the cooler climes of Scotland, relative to the United Kingdom in general. *Corydalis cashmeriana* should thrive in a cool, sheltered peat bed. A member of the poppy family, Papaveraceae, this corydalis produces an intriguing root system made up of congested, loosely scaly bulbs with swollen radish-like roots from the base. These may be lifted carefully in the autumn and teased apart as a vegetative means of propagation. Part of this plant's attraction is the finely dissected foliage which serves as the base to the dense short racemes of brilliant blue flowers in late spring to early summer. Once established the plants will spread by seed, showing little in the way of variation. I have no doubt this subject would feature highly in everyone's top ten choices for the peat garden. It owes its introduction to Ludlow and Sherriff in 1933 from western Bhutan.

In the late 1990s, another exciting species was discovered farther east than the typical location of *Corydalis cashmeriana*. From eastern Nepal through to Sikkim comes the little known *C. ecristata*, first introduced by

Codonopsis ovata, Schachen Garden, southern Germany   DIETER SCHACHT

the late George Smith, a true champion of the Nepalese flora and an enthusiastic plantsman so free with his vast knowledge and experience. I
have happy memories of viewing slides with him at his home where he
would brim over with excitement in telling of screes under the massif of
Makalu (27,800 ft.; 8480 m) dotted with the legendary *Gentiana urnula*,
or of meadows in eastern Nepal with a spectacular form of *Primula calderiana*, a sumptuous burgundy-wine colour alongside forests of *Rhododendron cinnabarinum*. While implanting the desire to travel to the Himalaya,
these descriptions should give greater insight into the growing of these
wonderful plants. *Corydalis ecristata* is still hardly established in gardens.

Corydalis cashmeriana, Schachen Garden, southern Germany DIETER SCHACHT

Once available, this miniature twin of *C. cashmeriana* with its equally eye-catching, deep blue flowers should settle down nicely in the peat garden.

ANEMONE, PRIMULA & OTHER GENERA

Supporting a balanced view of continued plant hunting in the Himalaya is the impact on horticulture made by the late-twentieth-century introductions of members of the buttercup family, Ranunculaceae. Further field study of *Anemone* is required to clarify the picture of the complex group in the section *Obtusiloba* (*Trullifolia*). These species are ideal subjects for the peat garden where a reasonable amount of light is guaranteed. They can be easily propagated and will provide important flower colour over a long period of time. Anemones are a classic example of plants' adaptability to differing climates. Though they are generally encountered in the subalpine zone, anemones fit admirably in the peat garden, which provides conditions closely resembling those of the temperate zone. This kind of cross-over is frequently experienced in the garden.

Anemone obtusiloba is a clump-forming perennial found throughout the Himalaya as an alpine meadow plant with soft hairy foliage made up of three to five toothed or cut lobes. The lobes seem to vary considerably and I have not been able to sort out the proper identification of a form widely available in commerce, a dwarf form with hairless foliage. The flower colour is equally variable with white and blue predominating. A very fine sulphur-yellow form, which is commonly found in the western Himalaya, has been introduced by plantsman Ron McBeath and now is offered in the nursery trade as *A. obtusiloba* var. *sulphurea*. A firm favourite of mine is *A. obtusiloba* var. *patula* which I first remember seeing in a raised bed at that great enterprise for alpine plants, Ingwersen's nursery in Sussex. It has radiating flower stems bearing a seemingly unending supply of deep blue flowers. This is clearly an early introduction, I believe one of Kingdon Ward's from Upper Burma, though few records exist. How sad that this area and others like it have received little or no attention from plant hunters for so many decades due to political uncertainties. A wonderful opportunity beckons when people of varying ethnic groups can once again enjoy mutual trust and move freely amongst one another sharing the plant heritage given to us to enjoy.

One of the finest introductions from the botanical expedition to Cang-shan in 1981 was *Anemone trullifolia* (S.B.E. 797). This is clearly a close relative of *A. obtusiloba;* the most obvious difference is *A. trullifolia*'s un-stalked and wedge-shaped foliage with three main lobes and little or no toothing. The flowers commence in April and are always evident on es-tablished clumps throughout the growing season. White flowers seem to predominate over blue, which my daughter, fresh from a botany lesson at school, explained is to be expected due to the effects of a dominant and recessive gene. Her formula for figuring the percentage of white and blue is remarkably accurate, and in addition to giving her a lot of pleasure caused me to marvel at this positive aspect of science that has made such

Anemone obtusiloba, Kashmir DIETER SCHACHT

an impact in plant breeding. The white flowers generally have a blue back, and the powder-blue-coloured forms are more subtle and deserve some encouragement by reducing the white forms. The free production of seed is remarkable; it seems as if within a few days of flowering the ovaries are swelling and seeds, really achenes—fruiting bodies made up of fleshy seeds—are sitting waiting to be nudged from their seats. As with most buttercups, the seed should be collected when ripe and sown the same day in a loam-based seed compost. Germination will generally take place the following spring.

As private treks begin to be organised into Tibet, the exciting prospect arises of making limited seed collections of entirely new species or reintroductions of material known only in the literature or as herbarium specimens. A new plant was introduced from Tsari, south-eastern Tibet, in 1998, a botanical variant to the now popular *Anemone trullifolia*. The superb golden yellow–flowered form named *A. trullifolia* var. *linearis* will undoubtedly prove to be an extremely valuable introduction to horticulture and peat gardens.

An early-flowering member of the same family is *Adonis brevistyla,* now well established in gardens from its wide distribution in the Himalaya and western China. It is often found in open woodland growing in dark humus-rich soils. A deciduous, clump-forming species with characteristic dark green, ferny foliage, the plant has showy flowers in early spring that give it such value for the peat bed. Its 6-in. (15-cm) stems carry large, white buttercup flowers with a mauve tint to the back of the petals. I would not recommend lifting species of *Adonis* for division. Instead, look for seed which ripens in the same way as that of the anemones but with a tighter head of achenes which can be gently removed when ripe and again sown immediately to ensure success.

The peat bed is certainly an ideal home for a variety of Himalayan species of *Primula,* and it is going to be a challenge to know where to draw the line so as not to dominate the planting with too great a number of these lovely plants. Do excercise will power, because to tip the balance of genera in one direction, notably with the genus *Primula,* is very dangerous to the health of the entire garden. The well-known pest called the vine weevil has become a great problem in horticulture, occupying much of scientists' and nursery managers' time in the search for a safe and effective control. This appalling pest is most dangerous at the larval stage when the tiny grubs will ravage collections of plants, particularly primulas, in the space of months as they eat the roots of the plants to destruction. Chapter 7 discusses various types of control, but do take great care not to welcome the pest in a needless way by overplanting primulas.

Though primulas figure throughout this book, readers will no doubt find a brief description of the breakdown of sections in this vast genus *Primula* helpful here in this chapter. The species and section names familiar to most gardeners are those proposed in the classification of the genus as carried out in 1948 by Wright Smith and Fletcher. The work carried out in 1961 by Wendelbo is equally scholarly and follows a viewpoint based on the evolutionary chain. I choose to follow the more popular and more easily understood version by Wright Smith and Fletcher. To help familiarise readers with this classification, the botanical sections are given in the following headings, with Wendelbo's names in parentheses when appropriate.

SECTION *NIVALES* (*Crystallophlomis*)

The species belonging to the section *Nivales* are marked by their large, mealy overwintering, or resting, buds. The flowers generally form an umbel on a stout stem. Many species are challenging to grow, but the peat garden presents a fine opportunity for them. Finding a substitute for the winter snow cover that they experience in the Himalaya is a difficulty, and some will benefit from a cloche cover to protect the resting buds from winter wet.

Where space provides, I would plant a group of *Primula chionantha* and *P. chionantha* subsp. *sinopurpurea*. If planted together they will be sure to hybridise. The species is one of the largest and easiest to grow, with typically spear-shaped leaves, flower stems up to 18 in. (46 cm), and one or more whorls of pure white flowers. The flowers are purple-pink in the subspecies. Both these fine forms are commonly found in China in the provinces of Yunnan and Sichuan.

A widely distributed species found in Kashmir, Nepal and Sikkim is *Primula macrophylla,* a lovely species amenable to the peat garden. It is

Primula chionantha subsp. *sinopurpurea*, Schachen Garden, southern Germany
DIETER SCHACHT

more slender than *P. chionantha* but in its best forms has white, mealy foliage and 9- to 12-in. (23- to 30-cm) stems carrying an umbel of several blue to purplish flowers often with a dark eye. At high altitude in the western Himalaya, notably in Kashmir, is a dwarfer variety named *P. macrophylla* var. *moorcroftiana* well worth looking out for in seed exchanges.

Due to the wide distribution of *Primula obliqua* from eastern Nepal and Sikkim into Bhutan, it is only a matter of time before this species be-

Primula macrophylla, Schachen Garden, southern Germany DIETER SCHACHT

comes established in gardens. The peat bed is the ideal spot for it, for this species is tricky and resents disturbance. It will need to be raised from seed as with all the members of this section, and at an early stage the established seedlings should be positioned between the blocks where they will settle and eventually form a congested clump of overwintering buds that resemble golf balls. In spring these erupt to produce attractive foliage and umbels of pendent cream-coloured flowers with a pink flush, very special indeed. Fairly closely related is the Nepalese species *P. stuartii,* found in the Lamjung Himal with distinctively toothed leaves, bold stems, and an umbel of yellow flowers. As with *P. obliqua* it will appreciate the cool confines of the peat blocks as it is the summer heat that invariably causes failure with this lovely section of spring-flowering primulas.

Primula obliqua, Barun, eastern Nepal GEORGE SMITH

Primula stuartii, Schachen Garden, southern Germany DIETER SCHACHT

SECTION *MUSCARIOIDES*

Although the species of the section *Muscarioides* are often short-lived, one or two have made great impact in horticulture and merit a place in the peat garden. They all are easily raised from seed and should be planted in the spring in groups of five to seven to create some impact. They form deciduous, leafless, tiny, green overwintering buds often just below the soil surface, opening up in late spring to early summer with 6- to 9-in.

Primula muscarioides, Schachen Garden, southern Germany   DIETER SCHACHT

(15- to 23-cm) stems carrying a clustered head or spike of flowers that are generally sweetly fragrant. Most of the species are distributed within the provinces of China, but many are also to be found from Sikkim eastward through Bhutan and south-eastern Tibet. Although not strictly Himalayan in the truest sense of the term, some of the Sino-Himalayan species provide useful summer colour in the peat garden. The type species, *Primula muscarioides,* is found most commonly in Yunnan growing in moist alpine meadows. The impressive deep purplish-blue blooms are formed as deflexed flowers in a spike. A favourite species of mine from the same province of Yunnan is the more diminutive *P. pinnatifida,* which does well in a cool position, ideally situated in the peat bed. Typically hairy foliage with shorter 3- to 6-in. (8- to 15-cm) stems bear a flared blue to mauve-pink boss of fragrant flowers.

One of the longest established members of the section and most striking of all primulas is *Primula vialii* from Yunnan and south-western Sichuan. Often growing in damp meadows, it was introduced into gardens by George Forrest under the name *P. littoniana.* But it formerly had been discovered by Abbé Delavay and described as *P. vialii.* In the peat garden it will take centre stage in July when it is utterly compelling with its soft lilac, red-topped spikes held on 12- to 18-in. (30- to 46-cm) stems like Chinese pagodas. After flowering and the spikes have turned golden brown, the stems may be cut and stored in paper bags, where the seed capsules will further ripen to be ready for winter sowing. Removing the fruiting stems will leave the plant with some vigour for several years of flowering, but the green resting buds are apt to be lifted out of the peaty soil by the frost and remain very susceptible to rotting. It is therefore helpful to cover the whole planting area of this primula with a generous supply of dry larch needles or peat and anchor this down with branches. The whole lot can be removed in the spring whereupon the buds will break forth into growth very late in May to repeat the flowering cycle.

SECTION *SOLDANELLOIDES*

The close affiliation between the sections *Soldanelloides* and *Muscarioides* gives a very clear indication of the development of the migration of the *Primula* species within this area of the Sino-Himalaya, the epicentre for the original movement of *Primula*. Yet how fascinating it is to observe the physical lines of demarcation built into each botanical section, preventing a disorderly, chaotic mish-mash amongst these lovely plants in this part of the world. Intra-sectional hybrids are known in horticulture but they are generally weak and short-lived. Such a hybrid arose during my time at Edrom Nurseries when an intermediate formed between *P. vialii* and *P. flaccida*.

The section *Soldanelloides* is more of an alpine group, more specialised, and the species very often grow in alpine turf or on moss-covered rocks. The inflorescence may be spicate or capitate but is generally made up of one or more nodding bell-shaped flowers. The powerful fragrance is prominent, and all may be easily raised from seed. The species are found from Kashmir through Nepal, south-eastern Tibet and western China. Due to their natural habitat, they should be protected from extremes of temperature in both summer and winter, and the overwintering buds must be kept dry during the winter months. Apart from these cautionary words they are amongst the finest of all plants for the peat bed, demanding the special care such aristocrats deserve.

An easy and robust plant from north-western Yunnan and south-western Sichuan growing in open pine forests and rocky pastures is *Primula flaccida*, formerly *P. nutans*. This superb species was introduced by George Forrest in 1914, and I believe it has not been reintroduced since, rather surprisingly given its distribution. The spike-like inflorescence gives it the close affinity to species of the section *Muscarioides*, yet here is a plant with wide-open flowers of a delicate lavender-blue emitting a heavenly fragrance. With qualities such as these, they belong in a bold grouping at the base of the peat walls, amongst a few dwarf rhododendrons.

If *Primula flaccida* is a special plant, the next is of crowning glory. *Primula reidii* var. *williamsii* was found and collected in central Nepal in a confined area of Dhaulagiri. The 1954 expedition, led by Williams and including Stainton and Sykes, was sponsored by the Royal Horticultural Society and the British Museum. For many gardeners this primula was the finest introduction from the whole expedition. In nature it grows in the shade of overhanging rocks in evergreen oak forests or in clearings, a diversity of habitat which might explain how amenable the plant has proved to be in cultivation. Tuck young plants on top of and between the peat blocks in vertical positions and allow them to establish themselves, seeding wherever they choose. The perfect simplicity of the flowers makes them so endearing. From a rosette of hairy leaves the scapes rise 4–6 in. (10–15 cm) carrying up to eight nodding flowers. The bell-shaped corolla is ice-blue with varying degrees of white towards the base, and the inside is coated with a heavy dusting of white farina. As if the flowers were not enough, they fill the air with the most exquisite fragrance of musk, notably in the evening hours when they attract night-flying moths to bring about pollination. The type species, *P. reidii,* is gen-

Primula reidii var. *williamsii,* Schachen Garden, southern Germany
DIETER SCHACHT

erally found farther west in the Himalaya and closely resembles *P. reidii* var. *williamsii* but displays purest white flowers. Although this species is amongst the easiest of the section *Soldanelloides* I would be prepared to cover the plants in the winter with a pane of glass or similar clear rigid material to protect the overwintering buds from extreme wet. Further members of this section and their propagation are discussed in relation to troughs in Chapter 5.

SECTION *CAPITATAE*

The type species of this section, *Primula capitata,* enjoys a wide distribution from eastern Nepal, through Sikkim, Bhutan, south-eastern Tibet and into Yunnan. Although a distinct species, it varies considerably in form. A very lovely plant it is, making a bold stand in the peat garden with its summer colour. The plants form deciduous clumps of generally heavily farinose, or meal-covered, foliage, and during the summer months 9- to 12-in. (23- to 30-cm) stems each carry a tight, disc-like head of fragrant deep blue to violet flowers. The plants are not long-lived but set plenty of seed for propagation.

Closely related is *Primula glomerata* from central and eastern Nepal, Sikkim and south-eastern Tibet. This species in its true form can be easily identified, though it bears a close resemblance to *P. capitata*. *Primula glomerata* holds its head of flowers in a vertical or nodding position, but *P. capitata* generally holds its flowers in a horizontal position. Also the foliage of *P. glomerata* shows little of the farinose characteristic that is so evident in the type species. Both are fine plants to have in bold groups.

SECTION *FARINOSAE*

Two species of this section, both within the subsection *Auriculatae* (*Oreophlomis*), should thrive in the peat bed. As with most primulas, sufficient light is essential from winter through to spring, with shade coming only from adjacent deciduous cover. A well-known species is *Primula clarkei,* from a very localised area around Poosiana in Kashmir. It was first found by Clarke in 1876, but all plants now grown presumably originate from seed sent from Kashmir in 1935. This creeping, mat-forming plant has very small orbicular foliage. Flowers, often borne singly on the shortest of stems, have a deep, carmine-pink corolla with a white centre. A splendid sight it is to enjoy a neat clump studded with the pink flowers in early spring. The one selection I am familiar with in cultivation is shy to set seed, which means careful division should be carried out every two or three years for established clumps. Divide whilst the plant is in full growth in a damp spell during June. It is very important never to lift and handle plants when they are under stress, but at any time if they have been ravaged by the infamous little horror of vine weevil, lift the clumps, wash them clean, divide them into little plantlets, and then carefully place them into a seed tray of coarse, washed river sand. The plants will generate new roots, and once acclimatised they can be replaced into the peat garden. Dividing sad-looking specimens and planting them into a peaty mix will generally spell a gradual rotting of the basal stems.

The second, lesser-known species in the subsection is *Primula elliptica,* also found in the north-western Himalaya. It has been much-admired by trekkers to the Indian Rohtang Pass where it is often found near the melting snow on hilly slopes and in the shade of boulders. As its name suggests the toothed foliage is elliptical with a one-sided umbel of two to seven violet- to mauve-coloured flowers with a golden eye. This species

Primula clarkei, Edrom Nurseries, Berwickshire JIM JERMYN

is very attractive and is just beginning to gain the attention it strongly deserves. It will become available in due course from seed collections, and I can strongly recommend a search for this fine plant.

SECTION *SIKKIMENSIS*

Some readers may be taken aback to find this section included as most of the species will clearly be too bold, strong-growing and out of place in

Primula sikkimensis var. *hopeana*, Schachen Garden, southern Germany
DIETER SCHACHT

the peat garden. One species, though, which I would always include in the peat garden is *Primula ioessa*. To my knowledge it has never been reintroduced since Ludlow and Sherriff's momentous collection from the Tsari district of south-eastern Tibet in 1938. It is a truly wonderful member of this section displaying typical umbels of two to eight flowers rang-

Primula ioessa, Schachen Garden, southern Germany DIETER SCHACHT

ing in colour from pinkish mauve to violet and rarely white with a distinct blackish calyx. The nodding flowers produced in early summer are beautifully fragrant as are those of *P. ioessa* var. *subpinnatifida* which I remember growing in lovely patches in the Schachen Garden above Garmisch Partenkirchen, an affiliate of the Munich Botanic Garden. In this variety the scapes are shorter, 6–9 in. (15–23 cm), and the flowers are a pleasing cream colour. Both will settle nicely into a moist pocket in the peat garden and can be propagated either by division of the clumps or from seed.

Primula ioessa var. *subpinnatifida,* Schachen Garden, southern Germany
DIETER SCHACHT

SECTION *CANDELABRA* (*Proliferae*)

Three of these species have a stature that places them in ideal company with *Primula ioessa* and a few species of *Meconopsis,* which I will mention following the primulas.

My concern is growing rapidly, as I am sure the reader's is too, as the selection of plants for our modest peat garden extends towards a dimension that may involve some careful decision-making. The decision-making requires even more care when a husband and wife with differing tastes arrive at the nursery preparing to purchase a selection of plants. I have many fond memories of trying to act as an impartial referee as various points of view were put forward to promote one particular plant over another. What a relief that we are not all cloned with the same tastes and outlook on life.

Reintroduced in the 1990s from north-western Yunnan by the excellent trip to Chungtien sponsored by the Royal Botanic Garden in Edinburgh (with collection numbers prefixed by C.L.D.) is *Primula serratifolia,* first introduced by Forrest in 1905. It is well established in horticulture where it shows a clear link with the section *Sikkimensis.* It produces semi-evergreen foliage and on 12-in. (30-cm) stems just one whorl, in my experience, of large, yellow, bell-shaped flowers with a distinct central orange bar on each petal lobe. This feature makes it a very attractive species. It is easily raised from seed. Another distinct member of this ever-popular section is *P. prenantha* which shows no signs of wanting to be typical of its relatives. Native to eastern Nepal, Sikkim, Bhutan and south-eastern Tibet this species is found amongst open, damp clearings in coniferous forest in the lower alpine zone. I am attracted to the elegance of this plant, dwarf in stature, seldom exceeding 9 in. (23 cm) in height, with an evergreen rosette and one, rarely two, whorls of four to eight nodding, brilliant yellow, bell-shaped flowers with a distinct red calyx. I hesitate to say that this species is easy to propagate from seed for I have found that the very small seed grains, by comparison to those of the other species within this section, are best sown fresh to ensure success. Division of the clumps seems best in early spring, prior to the first surge of growth.

My final choice amongst the candelabras would be *Primula cockburni-*

ana, confined to the wet alpine meadows of south-western Sichuan and introduced by Wilson in 1905. My experience suggests that this plant is shorter lived than most of its close relatives but sets an inordinate amount of seed given its meagre stature. I suspect that in nature it may tend to be close to biennial, certainly it is at its best in the second year and warrants regular replenishment. The gardener's work is well rewarded with a fine show from the slender mealy stems which bear up to three whorls of up to eight glowing, orange-scarlet, flat-faced flowers. The species cannot be confused with any of its orange-flowered relatives, but it has been parent to some fine hybrids. It merits a prominent planting in an open bed in the peat garden. Plants from this section enjoy an extra provision of moisture during the growing season.

SECTION *CORTUSOIDES*

This section is generally a group of stoloniferous or creeping perennials found in the forest zone. These are attractive species seldom offered in the trade. Two I recommend are the widespread *Primula geraniifolia* and the recently introduced *P. palmata,* brought back in the 1990s by Peter Cox from Sichuan. Both are ideal subjects to tuck between the peat blocks where they will run freely with attractively divided leaves and abundant drooping umbels of rose-purple flowers.

SECTION *PETIOLARES* (*Craibia*)

I wrote about the celebrated section *Petiolares* earlier in this chapter, recommending several species for the woodland garden. The peat garden also is a fine place to plant a variety of its species. A few species do not appreciate any disturbance once established and can generally be propagated satisfactorily from seed. Remember to sow the seed of the petiolarid species just after collecting it.

Primula calderiana subsp. *strumosa* is one of the most lovely of this group. Once classified as a species of its own, it has been sunk to subspecific rank under the umbrella of *P. calderiana* by the respected botanist Richards. I have no doubt that he is quite correct to draw this conclusion, strengthened by the observation made by Ludlow and Sherriff at Waitang, central Bhutan, in June 1949. Sherriff reported in his diary on

16 July 1949, "One day we marched in a north-westerly direction to the Monla Karchung La on the main Himalayan range and were quite certain we would meet up with *P. calderiana* once again as we could detect its 'fishy' smell up wind for at least 100 yards distant. Greatly to our surprise we were greeted not with masses of the purple *P. calderiana* but masses of

Primula calderiana, Schachen Garden, southern Germany DIETER SCHACHT

Primula calderiana, eastern Nepal GEORGE SMITH

the rich yellow *P. strumosa* which I realised had exactly the same odour as the purple one. At Pangotang and halfway between the two stations at Waitang there was a whole host of hybrids; powder-blue, violet, cream and the rest" (Fletcher 1975). So I am happily willing to bow to Richards's conclusion—how useful such field notes can prove to be. In the

Primula calderiana subsp. *strumosa,* Schachen Garden, southern Germany
DIETER SCHACHT

peat garden either the purple *P. calderiana* or its yellow subspecies, *P. calderiana* subsp. *strumosa,* will make a fine stand with strong 9- to 12-in. (23- to 30-cm) scapes carrying an umbel of six to twelve flowers. I hope that the close relatives of *P. calderiana* will be reintroduced, including *P. tsariensis* and *P. griffithii,* which have but a tenuous hold in cultivation at present.

Alongside the glorious genus *Primula* it seems appropriate to cover a very closely related and equally sensational genus: *Omphalogramma,* a name which in English means "marked navel." I think for the ugliness of the name alone I would prefer the genus to be merged with *Primula,* but there we are. A number of species within this genus occasionally make their way into the nursery trade, and I cannot recommend too highly planting them between the peat blocks. At no time should these plants be exposed to extremes of temperature. Tucked into the blocks, the solid overwintering crowns will receive just the protection they need, and during hot spells in the summer they can draw on the cooler temperatures at the base of the blocks of peat. Writing about the genus *Omphalogramma,* I am overwhelmingly reminded of that outstanding garden, Cluny, near Aberfeldy in Perthshire, Scotland. Laid out by the late Bobby Masterton and continued by one of his daughters and her husband, Wendy and John Mattingley, the conditions there are ideally suited to Himalayan plants. Enjoying extra humidity above the river Tay and a rich, moist, leafy soil, the situation is one to which few of us are privileged, and it is home to some fine stands of *Omphalogramma.*

Three species currently available with a little bit of a search are *Omphalogramma minus, O. vincaeflorum* and *O. elwesianum,* each bearing some resemblance in flower to the fine purple blooms of *Gloxinia.* All the species carry solitary, hanging, tubular flowers on short stems, except in *O. vincaeflorum* the stems may well reach 9–12 in. (23–30 cm). The sole means of propagation is by seed which, like the section *Cuneifolia* of *Primula,* is made up of curiously winged seeds which generally take as long as three to five years to grow and flower. Though this time period may strike readers as a negative trait, the plants of this species are probably the longest living of all hardy members of the Primulaceae. Clearly this is a group of plants for the seasoned gardener, but they will amply repay the efforts of those who can track them down and give them a place in the peat garden.

Not surprisingly the genus *Meconopsis* offers a few specialised species which will associate admirably with both the primulas and a number of liliaceous species described earlier. One of the finest species must be the monocarpic *M. integrifolia* with a wide distribution from eastern and south-eastern Tibet through Gansu, Sichuan and to north-western Yunnan. It is generally found in the higher mountains, most often seen in meadows amongst dwarf rhododendrons. Clearly it is a majestic plant in nature, standing out like a beacon of yellow and aptly named by Reginald Farrer the "lampshade poppy." I have met several individuals who have shared the privilege of encountering this spectacular species in nature and they all speak of its unmistakable grandeur—yet it is a plant that we can all enjoy in the peat garden.

Ludlow, Sherriff and Sir George Taylor were in south-eastern Tibet in June of 1938. They decided to leave the main range for a time and to cross to the other bank of the Tsangpo to the drier ranges behind the persistent monsoon screen, whence Kingdon Ward had reported such a rich flora in 1924–25. They found many exciting primulas, yet the spectacle of them was as nothing compared to that which greeted the plant hunters as they emerged from the mixed *Abies* and *Rhododendron* forest: "Our hearts gave a leap at the prospect before us; the rolling moorland was a billowy sea of dwarf rhododendrons and other shrubs. Spires of yellow poppy flowers [*Meconopsis integrifolia*] pierced this matting and all about were colonies of the sky-blue *Meconopsis simplicifolia*. Our admiration of the scene was unbounded and we pitched our tents on a broad exposed ridge in the midst of this glorious alpine garden about 200 feet [61 m] below the Sang La" (Taylor 1947). No other locality, except the neighbouring Nyima La, excelled nor indeed approached the Sang La for variety and profusion of *Meconopsis*.

What a joy that Taylor accompanied Ludlow and Sherriff on this trip—he was the foremost authority on *Meconopsis* and later wrote the botanical monograph on the genus. His words have had an impact on horticulture and explain a view we may adopt regarding *M. integrifolia* and its close relative *M. pseudointegrifolia*:

> The most conspicuous plant on the moorland was *Meconopsis integrifolia* whose fountain of yellow flowers rose elegantly through the carpet of *Rhododendron laudandum* and *Potentilla fruticosa* var. *grandiflora*. At this elevation about 13,000 feet [3970 m], the plants were up to 4 feet [1.2 m] in height and very monogeneous [of uniform nature in character]. All had prominent, slender, cylindrical styles and the ovaries were densely covered with golden-brown adpressed hairs. In sheltered pockets of black soil on the block boulder scree at 15,500 feet [4730 m] another form of *M. integrifolia* was found. This plant was barely 2 feet [60 cm] in height with up to twelve narrow petals and with the style so contracted that it was concealed by the dark brown hairs of the ovary. Such states have been treated as species by some authors but study of some hundreds of herbarium and cultivated specimens and examination in the field show that the forms of this polymorphic species merge and do not justify taxonomic separation.

The fact is that more than fifty years later a botanical paper has been published by Grey-Wilson splitting the species into two, *Meconopsis integrifolia* and *M. pseudointegrifolia* together with a few subspecies. Late-twentieth-century discoveries in north-western Yunnan would seem to support the idea that there is a reasonable botanical distinction between the two. In *M. integrifolia* the leaves are three veined whereas in *M. pseudointegrifolia* they are pinnately-veined. The rest of Grey-Wilson's prime characteristics I do not find to hold true, with the exception perhaps of the more poised flowers of *M. pseudointegrifolia*. The key to all this is Taylor's choice of the word "polymorphic," meaning the occurrence of more than one form of individual in a single species within an interbreeding population. If we accept this term in a practical sense we hold to Taylor's viewpoint. On the other hand, should we see that the plants' prime characters hold true through subsequent generations in our garden we may question this view. Though I may have belaboured this point, I feel strongly that most readers are down-to-earth gardeners like myself and deserve some sort of explanation of what the botanists are up to. Much botanical work is both helpful and necessary and I applaud

Meconopsis integrifolia, Schachen Garden, southern Germany
DIETER SCHACHT

it, but some occasions, and surely this is a prime example, present a need for balance.

In the peat garden both the *Meconopsis* and *Primula* species do benefit from a little additional fertiliser which should be applied at planting time. Remember that peat, where it is the dominant ingredient in the soil, is an inert material, devoid of the nutrients plants require. The hungrier plants will benefit from a supplementary fertiliser.

To accompany plants of *Meconopsis integrifolia* I would look out for good forms of *M. simplicifolia* with a distribution from central Nepal through Sikkim, Bhutan and into south-eastern Tibet. At its best this is a wonderful species, yet sadly many late-twentieth-century introductions have been rather disappointing. In its best perennial forms the leaves are narrow, entire, yet irregularly toothed or shallowly lobed and formed in a basal rosette. The erect leafless stems may rise up to 2 ft. (60 cm) but are generally shorter with a solitary, nodding, blue flower. Fine sky-blue-flowered forms are, sadly, monocarpic, flowering only once.

From the western Himalaya come two closely related monocarpic species, both performing well in the peat garden despite growing in scree-like material in nature. They are *Meconopsis latifolia* and *M. aculeata*. The former is endemic to Kashmir and is a bristly, spiny plant in all its parts. It has distinct basal leaves regularly toothed but not lobed and produces a spike-like cluster of sky-blue flowers on a stem often in excess of 3 ft. (90 cm). In cultivation it has been confused with *M. aculeata* which has a wider distribution in the western Himalaya, but this second species has foliage deeply cut and pinnately lobed. The flower formation and colour are very similar with the two producing fine hybrids in the garden. Protect young growth from marauding slugs in the spring, and propagate both by saving seed.

Rarely seen in gardens is the wonderful *Meconopsis sherriffii*, a pink-flowering relative of *M. integrifolia*. It may by polycarpic but generally dies after flowering. I hope this fine species will one day be reintroduced from its native Bhutan.

To bring this chapter and the planting of the peat garden to a conclusion, I would like to suggest from amongst the genera *Cyananthus*, *Gentiana* and *Sorbus* a few Himalayan subjects whose late-summer to autumn colour is their chief attraction. A number of *Cyananthus* species suit this situation, while others will do better in a trough or raised bed. The easiest to grow is *C. lobatus* and its many forms whose distribution extends

Meconopsis aculeata, Schachen Garden, southern Germany
DIETER SCHACHT

throughout the Himalaya, staining the open hillsides purple-blue in late August and September. Flowering at the same time in the garden, it is a mat-forming, herbaceous member of the campanula family, Campanulaceae, and responds well to an open sunny position between blocks of peat or at the corner of the bed where it can tumble down with its myriads of wide open, funnel-shaped flowers. The superb white form *C. lobatus* 'Albus' will brighten up a corner in the latter part of the year. Flowering a little early in August is the neater-growing *C. spathulifolius* from Bhutan, Tibet and north-western Yunnan. An elegant plant with typically

Cyananthus lobatus, Schachen Garden, southern Germany DIETER SCHACHT

a sprawling habit, fleshy growth and lemon-yellow flowers in abundance. This species easily can be raised from seed, yet all species of *Cyananthus* can be propagated from cuttings taken from well-established plants in the early spring when no more than 1 in. (2.5 cm) of growth has been made. Root the cuttings into a mix with a high proportion of washed sand, perlite and peat. Once the cuttings have rooted and are established, pinch out the stem tips to encourage lateral growth and the formation of a strong overwintering crown prior to the first winter. Being closely related to campanulas, they are always the favourite diet of slugs, which must be controlled.

Most autumn-flowering gentians, while enjoying the acid conditions of a peat garden, require a dedicated bed in full sun with a mineral soil base. I would though find a place for the wonderful species *Gentiana veitchiorum* which is found in south-eastern Tibet, Sichuan and Yunnan. It

Cyananthus lobatus 'Albus', Inshriach Alpine Nursery, Aviemore JIM JERMYN

commonly grows in somewhat dry meadows compared to its cousin *G. sino-ornata,* which nearly always prefers damp, marshy conditions. *Gentiana veitchiorum* is also reported to have been found in moist slopes and open woods. With this diversity of habitat one would have thought it would be quite amenable in gardens, but it is challenging. Likely too many plants have been started in pots which offers the least likelihood of success. Halda in his fine monograph of 1996 on gentians gives both Nepal and a site in the western Himalaya as a westerly distribution, and if this were the case it may shed further light on the interesting migration of this group of gentians. This species is generally compact in growth with broad foliage and a prominent overwintering rosette of leaves. The flower colour is clearly very variable, although this is apparently not the case in parts of Yunnan where the flowers are generally of a glowing violet-blue. Fine white forms are sometimes offered, and this species has been parent to some excellent hybrids. I will discuss these hybrids and more autumn-flowering gentians in Chapter 4.

And finally, two dwarf rowans of the genus *Sorbus* will provide some simple autumn colour in the form of attractive fruits and bright red foliage. *Sorbus reducta* was introduced by Kingdon Ward in 1943 and later was reintroduced from Yunnan where it forms ground cover around the Zhongdian Plateau with *Nomocharis aperta* growing through it. Generally suckering without becoming a nuisance the branches grow to 12 in. (30 cm) with large, deep pink fruits and orange-red autumn colour. A closely related species reported from Tibet and Yunnan is *S. poteriifolia,* a miniature shrub with dark green, glossy foliage and attractive pink flowers followed by reddish purple autumn foliage and white fruits. A fine all-round dwarf shrub for the peat garden.

The rich choice of both Himalayan and Sino-Himalayan species currently available in horticulture and suitable for inclusion in the peat garden should make apparent that the peat garden is an ideal feature to accompany or even substitute for the woodland in the modern garden. My experience and observation of established peat gardens—at such fine horticultural establishments as the Royal Botanic Garden in Edinburgh, Inverewe Gardens and Jack Drake's Nursery—leave no doubt that the scope is unlimited for creating interesting texture, outlines and colours for all tastes, with appeal at all times of the year. It is important to keep in mind the nutrition, most notably, of herbaceous subjects, to keep certain ericaceous subjects from spreading too far, and to take care before the winter to clear freshly fallen leaves away from plants positioned close to deciduous trees. Considering the aftercare and attention to detail that any specialised garden feature demands, the peat garden should play a valuable part in the Himalayan garden.

CHAPTER FOUR

Subalpine Zone

VERYONE WHO has ever walked or trekked through mountains, any mountains anywhere, must know that special feeling that grips the spirit upon emerging from a forest or thicket of bamboo and strolling out into open meadow. Here is freedom, a complete change in flora and fragrances, and a new dimension with the high mountains ahead and perhaps grazing animals nearby. This is the subalpine zone, which in the Himalaya covers elevations between 8000 and 13,000 ft. (2440–3970 m). From here emanate many of the most popular Himalayan plants and many that have made a profound impact in horticulture. At lower elevations, some of these plants have found a home in the bog garden, while others are better suited to a rock garden or raised bed. This chapter covers each of these features, plus a final part devoted to the autumn-flowering gentians.

Attempting to replicate in the garden the conditions of a Himalayan subalpine meadow is bound to require a variety of situations. The subalpine region contains many differing conditions in which plants grow, conditions which become clearer through an understanding of the particular part of the Himalaya to which each plant is endemic. For example, the point at which the tree-line gives way to a meadow flora varies from west to east. In the western Himalaya this may occur at around 12,000 ft. (3660 m), while in the east it is considerably higher at 13,000 ft. (3970 m).

Spring in Kashmir with *Primula rosea* and *Adonis chrysocyathus* DIETER SCHACHT

Because of such particularities, I will take each genus and suggest the ideal situation in the garden. For example, I may recommend that species found in stable scree conditions well above the subalpine zone be planted in the peat garden. Indeed the similarities abound between the flora of this meadow zone and the truly alpine one, to be covered in the next chapter.

In late July in central Nepal and at around 9800 ft. (2990 m) in the Marsyandi Valley, a trekker struck with that feeling of spaciousness looks with a keen eye across the dry, heavily-grazed meadows and can see the species remaining, clearly those unpalatable to grazing animals. Amongst the many exciting species encountered here is a classic Himalayan alpine plant, *Stellera chamaejasme,* rarely seen in gardens due in part, I guess, to the common misconception that choice or special plants are difficult to grow. I say in part, because this lovely member of the daphne family, Thymelaeaceae, is an example of a subject requiring great care and skill to effect a successful introduction. From deep taproots, bold clumps of simple stems up to 2 ft. (60 cm) are capped by a dense head of wonderfully fragrant, daphne-like flowers, red in bud, opening white. As with many Himalayan species the process of flowering, fertilisation, ripening and

Stellera chamaejasme, central Nepal GEORGE SMITH

Typical scene during monsoon with *Pedicularis longiflora* var. *tubiformis,* Langtang, central Nepal DIETER SCHACHT

subsequent seed dispersal is alarmingly quick, surely none more so than *S. chamaejasme,* making seed collection extremely challenging. A friend who led an expedition to Yunnan in the late 1990s emphasised this phenomenon when locating the same species in its yellow-flowering variety *S. chamaejasme* var. *chrysantha,* noting that within a few weeks of flowering the seed was not only ripe but actually germinating in the head of the flower. Clearly, in a situation such as this the cautious collector needs to avail him- or herself of a jar with damp tissue and place the seed, at whatever stage it has reached, carefully on the moist bed of tissue and look after it accordingly. My experience of this eastern form is a satisfactory one, having planted seedlings into a well-drained raised bed in full sun where the deep taproots can seek out a heavy loam into which they can anchor themselves. I have no doubt that the type species found commonly in central Nepal will grow quite happily in the same conditions. The key with so many of these meadow plants is that while they must not dry out in the severe heat of the summer, their roots should equally not sit in water, notably as they expect to enter dormancy in early autumn and not emerge until May.

In these introductory words on the subalpine zone and rich meadow habitats, I advise adapting the plants of this habitat in the main to a rock garden or a raised bed. So involved is the concept of constructing a genuine rock garden, that I recommend such a feature only for those who have the time, skill and care to ensure the often demanding maintenance. At the same time, a garden can have no finer aspect than a well-constructed, natural rock feature with a watercourse and pond. A rock garden with a natural look conjures up the words of the father of rock-gardening, Reginald Farrer, who wrote in *The English Rock Garden,* "to make a thing look 'natural' is by no means to imitate nature. Nature often looks more artificial than the worst forms of art. By making a rock garden look natural, then, we merely mean that it must have a firm and effortless harmony of hill or vale, cliff or slope. Conventionally 'natural' effects are best un-aimed at— rock gardening, like all arts, is not imitative, but selective and adaptive."

The advantage of a rock garden, however many or few rocks feature in the landscape, is the immediate provision of a cool, north-facing block of stone which so many Himalayan subjects will appreciate, not to mention the cool root run afforded by sunken rocks. The goal is to create a habitat for plants which appreciate, generally, maximum light, a cool root run and supplementary moisture during the growing season. The last requirement is for readers who garden in hot, dry areas or regions subject to little in the way of mean annual rainfall. Someone gardening on the west coast of Scotland or under Snowdonia in northern Wales will construct raised beds with more than the average proportion of drainage material. Here the annual rainfall is high, comparable with the Himalayan monsoon, together with the greatest asset of high summer humidity in a cooler climate. In this situation the surplus precipitation must drain away, whereas in the south-east of England the grower tries to retain moisture, having to supplement the natural rainfall and create artificially cooler aspects to compensate for the high summer temperatures.

In the Himalaya, plant hunters and trekkers rejoice at breaking out into meadows, screes and the higher alpine flora, but the challenge of growing these spectacular plants becomes ever greater the higher we climb. Each of these plants has adapted to the highly specialised conditions in which it grows, and at a certain stage we must look down at a group of plants, set up our tripod and camera, record the unique experience and leave it at that, because trying to re-enact these conditions at home would be impossible. Thankfully from the subalpine zone, most of the species can be grown quite satisfactorily in most gardens, with some care.

The ideal compromise for a full-blooded rock garden in a small to average-sized space is to construct a modestly sized raised bed. It could be designed to a height of perhaps 2 to 3 ft. (60–90 cm) and a width of up to 6 ft. (1.8 m) to allow, in the case of an island bed, ease of weeding from either side. Such an island bed could be a practical option to enable ease of handling for a disabled gardener. Raised beds can be situated in full sun or on the cooler, leeside of a wall to suit the choice of plants for such an aspect. The beauty of such a construction, whatever the situation, is the unique facility of acute drainage and the provision of low walls over which a variety of plants can tumble down to show off their trailing stems of flowers. By positioning a few well-placed rocks within the bed a number of cool corners and pockets can be created for species requiring the more delicate site that a north-facing rock can provide. The reader may well begin to object in the knowledge that such a freely drained bed, situated in full sun, will surely dry out, causing fleshy plants to expire without a fair chance. I hasten to add that at the time of construction I would always incorporate porous piping through the full stretch of raised bed, so that when the pipe is operational the seepage will run through to the needy roots. This method of irrigation is operational at very low pressure and uses very little water.

When it comes to the construction of a raised bed, the actual raising can be facilitated by means of stone, built in the form of a low wall, or possibly hardwood timber. I am personally drawn towards the practicalities of using wooden railway sleepers unless appropriate rock is available to construct dry stone walling. By whatever means the bed is constructed, remember that the walls are retaining a significant weight of soil behind them—the construction must be well built to allow for this weight. The soil constituents should ensure that both good drainage and moisture retention are considered. Install at least 6 in. (15 cm) of stones or similar drainage material at the bottom of the bed and cover with a 4- to 6-in. (10- to 15-cm) layer of humus in the form of very well-rotted manure that can be rubbed through a 1-in. (2.5-cm) sieve or a shredder. For the rest of the bed choose a soil type that is predominantly a good medium loam of neutral pH mixed with sphagnum peat and gritty sand: three parts by volume loam, one part peat and one part gritty sand. The porous-pipe for irrigation can be laid the full length of the bed at a sensible depth of about 6 to 9 in. (15–23 cm) below the soil surface, so as not to interfere with planting and maintenance, and some 6 in. (15 cm) from the wall. The open end of the pipe to which a ½-in. (1-cm) hose will be connected should be exposed by a few inches to allow for ease of connection without damaging plants. Firm the soil infill close to the walls, but avoid over compression, and fill the bed to a level higher than the walls to allow for several inches of sinkage. This is the time to place a few well-chosen rocks and stepping stones which will enable ease of planting and maintenance for wide beds.

While planting I generally have a bucket of fertiliser at hand to incorporate a light dusting into each hole. The fertiliser should be made up of all the required plant nutrients, though the available nitrogen, or nitrate level, should be relatively low so as not to promote too much vegetative growth. Our aim is to encourage strong, robust growth, particularly the root growth, to give the plant the best chance of coming through the first winter. A higher phosophate level will promote this aim. Each country offers its own brand names of garden fertilisers. In the United Kingdom, in terms of these three primary ingredients, I recommend two fertilisers: Vitax Q4 (5.3 N, 7.5 P, 10 K) or Enmag (5 N, 19 P, 10 K, plus 7.5 magnesium [Mg]). Both brands are currently available throughout the United Kingdom from recognised agricultural merchants.

Once the raised bed has been planted, carefully avoiding overcrowding at all cost, the plants should be well watered in from above. Following a short period of about a week for settlement, a top-dressing, or mulch, of pea-sized grit appropriate to the stone walls or in keeping with the look of the environment, can be applied to a depth of at least ½ in. (1 cm).

The plants mentioned in this chapter will enjoy the environment of a raised bed or rock garden. In the main they will prefer an open sunny aspect, but I will mention, where appropriate, subjects which prefer a cooler position, possibly on the north side of a rock.

It is fascinating to note the variation in growth habit exhibited by certain plants in the artificial garden situation, depending on the amount of light they are given. This may seem a rather arbitrary comment, yet in my experience it sheds light on one of the chief differences between long-term success or abject failure of many Himalayan subjects in the garden. Often significant plant growth and health can be enjoyed by offering a measure of shade to compromise for the cooler conditions provided in their natural habitat. Now, if the garden is positioned geographically so as to be able to grow the same plants in an open aspect together with a cool root run, then the species in question may assume a new appearance. The lax, softer growth in the shady site gives way to a more robust, compact and harder-looking plant. This open position may well provide the conditions for such a subject to survive a longer period and produce good-quality seed for propagation. A few genera that would respond in this way rapidly come to mind: *Anemone, Cremanthodium, Incarvillea* and *Gentiana*.

I hope that mentioning this significant variation in situation and the resulting growth habits will show readers the options available. But I also must stress that for these plants from the subalpine zone of the Himalaya, constant attention to detail will be required for their success in the garden. An astute watering regime managed and maintained throughout the growing season is perhaps the most significant detail.

The Raised Bed and Rock Garden

The arrival of spring will bring early signs of activity amongst deciduous clumps of *Anemone*. In Chapter 3 I mentioned a number of species suitable for the peat garden, yet in an open, sunny aspect the same plants will thrive and present a more robust characteristic. Whilst travelling in central Bhutan, Sherriff noted the extraordinary abundance of anemones on 21 May 1937: "On our return journey we soon met with a most lovely anemone, *Anemone obtusiloba*. It flowers both blue-violet and white, but looks as if it might come true from seed. I have never seen such a sight of anemones. For 100 yards or more the grassy hillside was thick with them, all jumbled together, a patch of blue, then joined on to a patch of white, and so on, a really beautiful sight. They were probably growing so profusely where the ground is rich with yak manure" (Fletcher 1975).

Few of us can provide a bed with yak manure, but a sunny, well-drained aspect we surely can. A variety of forms of *Anemone obtusiloba,* including the blue *A. obtusiloba* var. *patula* and *A. obtusiloba* var. *sulphurea* with its lovely lemon-yellow flowers, will provide valuable spring colour together with a regular supply of flowers throughout the season. A few weeks later to flower is the Sino-Himalayan *A. trullifolia*. Where space provides I would plant bold stands of this variable species in the rock garden, with drifts of individual colour forms flowing down like a mountain stream. The white form of *Anemone trullifolia,* as mentioned earlier, will predominate from seed when planted together with the blue variant, but it lends itself well to a large drift together with *Meconopsis horridula* and incarvilleas.

Plant association is very important in a rock garden if the landscape is to be more than a fine collection of plants. Consider the following marriage of species in a multi-partner format. The lovely evergreen shrub *Daphne retusa* provides height and form to accompany lower stands of the blue *Anemone trullifolia,* while several clumps of Roy Lancaster's early-flowering form of *Incarvillea mairei* (L. 2004) with its shrill, reddish-purple flowers add further colour to the scene.

Superior forms of familiar species observed in the field will continue to whet the appetites of keen plantsfolk. One such example is the well-known white-flowered Himalayan *Anemone demissa,* which to the casual observer looks like a large-flowered form of the European *A. narcissiflora.* But Ron McBeath, along with others who have explored the Marsyandi Valley in central Nepal, noted a superb form of this meadow species with a pale pink central band. The flowers are held in clusters on branched stems some 2 ft. (60 cm) in height. Clearly a fine introduction to be looked forward to in the rock garden.

An accommodating anemone making an occasional appearance in the nursery trade is *Anemone polyanthes,* often found in central Nepal. This species grows in clumps with up to six flowers of a stunning red to mauve held in umbels on 12- to 18-in. (30- to 46-cm) stems. In its best red forms, this is a superb subject for either the rock garden or raised bed, flowering in late spring.

Readers should know that many of the anemones, members of the buttercup family, Ranunculaceae, can be readily raised from seed, yet the seed carries a short period of viability. Keen growers may find that their favourite species becomes more frequently available from seed-collecting expeditions, those either privately sponsored or activated by the larger botanic gardens. With care the seeds of such genera as *Anemone* and *Ranunculus* can be stored in damp tissue in specialised containers. From a packet of a dozen seeds or more, it may be that only two or three will germinate. This should be seen, in the wider context, as a success, with the seedlings brought on to planting being a satisfactory start to cultivation and from which a fine crop of seeds should develop in subsequent years.

A final choice from this rewarding genus would be the widespread *Anemone rupicola,* often found in screes or in rocky outcrops in the meadow zone. This species must be grown in a lean mixture of soil, one low in available nutrients, notably nitrates, in order to encourage an abundance of the huge, solitary, pure white flowers which grow on 6- to 9-in. (15- to 23-cm) stems above attractive three-lobed leaves. I have ex-

Anemone rupicola, Schachen Garden, southern Germany DIETER SCHACHT

perienced a lack of flowers and plenty of growth from too rich a soil mixture and thus recommend positioning the plants between rocks in an open, sunny aspect. This species displays a different pattern of fruiting with the typical achenes, or seeds, held in a globular, white, woolly head.

I consider my two favourite Himalayan columbines, *Aquilegia nivalis* and *A. fragrans,* as challenging, with the rock garden or raised bed an ideal home for them. Both are to be found across the western Himalaya, notably in Kashmir and north-western India. *Aquilegia nivalis* is frequently found at altitudes from 9000 to 13,000 ft. (2750–3970 m), flowering between June and August. The foliage is very attractive and suggests an affinity to *Paraquilegia,* being divided into broad kidney-shaped, three-lobed leaflets. The flowers on 3- to 6-in. (8- to 15-cm) stems are stunning, solitary and deep-purple with almost blackish purple inner petals and short incurved spurs. In my view this species is a contender for the most beautiful Himalayan alpine. There is a case for tucking the taprooted plants between rocks in a cooler position without denying them light. I have found that they may take several years to flower, but the sight is well worth waiting for. As with all columbines, they may be propagated easily from seed. The best results come from sowing immediately after collection in a loam-based seed compost.

The second species, *Aquilegia fragrans* is taller growing, up to 2 ft. (60 cm) in height. A generous planting of this species in the rock garden would associate well with the flowers of *Anemone trullifolia* in its blue form. The lovely white to lemon-yellow flowers are pleasantly fragrant as the name suggests and several in number.

Belonging to the same family are two members of the genus *Delphinium, D. cashmerianum* and *D. viscosum.* Both are delightful plants worthy of a position in the rock garden. *Delphinium cashmerianum,* as its name suggests, is generally found in the western Himalaya at altitudes between 8800 and 14,000 ft. (2680–4270 m) in alpine meadows. It will form bold clumps of deeply lobed foliage and attractive purple-blue flowers on stems up to 9 in. (23 cm). The second species is less frequently encountered but quite distinct, with its greenish yellow flowers. Distributed from central Nepal to south-eastern Tibet this exciting plant is again found on alpine slopes. The flowers are held in a cluster on 6- to 9-in.

(15- to 23-cm) stems over attractively lobed leaves. Both species enjoy a sunny aspect flowering in late spring and may be propagated from seed sown soon after collection.

Although closely related, the members of *Trollius* are more easily grown than the delphiniums and deserve a place in any sunny rock garden that is not liable to dry out. The species *T. acaulis* is found across the

Aquilegia nivalis, Schachen Garden, southern Germany DIETER SCHACHT

Himalaya and into south-western China. Encountered on alpine slopes and in meadows this showy plant forms compact deciduous clumps of deeply cut foliage. The large, golden yellow flowers are solitary on 3- to 6-in. (8- to 15-cm) stems and resemble immense flat buttercups sitting up like saucers. It flowers in early summer and is easily propagated from seed.

Delphinium cashmerianum, Schachen Garden, southern Germany
DIETER SCHACHT

Trollius acaulis, Schachen Garden, southern Germany DIETER SCHACHT

The rock garden is the ideal spot for the spreading habit of *Bergenia purpurascens,* with its characteristic spring flowers held in nodding terminal clusters, a pleasing purple to rose-pink. In the autumn the hairless leaves assume vibrant red colours, livening an otherwise potentially dull corner.

A favourite subject for the raised bed and flowering through late May and June is the delightful *Geranium napuligerum.* This popular cranesbill is known more frequently as *G. farreri,* but it was first discovered by Delavay in Sichuan, China, and named *G. napuligerum* in reference to its somewhat turnip-like root. The former name therefore stands. It is found growing in rocky substrate between 13,000 and 14,000 ft. (3970–4270 m) where it forms neat clumps of attractively lobed, dark-green, kidney-shaped leaves. Three or four stems carry the delicate, soft pink flowers with black anthers. As with most species of *Geranium,* this one can be easily propagated by seed, but collecting the seed may prove challenging. Great care should be taken to judge the best time to cut off the fruiting heads before they curl up and catapult the seeds several feet from the mother plant. In such instances, practise makes perfect. This geranium is totally deciduous, so it may be beneficial to mark its position to aid winter maintenance when no aerial growth is evident.

Another species of *Geranium* responding well to a position in either the rock garden or raised bed is *G. donianum,* found growing widespread in Nepal. It forms neat clumps, and the blooms on this summer-flowering species are pinkish red on short stems amongst attractively lobed leaves.

Allium, or ornamental onions, made a huge impact in horticulture in the late 1900s, and readers may be surprised that a number of species are native to the Himalaya. It is their late-flowering nature that adds to their virtues for the rock garden. One of the most exciting plants for consideration is *A. wallichii,* a tuberous-rooted species with flowers on stems from 1 to 3 ft. (30–90 cm) in height. The stems are more typically around 18 in. (46 cm) tall with a lax, spherical head of crimson to dark purple flowers. Another species commonly found in Nepal is *A. humile,* flowering early in the garden and through late spring to early summer. Its white, star-shaped flowers are produced on short 4- to 6-in. (10- to 15-

cm) stems in the form of a lax umbel and, as with other white-flowering plants, benefit strongly from positioning amongst darker foliage subjects. The stems of this allium would happily pop up between the sprawling branches of *Salix calyculata* or *S. hylematica*.

It is not surprising that within the genus *Allium,* comprising some 700 or so species of onion found worldwide, confusion arises amongst some of the species. I suspect that a close link lies between the fairly wide-spread *A. sikkimensis* and *A. beesianum,* which is more frequently found in western China. Both are highly desirable garden plants and will provide valuable summer colour in the raised bed. *Allium sikkimensis,* given its taller stature, merits a bold planting in the rock garden where it will attain 12- to 18-in. (30- to 46-cm) stems with nodding umbels of pale blue flowers. From a horticultural point of view, *A. beesianum* is of immense importance, easily cultivated, flowering from mid- to late summer and easily propagated from seed. Sadly all too often British nurseries describe it in their catalogues, and then the plant they send turns out to be the distinct *A. cyaneum,* also a late-flowering, blue-flowered species, but not with bell-shaped flowers. The true *A. beesianum* is found fairly wide-spread in north-western Yunnan, south-western Sichuan and south-eastern Tibet where it grows in open, alpine meadows at altitudes between 10,500 and 14,000 ft. (3200–4270 m). It was first introduced from the Lichiang range in Yunnan by George Forrest in 1910 and eventually received a justified Award of Merit from the Royal Horticultural Society in 1981. When strong it will grow up to 12 in. (30 cm) in height with the most lovely sky-blue, nodding bells, each with a darker stripe along the center of the perianth segment. An albino form is also available. This outstanding allium can be propagated from seed, or superior forms may be divided as they come into growth in the spring.

The genus *Incarvillea* is of immense horticultural importance. So garden worthy and exotic in nature are the incarvilleas that they simply have to be given space in either the rock garden or a raised bed. I must emphasise how important it is, with the species under discussion here, that they all be given a position in full light and a soil that is freely drained and humus rich. The genus consists of eighteen species with a distribution from eastern Afghanistan through to north-western China. Their centre of migration clearly belongs to western China notably around north-western Yunnan. Christopher Grey-Wilson published a revision of the genus in 1998, and it is a thorough, clearly defined and practical work that I as a horticulturist find highly satisfactory. It does, though, leave the gardener with a few new names and alterations to cope with. In the 1990s several expeditions to western China, notably to Yunnan, opened a new window of opportunity, introducing a number of species from this sensational genus.

The broader geographic boundaries I have set out for this book will allow me to highlight a few species of *Incarvillea* distributed within the provinces of Yunnan and Sichuan. But first consider the one truly Himalayan species, *I. himalayensis*. This is a newly described species incorporating certain forms formerly of *I. mairei*. It is distributed from western Nepal, notably in the Barbung Sama, to northern Bhutan and southern Tibet, around the Nyoto Sama, at altitudes of 11,400 to 14,700 ft. (3480–4480 m). All the known sites for this species are located significantly in the drier regions to the north of the main Himalayan divide, in the rain shadow of the Indian monsoon that moves from Dolpo, Nepal, across to south-eastern Tibet. This habitat gives a clear indicator as to the plant's needs in the garden, for it simply resents too much winter wet and enjoys a good summer baking, a scenario that will appeal to gardeners in the dryer regions of both the United States and Europe. The species is perfectly at home on a raised bed filled with a high proportion of loam along with gritty sand and peat to retain moisture.

It is perhaps the exotic flowers that provide the greatest appeal within this genus, and *Incarvillea himalayensis* offers some of the finest flowers of all. In this variable species the gloxinia-like flowers are reddish pink, with a white throat and two white flares at the base of each corolla lobe. The flowers may attain some 3 in. (8 cm) across and are represented at their best in two well-known cultivars, *I. himalayensis* 'Nyoto Sama' and 'Frank Ludlow'. The cultivar 'Nyoto Sama' was raised from a seed collection in south-eastern Tibet at a locality of the same name by Ludlow, Sherriff and Elliot (L.S.E. 15614). Ludlow's diary of 3 June 1947 describes the native habitat: "Pride of place must go to the *Incarvillea mairei* [now *himalayensis*] which at 12,000 feet [3660 m] plastered the rock faces and the stony hilltops with its flat rosettes of dark green pinnate leaves and with its great gloxinia-like reddish-pink, white striped flowers sometimes 3 inches [8 cm] in diameter" (Fletcher 1975). Today, more than fifty years later, this cultivar remains quite distinct, generally flowering on a stem up to 6 in. (15 cm) high, and can easily be raised from seed. After flowering the long angular capsule up to 3 in. (8 cm) in length will mature from a greenish, black-spotted colour to a uniform brown and begin to open up. At this stage the fruiting capsules should be cut off and placed in a carefully marked paper bag and hung up to dry. The capsules can be prised open in the autumn, September or October, to reveal the substantial, flat and winged seeds which should be sown in a loam-based seed compost and placed in a cold frame. The seedlings should be transplanted in the normal way into a loam-based potting compost and in a matter of a month a little tuber will form. Whilst in growth they should be well watered. Flowering may well take place within three years from sowing. I would not recommend disturbing the established tubers as they certainly do not respond well to division at any time.

The cultivar *Incarvillea himalayensis* 'Frank Ludlow' is quite wonderful. It is almost stemless at flowering. This cultivar was raised from a seed collection made in northern Bhutan by Ludlow, Sherriff and Hicks (L.S.H. 17250) in September 1949. Seed-raised material grown in cultivation shows little in the way of variation and clearly demonstrates the stability of this fine cultivar.

Other species which are widely available in horticulture, that will grow well in a raised bed, are *Incarvillea zhongdianensis* and *I. mairei*. Each of these species is distinct botanically, as Grey-Wilson's paper demonstrates, but gardeners will find some of the differences less apparent. I do agree with the latest clarification within the genus, but any changes made to familiar names can take a while to sink in, as many nurseries, either stubbornly or unwittingly, hold to their former labels. Again, the main centre of diversity within the genus is the Sino-Himalayan region within Yunnan and Sichuan. *Incarvillea zhongdianensis* was introduced in the late 1990s from the Zhongdian Plateau in north-western Yunnan. It grows on dry grassy hillsides and occasionally in rocky places, flowering in May and June. This species is now well established in horticulture and proving a wonderful introduction, producing solid, herbaceous clumps of pinnate foliage. The nature of the leaves is what makes this species so distinct, with five to nine pairs of lateral leaflets. The flowers, typically held on stems about 12 in. (30 cm) high, are deep magenta with a yellow throat and two white, oblong flares at the base of each corolla lobe. In the garden, as with all incarvilleas, the time of flowering is early June onwards, and this species also can be easily propagated by seed.

Incarvillea mairei is widely grown with its shrill carmine-pink flowers. And mention must be made of a lovely soft-pink-flowering form known in the trade as *I. mairei* 'Pink Form'. A great complement to the type species, it is well worth looking out for.

A genus becoming better known due to some fine new introductions is *Cyananthus*. This member of the campanula family is of immense importance amongst Himalayan introductions, with a number of species widely available in the horticultural trade. Although most of them are easily grown and blue-flowered, a few exciting species have yellow flow-

Incarvillea mairei, Edrom Nurseries, Berwickshire JIM JERMYN

ers. I always feel rewarded to find plants that lend themselves to planting at the edge of a raised bed where their spreading stems can flow down over the walls. Although many *Cyananthus* species are found competing with grasses amongst meadow flora, they seem quite at home on a raised bed. Perhaps the greatest difficulty facing gardeners is the apparent confusion surrounding the naming of the species, particularly amongst the Sino-Himalayan introductions of the late 1990s. No doubt botanists will soon turn their attention to this wonderful genus and thus help gardeners choose from a mass of plants that includes clearly more than the distinct species.

The late-flowering habit of the genus is of great benefit. *Cyananthus lobatus* is the best-known and most widely available species. In nature it occupies the alpine turf amongst dwarf rhododendrons throughout the Himalaya. From the thick, fleshy taproot rise many stems which radiate out to form neat, leafy mats. In August and September the mats become masses of large, blue, funnel-shaped flowers which terminate each trailing stem. Its succession of flowers makes this species valuable, and several cultivars add to the range of shades of blue as well as the clean, pure white *C. lobatus* 'Albus'.

Flowering in late summer and into the autumn is a welcome newcomer collected in Yunnan. *Cyananthus spathulifolius* (C.L.D. 1492) is now well established in horticulture and merits a position on the raised bed where it will form a tidy mat of neat foliage with marked reddish stems. The lemon-yellow flowers are produced in profusion, typically campanulate, terminating each shoot. Propagation is by means of seed or soft cuttings taken in the spring. After flowering, a bladder-like capsule containing the seed can be collected and stored in a paper bag until the seed is ready for cleaning and sowing at the beginning of the new year.

During the winter when we spend time tidying up the raised bed, we can carefully pull away the now decaying top growth of cyananthus to reveal a mass of tiny overwintering shoots nestling amongst the top-dressing of grit. As spring advances with added warmth, they will begin to sprout, and when about 1 in. (2.5 cm) of growth has been made, carefully sever several cuttings from the perimeter of the clump. Use a sharply pointed pair of scissors for the purpose. Some harmless, sappy milk will exude from the stems. Immediately insert the cuttings into a seed tray containing a mix of three parts by volume damp perlite to one part washed, gritty sand. Firm the mix and water in the cuttings, then cover them with a tent of polythene and inspect them every few days to ensure they never dry out or lack humidity. They should root within three to four weeks, then carefully transfer them to a less humid atmosphere under gentle shade. A weak liquid feed can be given now until the rooted cuttings are ready for potting. Once the new plants are established in the pots pinch out the main terminal shoots to promote a strong overwintering crown.

The species of *Cyananthus* most often encountered in horticulture after *C. lobatus* is the distinct, mat-forming *C. microphyllus*, widely distributed from the Indian Uttar Pradesh, through Nepal and into southeastern Tibet. In nature it flowers from August to October depending on altitude and the return of winter snows. It is frequently found on open slopes or amongst rocks at elevations up to 15,700 ft. (4790 m) where it forms stout rootstocks producing many branched and trailing leafy stems, each bearing a lilac-blue, funnel-shaped flower. This species produces seed and may be easily propagated from cuttings. I strongly recommend planting it at the perimeter of the raised bed where the trailing, leafy stems radiate out from a flat mat of glaucous foliage and, over a long period from August onwards, provide a mass of pale-blue flowers falling over the edge of the bed.

Similar to the foregoing yet clearly distinct due to at least two important features is *Cyananthus sherriffii*. Firstly, in early spring the new growth is covered with silvery hairs which differentiate this species from its less hirsute cousin. Secondly, *C. sherriffii* is not as easily cultivated and prefers to be tucked between rocks or positioned in a vertical crevice to combat extreme winter wet. These two features give evidence of its natural preference for dryer conditions, yet this lovely species has never failed to grow for me in either a trough or a raised bed. The flowers are tubular, bearded in the throat and the most lovely pale blue in colour. Altogether it is a rather fine plant and can be propagated by soft cuttings taken in the same way as described earlier.

In September 1936 whilst concluding a Tibetan expedition, Ludlow

and Sherriff spent several days in the Bimbi La. There above the trees the
great expanse of grassy hillside was carpeted with the mauve-violet *Cyananthus wardii* (L.S. 2557). Again in 1998 and 1999 trips were made
into south-eastern Tibet, and the travellers confirm the location of this
species. I hope that in the near future this superb meadow plant, akin to
a more amenable version of *C. sherriffii*, will be introduced successfully
into cultivation. Similar in habit is *C. incanus* which enjoys a wide distribution from central Nepal to south-western China. The showy flowers
are blue with long white hairs in the throat.

Cyananthus microphyllus, Schachen Garden, southern Germany DIETER SCHACHT

A genus deserving more attention both in our gardens and in horticulture is *Dracocephalum*, a member of the Labiatae. This genus of aromatic, perennial herbs includes a number of Himalayan species that merit a position on the raised bed or in a rock garden landscape. The descriptive generic name emanates from the Greek words "draco," dragon, and "cephale," head, aptly depicting the shape of the flowers. Two reasons for their importance horticulturally are that most dracocephalums flower in the summer season when colour is so valuable and they are easily grown. A species found stretching from the western Himalaya into Yunnan is *D. wallichii,* surely the most decorative of all. In my experience plants have formed low, woody shrublets up to 12 in. (30 cm) in height with aromatic, heart-shaped leaves and beautiful, large, pale-blue flowers formed as whorls in a dense head surrounded by upper leaves. Somewhat more erect growing with linear leaves is *D. forrestii* from the Sino-Himalaya with 1-ft.-high (30-cm) spikes of deepest blue flowers. After flowering, dracocephalums should be cut back to the ground to maintain a neat habit. Save the seed of these plants for the best means of propagation.

The Himalayan subalpine zone, including the lush meadows, hosts a number of valuable members of the genus *Potentilla*. The following few

Cyananthus incanus, Khumbu, eastern Nepal GEORGE SMITH

species fit nicely into the more traditional rock garden along with the practical raised bed.

To mention the name *Potentilla nepalensis* conjures up the well-known tall-growing herbaceous plant, *P. nepalensis* 'Miss Willmott', with its attractive crimson-coloured flowers. From northern Pakistan in the Karakoram range a fascinating number of plants are found, many growing in arid conditions at the most western limits of the Himalaya. On the Shogran Pass amongst a rich flora, Henrik Zetterlund, a member of the Swedish expedition to this area in 1983, found a very neat-growing form of the species, *P. nepalensis* (S.E.P. 249), which was later given the cultivar name 'Shogran' due to the significant impact it has made in horticulture. From tight overwintering clumps radiate adpressed branches of typically divided leaves with innumerable flowers of a delicate crimson. The flowers bloom over a long period from late summer onwards.

A highly variable species of great merit in the rock garden is *Potentilla atrosanguinea*. It ranges in flower colour from yellow through orange to outright red. In all its forms the pubescent foliage is a beautiful silvery colour, sharply toothed, and with flower stems varying in height from 6 to 12 in. (15–30 cm). A fine, early-summer-flowering subject found widespread throughout Nepal.

Finally for the rock garden, I recommend a useful and rewarding subject invaluable for its autumn colour, both for its flowers and foliage. *Polygonum vaccinifolium* — the genus was formerly *Bistorta* — is found from Kashmir through to south-eastern Tibet. Forming trailing mats, this one must be given space to spread amongst and over rock work. Keep it clear of the confines of a raised bed. Should it spread further than planned, a little surgery will resolve the problem. Slender racemes of soft pink flowers appear in late summer and autumn, and the small leaves assume lovely red tints in the autumn months.

The Ravine Garden

The ravine garden is a space that combines rock work together with a water feature. This type of situation is hard to create artificially, but some gardens may be blessed with a natural watercourse with rocks and pockets of soil laid on. In no way should this rocky landscape compete with the traditional bog feature, which is home to a wide variety of plants and which I will discuss in the next section of this chapter.

The plants from the subalpine meadow zone in the Himalaya all grow in full light. Some species prefer dry rocky areas, such as *Incarvillea*, but others are to be found in damp conditions amongst rocks in pockets of deep loamy soil. The specialised plants that demand such conditions are my recommendations for the ravine garden. Our goal is not only to grow them successfully, but also to allow them to perform in as natural a way as possible, encouraging such plants to flower in true character.

Surely one of the true Himalayan classics is *Rheum nobile,* indeed most aptly named the "nobility" of the rhubarb family, Polygonaceae. The species is rare in cultivation, but seed is often made available from seed expeditions and its demanding growing conditions can be met within the ravine garden. Often growing in screes above the subalpine meadow zone, *R. nobile* is widely distributed between 11,800 and 14,700 ft. (3600–4480 m) throughout the eastern Himalaya into Bhutan, Tibet and the provinces of western China.

The keys to success in cultivation are the provision of good light in addition to a cool, deep root run into a fairly rich, loamy soil with running water into which the taproots will penetrate. The several-feet-deep root run can be achieved by embedding decent-sized boulders—at least 3-ft. (90-cm) blocks—into the soil, providing pockets of soil where the plants will thrive while their deep taproots find protection by the sides of the rocks during hot spells.

Seedlings should be pricked out straight into deep pots, once known as "long toms," and not allowed to dry out during the growing season. The following spring, young plants should be planted out at least 2 ft. (60 cm) apart. The plants are totally herbaceous and reappear in late April, or early May on the east coast of Scotland. The most challenging part is to bring them to flower. These recommended growing conditions should ensure that some five to six years in the future, and probably only once, the typical rhubarb-like, 12-in. (30-cm), red-margined foliage will provide the base for the most striking, erect stems up to 3 to 4 ft. (0.9–1.2 m) in height with conical spikes of large, pale cream-coloured,

Rheum nobile, Bimbi La, southern Tibet ANNE CHAMBERS

rounded, bladder-like bracts concealing the numerous green flowers. As these stunning bracts decay, a mass of black, triangular seeds, technically nutlets, are left hanging and ready for collecting, storing and subsequent sowing at the turn of the year. Should the grower be successful in flowering this outstanding species, he or she will no doubt herald the success with a loud trumpet blast and, forgetting all rationality, contact appreciative friends to witness the spectacle!

An important genus symbolic of the Himalaya and presenting a challenge to horticulturists and gardeners is *Cremanthodium,* belonging to the composite family, Compositae. The generic name in its Greek origin suggests "kremao," to hang, and "anthodium," flower-head, referring to the pendent flower-heads which are reminiscent of miniature sunflowers. One or two species present few challenges, but in the main, encouraging seedlings on to flowering has proved difficult. I hope that a project such as that recommended here will prove to be the very conditions to suit this lovely genus. I am still trying.

Many of the species will be found within the alpine zone and occupy the higher stations in scree conditions. I will describe a few which grow in both subalpine meadow conditions and the alpine zone, where the roots are able to penetrate into firm soil beneath the rocks. The best way to obtain material of *Cremanthodium* is through seed-collecting expeditions to the Himalaya. Store the seed in an airtight container in the refrigerator, and sow in the spring as soon as the soil conditions are suitable. The seed may be sown in situ, which involves preparing a seed bed by gently raking a few square feet of soil and sowing the seed singly on the surface, a few inches apart. Cover the seed with a thin layer of soil spread through a sieve, then add a further layer of coarse, gritty sand to stabilise the seed and protect the necks of the germinating seedlings. Water in well. Though this all may sound a little complicated, these plants resent root disturbance and therefore should establish more easily through this method.

An alternative method of raising plants is to sow the seed in a loam-based seed compost, utilising cellular trays or small 1- to 2-in. (2.5- to 5-cm) pots. Sow the seeds singly, covering them the same way with soil and gritty sand. Ensure the seed containers remain moist but not wet. Once germination takes place and the resulting seedlings have established, plant them along with their cells of soil in a prepared bed. This method obviates the need for pricking out and the inevitable root disturbance which generally causes their death.

The easiest species to grow and one often available in commerce is *Cremanthodium arnicoides,* found fairly widespread across the Himalaya in rich meadows. As with all the species, this one forms a herbaceous crown of basal leaves producing flowering stems up to 2 ft. (60 cm) with several nodding, glowing-yellow flower-heads up to 2 in. (5 cm) across. This species will prove to be the most satisfactory in the garden, thriving in the cool, rocky habitat with good light.

Cremanthodium arnicoides, Schachen Garden, southern Germany DIETER SCHACHT

A further two species which may require some seeking out are *Cremanthodium decaisnei* and *C. reniforme*, both found in more stable situations amongst alpine turf or rock outcrops where the roots are able to penetrate soil. So stunning are the flowers of these species, every attempt should be made to locate seed and provide the right home for them. With *C. decaisnei*, 4- to 6-in. (10- to 15-cm) stems produce nodding, yellow flowers with a well-developed calyx of brown overlapping sepals forming a cone at the back of the flower like some quaint bonnet—surely it is one of the most exquisite of all Himalayan flowers. *Cremanthodium reniforme*, as its name suggests, has kidney-shaped leaves and solitary, nodding, yellow flowers on 9- to 12-in. (23- to 30-cm) stems.

Cremanthodium reniforme, Langtang, central Nepal DIETER SCHACHT

The Bog Garden

Clearly the provision of a watercourse offers great possibilities for the Himalayan garden. What greater bonus could a gardener receive than to enjoy a natural supply of water running through the garden! In Scotland we call a stream a "burn." A boggy area, whether it be naturally occurring or artificially created is often associated with poorly drained soil, possibly involving a clay or otherwise heavy substrate. But in fact, as long as the water area is not stagnant and is acid in nature, the site can be developed to incorporate a wide variety of plants, both woody and herbaceous. The differences betweeen the ravine and bog gardens may seem minimal. Both can be naturally occurring. The ravine involves water and a natural rock outcrop, while the bog is an area that either naturally or by human intervention provides a source of permanently moist soil.

Of course the taller-growing primulas of the sections *Candelabra* and *Sikkimensis* come to mind for the bog garden. Tastefulness, though, calls for a variety of plants to flower at various times in the season to enhance the garden landscape.

At the edge of a burn or around the margins of the bog garden, early-spring colour can be assured by a mixed planting of *Caltha*, the marsh marigold, and a variety of primulas. This is a natural association often experienced by visitors to the mountains of Kashmir and the western Himalaya. The caltha found in those parts is *C. palustris* var. *himalensis*, displaying its typical lush, glossy foliage with bold, terminal clusters of golden yellow or occasionally white flowers. It will flower in the early spring in gardens at the same time as the brightly coloured and easily grown *Primula rosea*, found abundantly by running water in the western Himalaya. This primula is easily grown, producing its distinctive lax umbel of rose-pink to red flowers on 6- to 9-in. (15- to 23-cm) stems. As with most primulas in the *Farinosae* section, this one is easily propagated from seed, but in this case I recommend sowing the seed as soon as it is collected, to greatly improve germination.

To this association add the bold clumps of *Primula denticulata*, the drumstick primula, and there can be no finer sight in the bog garden. Once again easily grown, it is highly variable, offering a variety of colours which can be enjoyed in drifts broken up by the yellow flowers of the marsh marigolds. To propagate a favourite colour form or named cultivar, regular division is the simplest method, carried out after flowering or during the period of dormancy in the autumn. Saving seed from good colour forms will not guarantee a further generation of such colours. Shades of mauve-blue predominate together with good reds and a pure white.

A range of the Sino-Himalayan *Iris* species will prove rewarding in such a damp area, associating well with the taller primulas. Try the blue to purple-flowered *Iris* species, such as *I. bulleyana,* which ranges from pale to deep blue, or *I. clarkei* in its dark purple form or *I. chrysographes* in purple to black. Of the candelabras, *Primula helodoxa* is the supreme choice with lovely golden yellow flowers. From the section *Sikkimensis, Primula alpicola* in its lemon-yellow form or the type species *P. sikkimensis* with its fragrant, yellow flowers would provide the ideal contrast beside the various hues of purple-blue irises.

Trollius acaulis with *Primula rosea,* Kashmir DIETER SCHACHT

One of my favourite herbaceous subjects for the bog garden is the stately rhubarb from the Sino-Himalaya, *Rheum alexandrae,* showing its best in early summer. Commonly found in the mountains of western China and Tibet, growing in swampy areas often amongst willows, the plants are made up of rather large, leathery foliage forming bold rosettes. The inflorescence is handsome, attaining some 3 ft. (90 cm) at best, forming a solid stem shrouded in creamy-yellow pendent, leaf-like bracts that hide the flowers. This exciting species may be propagated by seed, or nutlets, which can be collected as the whole plant begins to decay in the early autumn. A bold planting of this subject would associate well with drifts of bog primula such as the superb *Primula secundiflora* with its nodding umbels of wine-red-coloured flowers, or with the candelabra prim-

Primula rosea, Kashmir DIETER SCHACHT

ulas, including a mixed planting in pastel shades of *P. bulleyana* in orange, *P. pulverulenta* in plum-red and *P. chungensis* in yellow-orange. A marriage of these candelabra species will bring about a natural range of hybrids, producing a lovely blend of pastel colours to make the boggy area a chief delight during summer months.

Primula denticulata, Kashmir DIETER SCHACHT

Primula alpicola with *P. alpicola* var. *violacea* in the foreground, Schachen Garden, southern Germany DIETER SCHACHT

Primula sikkimensis, Langtang, central Nepal DIETER SCHACHT

Some of the more vigorous blue poppies will grow well in this situation, whether in full sun or dappled shade. The best ones to choose would be the vigorous *Meconopsis* George Sherriff Group along with the sumptuous turquoise-blue *M.* ×*sheldonii*. I cannot overlook a personal favourite, *M. quintuplinervia,* Farrer's harebell poppy, found in western

Meconopsis ×*sheldonii,* Edrom Nurseries, Berwickshire JIM JERMYN

China and Tibet. This is a spreading perennial sending out underground stolons. It loves a damp situation and produces 6- to 9-in. (15- to 23-cm) stems, each bearing a pendulous, pale lavender flower. Stately plants that blend very well with the primulas and meconopses are a number of *Rodgersia* species, including the exciting *R. pinnata* from western China and *R. nepalensis* from eastern Nepal. Both form herbaceous clumps with bold, pinnate foliage and flowering stems up to 3 ft. (90 cm) in height. The lovely spike-like flowers are in the case of *R. pinnata* deep pink and in *R. nepalensis* creamy white. Rodgersias may be propagated quite satisfactorily from seed.

To conclude, a subject providing useful colour in the boggy situation would be an edging or marginal planting of the spreading *Polygonum affine*. This species is seen at its best in either of the superior forms *P. affine* 'Donald Lowndes' or 'Darjeeling Red', both spreading into wide mats. The pale-pink to reddish flowers are borne on a cylindrical spike in the late summer, lasting well into the autumn when the foliage assumes superb reddish tints.

Autumn-Flowering Gentians

Readers may be surprised to learn that many popular autumn-flowering gentians, notably *Gentiana sino-ornata* occupy distinctly marshy conditions in nature. Their preference for open, damp meadow conditions brings me to devote this section to these sensational plants. But compiling this section has presented a serious challenge, for the many Himalayan and Sino-Himalayan gentians with horticultural merit and garden worthiness make it difficult to choose which species and cultivars to plant in the garden.

Of the 360 species of *Gentiana* recorded in science, some 248 species are native to China, giving a clear picture as to the source of the genus and from where they originally migrated. For such a large and valuable genus a comprehensive classification was needed early on, to bring about some botanical order. So it was that in 1894 the Russian botanist Kusnezow undertook a major work on the genus, although at that time few of the many Chinese species were known to him or science.

In subsequent years several botanists have worked on *Gentiana,* notably Marquand in 1937, but the definitive work now available was published in 1995 by the Science Press of Beijing in *Flora of China.* This is a thorough and absolutely comprehensive work that covers most of the species of all the genera relevant to this title. To be truly specific about geographic boundaries, relatively few species of *Gentiana* are found in the Himalayan massif. Yet, by comparison to the massive horticultural importance of gentians in the Sino-Himalayan context, I make no apologies for "widening the net."

The taxonomic classification of *Gentiana,* in order to cope with the tremendous diversity within the genus, defines a number of sections which bring together species according to their scientific makeup. The five sections that cover plants from the Sino-Himalaya are *Kudoa, Frigida, Pneumonanthe, Phyllocalyx* and *Isomeria.* This chapter highlighting the subalpine meadow zone concerns species from the section *Kudoa.* The following paragraphs discuss their impact in horticulture together with the hybridisation that has taken place, and of course their successful cultivation in the garden. The other sections will be covered in Chapter 5 as we rise higher in altitude to the alpine zone. Most of the subjects discussed here present few challenges to the gardener, but the truly alpine species will test the skills of the cultivator.

The one single species of *Gentiana* that has made the greatest impact in horticulture during the twentieth century is *G. sino-ornata,* first collected by Forrest in north-western Yunnan in 1904. What is so extraordinary about this notable introduction is its persistence in horticulture for nearly a century. This length of time is significant because so many gardens in which this species grows simply cannot provide the ideal conditions, thus endangering its survival. But survive it has, setting very little seed over the years due to its late flowering in September and October, giving the fertilised ovary little time to ripen before the decaying trumpets fill up with rain water and rot away.

Not until 1991 and the highly successful expedition to Yunnan, carried out in part by the Royal Botanic Garden in Edinburgh, was this species re-collected and brought back to gardens. Of great interest, both horticulturally and to science, is that the resulting material (the collection numbers carry the prefix C.L.D.) displayed a fundamentally different habit to Forrest's collection. The C.L.D. collections show a marked stoloniferous habit with slender growth, while Forrest's original material is of a more compact nature, making it more desirable as a potted plant in the nursery trade.

Gentiana sino-ornata is found in Sichuan and north-western Yunnan and forms a central rosette from which radiate many spreading stolons which root at the nodes. The stolons measure typically up to 8 in. (20 cm) in length. The narrow leaves are in pairs and form a tube around the stem, making a pleasant carpeting effect. At the end of each stolon the solitary flowers are borne in the form of striking trumpets beautifully striped on the outside. The colour varies immensely in nature, but Forrest's form still rightly forms a benchmark with which new material can be compared—his original introduction is a glorious royal blue. The species offers a white form, *G. sino-ornata* var. *alba,* and one of the newer in-

Gentiana sino-ornata, Yunnan, China DAVID MILLWARD

troductions with a strong stoloniferous habit is *G. sino-ornata* (C.L.D. 476b) with slate-white flowers and brown markings on the outside.

The typical habitat for this species in China is wet meadows or river banks and alpine meadows. It clearly prefers a lime-free, moisture-retentive bed in an open aspect. To create a bed for this gentian and its relatives is really a simple matter, provided the garden is not subject to a blatantly alkaline, or limy, or overly hot and dry aspect. I recommend creating a bed of any suitable proportion, possibly an island bed of uneven shape either on a gentle slope or on the level. The position should allow full exposure to light. If the natural soil is neutral to acid this is an ideal basis from which to work. If on the other hand the pH is slightly alkaline it may be practical to import an acid soil and excavate to a sufficient depth, say to 18 in. (46 cm), and replace the soil, adding a generous amount of sphagnum peat. This is a worthless excercise if the natural soil is very alkaline, or chalky, as the chalk will leach back into the supplementary material, or if the water supply is highly alkaline. Gentians are not great feeders, which makes it inadvisable to add fertilisers to the soil. If the soil is particularly impoverished, however, apply at planting a little general fertiliser with low available nitrates and some extra magnesium, such as Enmag in the United Kingdom, which includes 5 N, 19 P, 10 K, 7.5 Mg.

To enhance the display of autumn gentians, which are predominantly blue, I recommend incorporating a few woody specimens in the form of slow-growing trees and shrubs to balance the autumn display. Although not necessarily of Himalayan origin, a specimen of the sweet gum, *Liquidamber styraciflua* 'Worplesdon', will form a tree with maple-like foliage and superb autumn colour. Other smaller shrubs suitable in a modest-sized bed would be *Fothergilla major* or *Enkianthus cernuus* f. *rubens,* both displaying wonderful autumnal tints.

The gentians are widely available from specialist nurseries and are best planted in late spring to allow a full season for them to establish. Inevitably most normal people will be moved to purchase gentians in the autumn when they are in flower. This is not the best time to plant them in the garden as they will not establish a root system prior to the coming winter. By all means purchase the plants in flower but retain them in their pots, keeping them well watered until the foliage turns brown. The plants will overwinter outside quite satisfactorily, being ready for planting as the weather allows the following spring. The more vigorous species and hybrids should be planted with enough space to spread out. The ideal planting distance is some 9–12 in. (23–30 cm) apart. A careful mix of both species and hybrids planted together in bold groups will create a display of colour commencing, typical of a Scottish climate, in early August right through to early November.

It is very important in the first growing season, from May through to late July, that the newly established plants do not dry out. Water the gentians infrequently but thoroughly, ensuring that the plants are soaked either early in the day or last thing at night. Frequent damping down in a half-hearted approach will simply encourage the young plants to send out feeder roots near the surface, thus failing to produce strong anchoring roots. This kind of development will result in inevitable death if the watering suddenly ceases in a hot dry spell.

After flowering, the gentians will not need deadheading, unless the gardener plans to save seed, which is an easy operation. After pollination and fertilisation, the ovary, or seed capsule, extends out of the decaying trumpet, exposing itself to enable successful dispersal of seed. As the capsules turn brown and begin to open slightly they can be detached and placed into a paper bag to dry out. Once dry, they are ready for cleaning and sowing at the turn of the year in an acid loam-based seed compost.

In late March or early April, all the previous season's growth can be pulled away from the central rosette and discarded, allowing the new growth to proceed. This is a good time to weed the bed thoroughly and top-dress with a thin layer of sphagnum peat. After three to five years of growth the gentians will need to be lifted and divided at this time in early spring, just as the plants are breaking out of dormancy. Lift each of the fat clumps and remove any excess soil, carefully keeping the varieties separate. Simply loosen the clumps gently and the thong-like roots will fall apart. It is important to grade them out on a bench retaining only the plants with strong and healthy roots. Plant the very best quality ones back into the bed with some fresh soil, rotted compost and peat. The plants of secondary quality can be given away or potted up in an acid potting compost to await future planting. Water in the fresh planting thoroughly. Experience will show which species and varieties are more vigorous, some needing more frequent division and others rarely bulking up at all. If beds are neglected, though, the quality of flowering will recede and plants will become impoverished and eventually die.

An exciting aspect of this section *Kudoa* of *Gentiana* is that beginning with just some seven species, and a rational number of cultivars, the yield results in a great range of blues and some lovely pure whites, thus creating a magnificent display—perhaps one of the highlights in the Himalayan garden. A magnificent plant becoming better understood with late 1990s exploration of north-western Yunnan is *Gentiana veitchiorum*. This is a highly variable species found over a wide area including north-western Yunnan, south-eastern Tibet, Gansu and Bhutan. This is a distinct plant often rhizomatous in habit and therefore proving less generous from division. Its more compact habit is endearing in the garden, with a typical basal rosette and much broader leaves than *G. sino-ornata*. I have observed that the material available in horticulture, including the now rather tired specimens of *G. veitchiorum* (L.S. 13321), have a marked tendency to branching, a desirable asset when searching for free-flowering, compact hybrids with a deep blue flower. These characteristics also show up in the *G. ×stevenagensis* hybrids such as 'Frank Barker', the outstanding 'David Tuckwell' and 'Shot Silk'.

In north-western Yunnan Ron McBeath found *Gentiana veitchiorum* growing in alpine meadows, turf banks and amongst open scrub, in stark contrast to the marsh situations of *G. sino-ornata*. He noted that the flowers varied little, being almost always a deep violet-blue. This rather constant flower seems to hold true in cultivated forms from this area. In other regions, including river banks and alpine meadows, the habitat of the species is more versatile, showing great variation in flower colour and form. The species was first discovered in 1915 by Wilson in Sichuan, his expedition sponsored by the well-known firm, Veitch, hence the specific name. Certainly more will be learned of this superb species as plant exploration continues, but it has already made a great impact in horticulture and deserves to be sought out by keen plantsfolk.

With a thoroughly confused scientific history comes the glorious species *Gentiana lawrencei*, known to most gardeners as *G. farreri*. The thorough *Flora of China* identifies two varieties, firstly *G. lawrencei* var. *lawrencei;* they note the distribution as south-western Gansu, Qinghai and western Sichuan, mentioning correctly that it was first described from a garden plant grown from seed collected by Brocheral in 1905 near Lake Baikal in Mongolia. The second variety recognised by the *Flora of China* is *G. lawrencei* var. *farreri,* found in alpine meadows also from south-western Gansu, Qinghai and western Sichuan. The botanical difference between the two varieties is stated to be the length of the calyx lobes, the long whiskers situated behind the flower, which are much longer in *G. lawrencei* var. *farreri.* My personal feeling, based on my own experience of it in cultivation and on accounts from those who have been privileged to encounter the plant in nature, is that *G. farreri* is a variable species stretching over a very wide distribution with a possible diminutive form in Mongolia. It is apparently very common on the Tibetan Plateau and reports from Ludlow and Sherriff suggest that another form is to be found around Lhasa.

To that great alpinist Reginald Farrer, a Yorkshireman of true character, I must now turn for a flavour of the intense excitement to be derived upon first seeing *Gentiana lawrencei* var. *farreri.* On a trip in 1914 to the Da-Tang mountain in northern Gansu Farrer wrote, "In the fine turf that crowned the top of a sloping boulder there stared at me a new gentian, a gentian that obliterates all others of its race. I gave tongue for Bill [Purdom] and, together, in reverent silence, we contemplated that marvel of luminous loveliness" (1919). Farrer described it as having "a subtle swell to the chalice, that is streaked outside in heavy lines of black and purple that divide long vandykes of dim periwinkle blue, with panels of Nankeen buff between: inside, the tube and throat are white but the mouth and the bold fingers are so luminous and intense a light azure that one blossom of it will blaze out at you among the grass on the other side of the valley. It literally burns in the alpine turf like an electric jewel, an incandescent turquoise." Farrer collected seed of this fine form displaying Cambridge-blue-coloured flowers. The seed germinated at the Royal Botanic Garden in Edinburgh, and flowering plants were sent on to Farrer in 1916. What great joy this brought him and deservedly so. He was to die of illness when still a young man while on a botanical trip to China in 1920.

I can share a little of his joy as I still grow material related to the original introduction, carefully selected from seed. One interesting, rarely mentioned fact about this variety is that along with several other well-known plants from the mountains of the Sino-Himalaya, it can tolerate a significant amount of magnesium limestone, or dolomite, in the soil and indeed seems to thrive with some added dolomite incorporated into an acid soil. This does not mean that such plants will thrive in dry, chalky soils. It is this rather significant fact that I believe may have helped to maintain this wonderful plant in cultivation for so many years. While I was doing my apprenticeship under Will Ingwersen in Sussex in 1971, a consignment of plants arrived at the nursery from Joe Elliot, another great plantsman who ran an inspirational establishment in the Cotswolds. The endemic soil at Elliot's nursery was of course Cotswold limestone and he told me that the only autumn-flowering gentian he could grow was *Gentiana lawrencei* var. *farreri*. So fine were the flowers on his

Gentiana lawrencei var. *farreri*, Edrom Nurseries, Berwickshire JIM JERMYN

plants when delivered to the Sussex nursery that my eyes were fixed on them, so Ingwersen gave me one when I left my assignment with him. I have never lost this material nor forgotten its origin and am sure many other fortunate gardeners still grow this original form which fits exactly Farrer's rather poetic description.

Gentiana lawrencei var. *farreri* grows very well in a cool yet open bed or trough with added dolomite, and in my experience is not as happy in a peaty bed as the other *Gentiana* species, although still appreciating plenty of moisture during the growing season. One of the first plants to flower at the beginning of August, the variety is of more lax habit than other species with leaves a bright green in colour, long and narrow and distinctly recurved. The long calyx lobes are a strong characteristic, but both in the wild and resulting cultivated seedlings display a variable flower colour, from the distinctive Cambridge-blue through to deeper colours. In its best form this is surely one of the finest species and has been parent to some of the finest hybrids in cultivation. It may be divided as with the other species but it has not proved to be so prolific in bulking up, yet does set plenty of seed. This may be collected and stored and sown as suggested before. The resulting seedlings will show variation and with a little experience it will soon become apparent which are the seedlings to put aside as hybrids for further trial, aiming to retain those of similar character to maintain some purity and at the same time ensuring renewed vigour.

This brief description of an outstanding garden plant shows just how wonderful this hobby of gardening and growing challenging plants is. A number of horticultural characters have appeared through the generations and have given so much with their explorations, committing their experiences to such descriptive prose. Added to these are a number of celebrated growers who over the years have shared their knowledge and expertise with keen students like myself, eager to try and piece together the horticultural jigsaw puzzle. Indeed we owe all those individuals a great deal, and the best way to show our appreciation is of course to continue sharing our experiences.

In our modern era this is just what individuals such as Roy Lancaster have done. He, along with his colleagues in the Sino-British expedition to Yunnan in 1981, was instrumental in introducing another species of horticultural merit. *Gentiana ternifolia* was introduced as *G. ternifolia* (S.B.E. 1053), possibly in the form of two separate clones later named 'Cangshan' and 'Dali'. They were collected from the damp meadows of Dali. This species is extremely prolific, spreading quickly and flowering freely when given plenty of light. It hybridises freely with its close relatives and is sure to be parent to some lovely compact hybrids in years to come. It is a great choice for edging a bed, with a compact habit and sky-blue flowers appearing towards the end of the season in September and October. With such a vigorous habit it easily bulks up from division, perhaps as soon as after three seasons.

Two species well worth including in the bed of gentians, while being less vigorous in habit and quite distinct in flower, are *Gentiana hexaphylla* and *G. prolata*. The former was introduced by Farrer from Gansu in 1914 and has remained in cultivation somewhat precariously until the reintroduction by the very successful seed-collecting trip organised by the Alpine Garden Society to north-western Yunnan in 1994 (having collection numbers prefixed by A.C.E.). Once again one of the members partaking in this trip, Ron McBeath, noted that on the summit pass of the Beima Shan he and the party were overwhelmed at the short turf full of *G. hexaphylla* (A.C.E. 1692) in full flower. At 13,700 ft. (4180 m) the well-drained turf would receive ample moisture from the monsoon rains. The colour varied little, most flowers being pale blue with petals flared wide open. The foliage of this species is distinct, with grey-green, rather glaucous leaves in dense whorls of three to seven leaves per node. Often flowering in August in our eastern Scottish climate, it may serve as an attractive parent to hybrids as it becomes re-established in horticulture. In 1931 A.G. Weeks crossed *G. farreri,* meaning *G. lawrencei* var. *farreri,* with material from Farrer's introduction of *G. hexaphylla* producing *G. ×hexa-farreri.*

Gentiana prolata is another species flowering early in August. It is most attractive with neat foliage and narrow tubular flowers. It has a wide distribution, taking in south-eastern Tibet, Bhutan, Nepal and Sikkim. Beer introduced a fine form from eastern Nepal that has persisted well in gardens, forming a basal rosette and short flowering stems bearing bright blue, tubular inflorescences with a marked white throat and spotting within. This species is easily propagated from seed and will prove a popular plant in the gentian bed.

Several species introduced in the late 1990s may well become known to horticulture through the coming years as they begin to filter into the trade, but it is to the multitude of hybrids that we now turn our attention.

Gentian Hybrids

Most keen growers of gentians have quickly perceived the plants' willingness to hybridise readily and form exciting new plants with admirable qualities for the garden. Venturing into hybridising requires little in the way of scientific training. Just carry out the purpose in an orderly fashion using a small, soft paint brush to pass the pollen from the male plant to the chosen female species. Choose a female parent and cut open its large buds and remove the stamens with a pair of forceps (see figure). The plant must now be protected or covered to keep off unwanted insects until the stigmas have recoiled and become receptive. Then apply pollen from newly dehisced anthers of the chosen male parent. It is important to tag the pollinated flowers with details of the parentage and date of pollination. After pollination has been carried out hopefully fertilisation will soon take place. For a few weeks until the capsules begin to ripen, the female plant should be covered up again with a tent of muslin. This is the method for the organised hybridist, but nature can also take its course, and an eager eye can easily pick out a hybrid from a batch of seedlings as they begin to produce their first set of true leaves. Nature may produce some of the finest hybrids showing the best constitution—a sharp eye will spot them. In my experience it is a species of hoverfly, or wasp, that is the chief natural agent to this process here in Scotland.

I have no intention of giving a comprehensive list of available hybrids. The many nursery catalogues specialising in autumn-flowering gentians from the United Kingdom, Germany, Switzerland and the United States will serve the reader admirably. I mean to present some of the finest that I have grown and that other gardeners have much admired.

The first serious hybridisation of autumn-flowering gentians commenced in Britain around 1930 utilising the few known species available in horticulture. A number of the early hybrids proved much easier than the species to cultivate in less amenable growing conditions. One of the first hybridists was R. H. Macaulay of Lochgilphead, Argyll, Scotland, who crossed *Gentiana sino-ornata* with *G. lawrencei* var. *farreri* to produce *G. ×macaulayi*. This hybrid proved of immense importance to gardeners the world over. Of the five or so seedlings Macaulay raised from this cross, one was chosen and named *G. ×macaulayi*, and divisions of it and the others were distributed to his friends, amongst whom was R.D. Trotter of Brin, near Inverness, Scotland, a fine gardener and close friend of Jack Drake. It was Drake who told me the story of the five or so seedlings. Drake recalled visiting Trotter's garden in the autumn of about

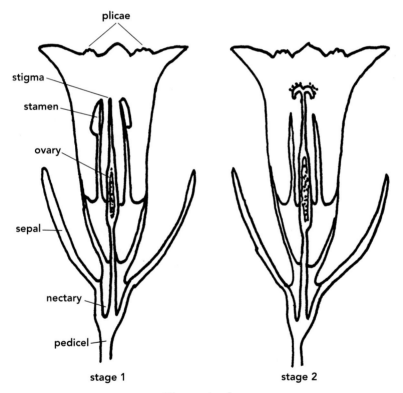

The gentian flower

1959, and seeing each of the seedlings in full flower, he felt that apart from the already named *G. ×macaulayi,* only one other was an outstanding seedling. Drake was given a clump of the second outstanding one, and in due course *G. ×macaulayi* 'Kingfisher' was born. It has proved to be one of the finest of all our autumn-flowering garden plants. It is very close to *G. sino-ornata,* being slightly paler when seen en masse, and flowers at least a fortnight earlier. The name 'Kingfisher', besides describing the glorious blue, also highlights the flowers' marked orange anthers prior to pollination. Some hybrid seedlings resemble one parent more closely than the other, and the original *G. ×macaulayi* resembles *G. lawrencei* var. *farreri* more closely than its other parent. It has proved to be a vigorous hybrid and may still be in cultivation, though I know of no nurseries offering it.

A little later, in 1934, Macaulay created the popular hybrid *Gentiana ×carolii* from *G. lawrencei* var. *farreri* and *G. lawrencei.* Looking at this hybrid, which is still widely grown in gardens today, it looks to me much more as if the two parents are *G. lawrencei* var. *farreri* and *G. prolata,* but one must respect the records from the hybridist. It is the first autumn gentian to flower, often at the end of July. It is a free-flowering hybrid, neat in habit with narrow tubular flowers, pale turquoise blue in colour. In my experience this is a sterile hybrid, which sets no seed. This plant needs division every few years both to rejuvenate and to provide a means of propagation.

At the same time Macaulay made another pioneering cross using *Gentiana veitchiorum* and *G. sino-ornata,* producing the excellent *G. ×bernardii,* later renamed *G. ×stevenagensis* 'Bernardii'. It is another fine compact grower, flowering later on in September, with dark blue flowers with purple bands within.

In 1938 W. E. Mackenzie, while a member of staff at the Royal Botanic Garden in Edinburgh, made an important cross between *Gentiana lawrencei* var. *farreri* and *G. veitchiorum,* producing one of the most famous, and in my opinion one of the finest, hybrids, namely *G.* 'Inverleith'. This one has the rather spindly habit of *G. lawrencei* var. *farreri* but a stunning flower colour, perhaps the best of all, real Gentian-blue—appearing early in August. I strongly recommend this cultivar to any grower of these lovely plants, although it has become rather difficult to obtain in its true form. One or two cultivars have appeared in the trade as imposters under this celebrated name, so be careful to check the origin of material under offer.

Two outstanding cultivars which have become rare are *Gentiana* 'Devonhall' and 'Glendevon', both raised by Andrew Harley. The lovely high-altitude species *Gentiana ornata*, from Nepal, was utilised in both cases. (I will describe this species in more detail amongst the gentians discussed in Chapter 5.) For 'Devonhall', *G. ornata* was crossed with *G. lawrencei* var. *farreri* to produce a compact plant with pale blue flowers. 'Glendevon' involved *G. ornata* and *G. sino-ornata,* but the resulting hybrid barely differs from *G. ornata* with its neat habit and dumpy, turquoise-blue flowers.

Having lived for a while in Hertfordshire, a county in the south-east of England which is relatively dry and often subject to soil of relatively high pH, I always marvel at the ability of Clarence Elliot (father of Joe Elliot), who ran an alpine plant nursery in Stevenage, to grow these gentians. His nursery manager, Frank Barker grew some autumn gentians very well and made a cross between *Gentiana sino-ornata* and *G. veitchiorum,* producing the compact, late-flowering hybrid called *G. ×stevenagensis* 'Frank Barker' with lovely dark purple-blue flowers.

These are a few of the pioneer crosses made with the species then known in cultivation. In the late 1900s many well-known hybridists in some cases repeated the crosses, perhaps using newly introduced species, but in the main resulted with already-known cultivars. Clearly as the years go by the sky is the limit for possibilities open to the modern hybridist. Garden centres can hardly keep up with the glut of new names, but if only the majority of the newly named cultivars were worth the names appended to them. A good all-round modern hybrid needs to have, above all, a sound constitution to cope with the changing climate. It needs to be free-flowering, a good clean colour and above all absolutely distinct so that if you choose to name the hybrid after your daughter, it will live up to her name and continue as a fine garden plant for a long time.

Some of the finest modern hybrids owe their origin to famous nurseries in Scotland, Wales, Germany and Switzerland, and it would be silly to start naming them and then sadly miss a few. Surely as I write others will have commenced this interesting work of hybridising. The following are a few of my personal favourites that my gentian bed just could not do without. The exact origin of some of the finest hybrids is a little obscure, so unless I am absolutely sure, I will not attempt to offer a suggestion as to the parents.

One gentian that must rank as the most free-flowering of all is the dark blue, multi-headed cultivar *Gentiana* 'David Tuckwell', formerly known under the invalid name of 'Multiflora' (cultivar names should not be Latinised). The name commemorates its raiser.

Jack Drake's nursery since about 1950 has been responsible for disseminating many fine gentians. While training there I not only fell in love with this part of the highlands of Scotland, near to Aviemore, but also chose my career under the inspiration of the range of plants grown at the nursery. A distinct cultivar, selected as an Inverleith seedling, was *Gentiana* 'Susan Jane', named after then-proprietor John Lawson's youngest daughter. This hybrid has a fine compact habit with beautifully striped, turquoise-blue trumpets.

George Sturrock who set up a family business specialising in autumn-flowering gentians for the wholesale market in Angus, Scotland, put a name to a very fine Devonhall seedling, *Gentiana* 'Blue Bonnets', again free-flowering, mid-blue and easily grown. He has raised many fine seedlings, two of which I purchased in a mixed bunch. They have proved of such great quality that I named them while still running Edrom Nurseries and exhibited them at several Royal Horticultural Society shows. *Gentiana* 'Soutra' is a pure white, compact-growing plant with dark-green foliage, sound in habit and easily grown. The other, *G.* 'Sheryl Louise', is a vibrant deep-blue-flowering cultivar which I named after my daughter, who has loved helping at the shows over the years and enjoys meeting the public at large.

Another fine nursery, established in northern Wales and rising to prominence in the 1990s, is Aberconwy Nursery, run by Keith and Rachel Lever. Amongst a whole host of cultivars raised by Keith is one which deserves particular mention. It is *Gentiana* 'Shot Silk' which is compact in habit resembling a more free-flowering version of *G.* ×*stevenagensis* 'Frank Barker', with deep blue flowers with attractive bands of violet blue.

Gentiana 'Blue Bonnets', Edrom Nurseries, Berwickshire JIM JERMYN

To conclude, I would have to go back in time to a batch of cultivars raised by Neil Lyle of Maryfield Nursery in Fife, Scotland. His first batch of hybrids were named in commemoration of Queen Elizabeth's coronation in 1953. Three of these are *Gentiana* 'Elizabeth', 'Coronation' and 'Edinburgh'. This last is my favourite, compact in habit with stunning turquoise-blue flowers produced over a long period of time in mid-autumn.

Gardeners can select and combine their favourite species and hybrids to give the garden a balanced look, with both vigorous and compact plants in the bed, giving colour right through August on to the end of October and the beginning of the frosts. As long as the main requirements are adhered to, namely, an open situation, an acid soil and most importantly the provision of plenty of moisture during the growing season, the autumn-flowering gentians should give years of pleasure highlighting the year-round appeal of the Himalayan garden.

CHAPTER FIVE

Alpine Zone

To reach any conclusion in a written work suggests approaching a climax or crescendo, a moment of extreme excitement. This chapter is no exception, for we have reached the alpine zone, the height at which the adrenaline levels are surely at their peak. For me, and for many, having concentrated on the cultivation of these extraordinary plants without having first-hand knowledge of their location in nature, the excitement and challenges presented by the different zones might seem to be represented fairly equally at any altitude, but still something is special about this true alpine zone. Perhaps it is the knowledge that few have scaled these heights, some 12,000–16,400 ft. (3660–5000 m), and seen these specialised plants. Whatever the draw, so many of us crave the opportunity to try and grow them, whether the natural conditions available are conducive to their cultivation or not.

Few plant explorers would disagree with the observation that the richest diversity of choice alpines is to be found in a broad band along the upper edge of the alpine meadows and the base of the extensive screes at varying altitudes depending on the Himalayan region. Well-known plant hunter Ron McBeath noted, "It is impossible to describe the excitement felt when you are labouring your way steadily upwards and come across first one *Primula wigramiana* in perfect flower, then a few, followed by a hillside dominated by this beautiful species" (1985). In this band or zone, so affected by the monsoon, frequent springs are fed by the melting snows which irrigate the upper meadows and screes, providing conditions that are practically impossible for mortal gardeners to simulate at low altitude. With this sobering fact in mind I embark on this exciting chapter.

I have been privileged to know individuals who have shown such generosity in their willingness to impart time and knowledge, often in the form of private slide shows, to the point where I have felt almost sure that part of me was there in the Himalaya with them. The late George Smith was one such friend who often invited me to stay overnight after lecturing nearby or when passing through the area. Always, out came the projector and then hours of sensational slides from a region of Nepal, a country with which he was so familiar. I most profoundly remember slides of an extraordinary gentian. First we saw views of the snow-capped Himalayan peak of Makalu, breathtaking indeed; then the perspective zoomed in to the glacial screes but showed no plant life; then closer still, the slides just barely showed some marks of vegetation between the boulders. Finally came the most perfect clumps of gentian, the likes of which I had never seen before. I asked what they were, and Smith roared with laughter, almost falling backwards off the chair. That I had no idea of the answer to my question appealed to him so greatly—I was simply speechless. The best was yet to come, for the final slide was a close-up of the most exquisite, slate-blue urns sitting between the stones of the scree in all their imperial beauty. It was *Gentiana urnula*, epitomising the challenges of not only trekking to such heights in east-central Nepal but also of finding such a wonderful plant and recording the event with lovely slides. Smith was a master.

Other individuals who have helped and motivated me in a similar fashion are Dieter Schacht under whom I trained at the Munich Botanic Garden; Ron McBeath who has been involved in many expeditions with the Royal Botanic Garden in Edinburgh to both Nepal and China; together with Henry and Margaret Taylor who are superb growers of alpine plants and have shared their knowledge and experience of many expeditions, notably to India and the western Himalaya.

Since the 1990s exploration to some parts of the Himalaya has not been easy, particularly due to the political unrest in Kashmir and the uncertainties linked with the borders of China and Tibet. I have been very thankful and excited to learn of trips carried out in the late 1990s by Peter Cox, his son Kenneth and my good friend Graham Rugman to this sensitive area in south-eastern Tibet. What a thrill they have experienced returning in the footsteps of Ludlow, Sherriff and Kingdon Ward. It is surely just a matter of time before we can enjoy growing a few more of the plants we have only been able to read about, as they make their way back into cultivation by carefully organised seed collections.

If we are able to obtain plants of the alpine zone from specialist nurseries, friends or seed exchanges we should consider pot culture for the early stages of their cultivation. Using pot culture is both normal and

Gentiana urnula, Khumbu, eastern Nepal GEORGE SMITH

prudent, yet an extended period of containerisation could well mean the plants' eventual downfall. This I say with many years of experience in the nursery trade where due to necessity, container-growing is a routine. When plants are given day to day care, not only can they survive but also thrive and produce healthy mother plants while in the pots, provided the roots are allowed to reach into a free-draining soil.

The best eventual site for these higher alpines may well be the raised bed or trough. The majority of these species will accept nothing but good mineral soil of acid to neutral pH. In the exceptional circumstance when a subject prefers an alkaline soil, a measure of coarse dolomite grit can be added around the individual plant. Indeed, for such subjects, a dedicated trough could be prepared with just such a specialised soil.

In the main, plants from this alpine zone will appreciate all the natural light they can get, and at the same time they must not dry out during their growing season. In some cases, notably amongst the primulas, the preferable position for the plants is dappled shade, but at least protect them from the fiercest early-afternoon heat. However, these are very much the exception to the rule.

Although I am proposing to highlight some of the most exciting species found in this zone throughout the vast Himalaya, readers must realise that many of these plants will only be available with diligent search through specialist nursery catalogues and annually produced seed lists. The Appendix lists sources to watch. I can, however, assure readers that once successful in locating a much sought-after plant and once successful in cultivating it, they will find the reward unsurpassed even though the plants may not live long.

The Ranunculaceae

A genus that always has appealed to me personally is *Adonis.* Most of the species hail from Europe, but a lovely one is from the western Himalaya. The species is *A. chrysocyathus,* found predominantly in Kashmir, and once located it often is found to be locally common. A member of the buttercup family, Ranunculaceae, it is early to flower, forming strong, perennial clumps of deciduous foliage. These plants burst into flower before the feathery leaves have fully formed. Golden yellow flowers are produced in profusion on stout 6- to 9-in. (15- to 23-cm) stems. Once established the clumps should be left alone and the plants propagated by seed collected when green, identifiable in achenes, or single-seeded fruits, with a hooked beak which when ripe will fall away when gently rubbed. Once collected, the seed should be sown immediately and may take several years to germinate. As with other members of this family it is important not to be too hasty to prick out the seedlings, rather leaving them in the seed pot to mature for another year, feeding them with a weak,

Adonis chrysocyathus, Zoji-La, Kashmir DIETER SCHACHT

balanced liquid fertiliser at frequent intervals while they are in full growth.

Another member of the buttercup family is the wonderful dwarf monkshood, *Aconitum hookeri,* found at high levels in alpine turf from central Nepal through Sikkim into western China at around 13,700 ft. (4180 m). This is a species well worth seeking out. It requires care to establish successfully, but once this is achieved will reward with years of typical eye-catching purple cowls held on 4-in. (10-cm) stems above attractive dark green, dissected leaves. This choice species spreads by underground stolons emanating from tiny little dark-coloured tubers. It grows admirably in a humus-rich, gritty soil, associating well with a dwarf vaccinium or similar subject which will allow the stems of the aconitum to pop up amongst the evergreen foliage, providing both support and protection at the root for the fragile tubers. These little tubers are utterly resentful of winter water-logging and often rot when grown in a pot. The stunning flowers appear in the summer and often provide a generous amount of seed, which should be collected and sown at once.

The stable screes provide an abundance of exciting plants which require great care when cultivating them in our own low-altitude gardens. Notably, such plants found in screes are growing in pockets of accumulated mineral soil into which the plants can establish their roots. Remember that in most cases these screes are fed with an almost constant supply of snow melt, except in the few cases where the area is affected by a rain shadow and experiences dryer conditions, such as parts of the Tibetan Plateau and the Dolpo area in central Nepal. Under our low-altitude conditions, those plants from screes strongly influenced by the monsoon will simply resent drying out during the growing season. In most cases, they also will prefer an open sunny aspect, making the whole project of growing these a plausible challenge.

The high-altitude *Delphinium* species, closely related to the foregoing aconitums, love to get their roots down into an open, gritty, mineral soil and in these conditions may form established, deciduous clumps, thriving for many years. Sadly it is the gritty element that provides the essential drainage, which, at the same time, can so easily cause the immediate drying out. Drying out may lead to death during a protracted spell of hot dry weather during the growing season when the roots are in search of moisture. I find it worth belabouring this point to assure readers that these high Himalayan alpines are not out of reach of cultivation, but success is attainable only with care and attention to detail, especially watering when the plants require it.

Delphinium brunonianum is found from the western Himalaya across to south-eastern Tibet in the alpine turf and stable scree. It is somewhat variable in flower and can be identified by its strong musky fragrance. Attractive blue-purple flowers with a woolly appearance are borne in a dense cluster on stems no more than 8 in. (20 cm) tall over typically lobed foliage.

A lovely little species I have grown on and off for several decades now is the Ludlow and Sherriff introduction *Delphinium muscosum* (L.S. 19375) which will grow well tucked between small rocks in a raised bed. This species is in no way inhibited when given some extra dolomite and may indeed prefer the presence of a little magnesium. The collector found it growing in stoney or slaty scree at 15,500 ft. (4730 m) in central Bhutan. Forming neat clumps of dissected foliage, the flowers are a rich violet-blue sometimes with a white beard on short 2- to 3-in. (5- to 8-cm) stems. As with all delphiniums, division, while sometimes possible, is not recommended, but propagation is by seed, sown as soon as it is ripe.

Two rather rare species found in similar scree-like conditions are the closely related *Delphinium glaciale* and *D. nepalense*. The former is a treasure found in the upper limit of vegetation in Nepal and Sikkim where it forms a cluster of tiny, hirsute leaves and disproportionately large flowers a stunning misty blue held in twos or threes. *Delphinium nepalense,* recorded from north-western Nepal around Dolpo, has bright blue flowers over grey-green foliage of similar habit to its cousins. These are exciting species worth hunting for and giving pride of place in the garden.

No less demanding are species of *Paraquilegia*. This is the final member of the Ranunculaceae I would like to highlight, one of the many gems, found exclusively in cliffs or rock-crevices at high altitude from the western Himalaya into the rich flora of Yunnan. The species we have come to be most familiar with is *P. grandiflora* (synonym *P. anemonoides*).

In the western limits it is often smaller flowered and pale pink to white in colour, a variant that is often considered to be the separate species *P. microphylla*. Throughout the vast Himalaya collectors have been united in awe of this true alpine aristocrat. While exploring in Bhutan in 1934, Ludlow and Sherriff encountered the finest specimens they had ever seen. Sherriff's diary for 14 July 1934 describes, "Hanging from the cliffs north of the camp were dozens of aged clumps, some of them 2 feet [60 cm] across, *Paraquilegia grandiflora* [L.S. 678], delicate bluish-green deeply cut foliage blending beautifully with the large deep-violet, sometimes lilac, fragile, ever trembling flowers" (Fletcher 1975). Later, in

Delphinium glaciale, eastern Nepal GEORGE SMITH

1938 when collecting with Ludlow and Sherriff, George Taylor found a superb Tibetan form, again in cliffs at around 12,000 ft. (3660 m). He said, "For all its sheer delicacy, poise and refinement it must be supreme."

Paraquilegia grandiflora is readily available from specialist nurseries and its cultivation is not too demanding, either in a garden or in a pot under glass. The best way to simulate its natural conditions is to grow it in a trough or raised bed in a partly shaded aspect. The trough, about 36 by 18 in. (90 by 46 cm), should be of reasonable depth providing at least 12–18 in. (30–46 cm) of soil for a deep root run. Tufa rock is the favourite material to provide crevices in which to plant this species. Bury tufa blocks roughly 12 in. (30 cm) square at least 6 in. (15 cm) into the gritty soil which has been used to fill the trough.

The formation of tufa rock commences with rainfall which dissolves and carries calcium carbonates. The water passes through pervious, or open to penetration, layers of limestone, eventually reaching impervious layers and emerging as springs. As the water passes through layers of decaying organic matter including roots and moss, deposits of calcium carbonate form around this material and gradually develop into porous incrustations. As the deposits increase, the rock "grows" upwards. Over the period of many decades the rock known as "tufa" forms and can eventually be quarried as a soft, porous rock. Once exposed to the air, its surface hardens into an extremely solid stone. I remember visiting a splendid tufa quarry in the south of Germany and being thrilled to see that even the village church was constructed of tufa. Although tufa is often made up of over 90 percent calcium carbonate, the porosity of the rock allows all available lime to drain away. In practical terms, obtaining weathered tufa or carrying out the weathering process ourselves by watering it from time to time and exposing all of it to air, will enable the rock to be utilised in the garden as a prime means of growing crevice dwellers, whether lime lovers or not.

Paraquilegias are often found on calcareous formations in the Himalaya and like to be wedged between pieces of tufa in the garden. In such conditions the plants should thrive and establish clumps, flowering profusely in late spring. Although propagation can be carried out by stem cuttings, I recommend hand-pollinating the flowers by gently transferring pollen from one bloom to another with a soft paint brush. Once the little capsules have formed and begin to turn orange-brown, collect them and remove the seed. As with its relatives in the Ranunculaceae, sow the seed right away for successful germination.

Androsace

One of the highlights of this alpine zone is the numerous members of the primula family, Primulaceae, of which the genus *Androsace* proves quite outstanding. The tireless work of both George Smith and Duncan Lowe comes to mind immediately when we discuss this wonderful genus. Their work on the subject, *Androsaces,* published in 1977 and later revised, has proved invaluable in both identifying and growing the plants. Both men died before witnessing the benefit their volume will give to horticulture. As I stated early in this book, growing many of the high Himalayan alpines successfully is only possible through a basic understanding of their habitat in nature. George Smith studied the native habitat in great detail, and Duncan Lowe put the information into practice, growing many of the plants to perfection in raised beds in his Lancastrian garden on the west coast of northern England. The passing of these two men in the late 1990s is a reminder of the legacy such individuals leave, from which future generations may benefit.

My aim here is to write about a few of the finest species I have grown satisfactorily, and to draw readers' attention to some exciting androsaces which will surely be making their appearance in specialist nursery catalogues in the future. Most of them are spring-flowering in cultivation.

A significant factor in growing Himalayan androsaces successfully is recognising their need, with a few exceptions, for snow cover from November to March, a requirement which we cannot offer in our low-altitude gardens. A trough or section of a raised bed can, though, be covered artificially during this period by placing a stabilised structure of either glass or some satisfactory substitute such as polycorbonate over the plants in question so that the hirsute cushions do not rot with the effects of winter wet or rolling winter fogs, such as we are subjected to on the east coast of Scotland. Having mentioned more protective measures,

I have never seen any ill effects attend the lovely and rewarding species from the western Himalaya, *Androsace sempervivoides*. Here is a plant that can immediately be recommended for a trough or raised bed, where it should be positioned to enable the loose mats of spreading runners, sprouting from neat rosettes, to fall over the perimeter. Neat umbels on short stems of 1 to 2 in. (2.5–5 cm) carry showy deep-pink flowers with a crimson eye, flowering in spring.

Androsace sempervivoides, Schachen Garden, southern Germany JIM JERMYN

Androsace mucronifolia is another species native exclusively to the western Himalaya. It is accommodating, being none too fussy concerning winter protection of the rosettes. It was first found in its true form in Kashmir by Dieter Schacht and then later collected by the Swedish expedition to the Karakoram in north-western Pakistan in 1983 (the collection numbers are prefixed by S.E.P.). The leaf rosettes are much smaller than those of *A. sempervivoides,* and this species forms a tight mound from a central rootstock. The short umbels carry two to six pale pink, sweetly scented flowers. A trough is its ideal home, and as with *A. sempervivoides,* cuttings may be taken after flowering and will root easily in a sandy mixture.

Androsace mucronifolia, Kashmir DIETER SCHACHT

One of the most rewarding amongst these spring-flowering andro-saces producing fine umbels of flowers is the much confused *Androsace studiosorum* (synonym *A. primuloides*). It too is found in the western Hi-malaya, notably in Kashmir and north-western India. In the late 1990s Henry and Margaret Taylor found fine forms in a rich valley named the Doksa in north-western India, where it grows in turfy hollows. The flowers are usually pink, but sometimes pure white, held on dense, hairy umbels over woolly rosettes sending out stolons 2–3 in. (5–8 cm) in length, rooting as they go. I have found, even on the dryer east coast of Scotland that these woolly rosettes are apt to rot in the winter unless they are given some protection from the wet. In its best forms this is one of the finer species. Closely related, and frequently confused with *A. studio-sorum* is *A. sarmentosa;* possibly the two would best be merged into one variable species. *Androsace sarmentosa* enjoys a wider distribution, occur-ring across Nepal and into Sikkim. It is represented by some fine forms in cultivation, surely the finest being the vibrant carmine-pink *A. sar-mentosa* 'Chumbyi'.

Flowering late in June and July is a personal favourite from the north-western Himalaya, *Androsace lanuginosa,* growing on earthy banks and open hillsides. It forms wide, loose mats of interlacing stems and looks best trailing between rocks or pouring down from a dry stone wall. Aris-ing from the leaf axils, often at the same time as the production of new rosettes, are umbels of up to fifteen flowers of a distinct lilac-pink col-our. A pure white form is named *A. lanuginosa* var. *leichtlinii.* All forms are best given some winter protection.

As the altitude increases, the *Androsace* species begin to take on a diff-erent look, with a tighter cushion or mat form. The higher the altitude the more refined is the adaptation of the plant, yet it is interesting to note that some species occur both in central Nepal and in south-western China. Much farther east in the province of Yunnan androsaces grow at a lower altitude and may display a different habit as a result. For this rea-son we should not generalise about the appropriate habitat for a species; an accurate appraisal of the true habitat of the plant in question together with its geographic location needs to be understood.

George Smith spent much time trying to sort out the confusion surrounding the taxonomy of *Androsace muscoidea* for his revision of the genus. The species and varieties which seem to cause difficulty for both the horticulturist and taxonomist are *A. muscoidea, A. robusta* and *A. villosa* var. *jacquemontii*. The androsace endemic to the north-western Himalaya, displaying tight mats of congested woolly rosettes, seems to be the variable *A. muscoidea*. Smith believed that the popular plant found in the western Himalaya in 1952 and named *A. villosa* var. *jacquemontii* has a closer affinity to *A. muscoidea*. As a horticulturist I strongly agree, especially considering the Taylors' notes on plants found in the Rohtang La area of north-western India. Another subject requiring winter protection, *A. muscoidea* has either pure white or pink flowers scenting the air with honey. A superb white-flowering form was found in the valley

Androsace muscoidea, Kashmir DIETER SCHACHT

north of Dhaulagiri in Nepal in early June at an altitude of 15,900 ft. (4850 m). It has been named *A. muscoidea* 'Dhaulagiri'.

Several plant hunters who have climbed to the head of the Marsyandi Valley or botanised the upper part of the Kali Gandaki Valley, both in west-central Nepal, note the stunning display of rich rose-purple flowers belonging to the as recently as 1999 described *Androsace robusta* subsp. *purpurea*. I find it rather intriguing that the lovely *A. muscoidea* 'Dhaulagiri' was found at an altitude of 15,900 ft. (4850 m) in the same region as the *A. robusta* subsp. *purpurea,* while the latter seems to enjoy higher elevations, to around 16,400 ft. (5000 m). Another difference between the two is that the *A. muscoidea* 'Dhaulagiri' appears to flower in early June, while the brightly coloured *A. robusta* subsp. *purpurea* flowers from the middle of June on to the end of July. To grow these glorious alpines successfully, a trough or raised bed with overhead winter protection will provide the best chance of success. Ron McBeath recalls the sight of this rose-purple-flowered form of *A. robusta* growing on "gentle sloping scree with an easterly aspect, acre after acre was coloured a rich, rose-purple with the androsace" (1985). Mat-forming with quite small rosettes of incurving hairy leaves, *A. robusta* has relatively large flowers held in an umbel on a stem no more that 1 in. (2.5 cm) in length. Little variation occurs in this region of central Nepal where the flowers display this stunningly rich rose-purple. Surely this is a true Himalayan treasure worth seeking that presents the keen grower no great challenge.

Now though, we enter the realms of a challenge. This in no way suggests impossibility, rather a more intense need for attention to detail. A number of mat-forming and cushion androsaces occur at high levels in this alpine zone. Following are three of the finest as well as some exciting species for the collector.

Only as a result of Nepal becoming more accessible to trekkers and plant hunters since the 1950s have many of the exciting plants I am able to describe here become known to horticulture. As mentioned earlier, it was Polunin, Stainton, Sykes and Williams who made early expeditions and introductions, while Lowndes, Beer and since the late 1970s Smith, McBeath and other collectors have discovered and introduced these exciting high-altitude androsaces.

Widely distributed across the Himalaya and into northern Yunnan is the desirable *Androsace zambalensis*. It is found between 15,000 and 17,000 ft. (4580–5190 m) growing on open stony ground and shale slopes, but significantly not enjoying the wetter extremes of the eastern Himalaya and Sikkim. It makes flat mats of tightly packed, globular rosettes up to 1 ft. (30 cm) across. Each rosette produces a very short scape of three to five flowers, white with a yellow eye, but as the flowers age the eye turns red. This will rank as one of the finest of all androsaces. It is fairly amenable in a trough or raised bed, as long as the substrate in the artificial habitat contains good organic soil with plenty of shaly drainage material, both through the mix and on the surface around the cushions. Do not allow these plants to become desiccated during the growing season by the combination of heat and drought.

A firm favourite of many alpine growers is *Androsace globifera*, occupying the south side of the long Himalayan range. It is found between 11,000 and 15,000 ft. (3360–4580 m), generally on the wet, exposed side of the mountains. It can form enormous mats and cushions which cover themselves with the most wonderful lilac flowers. In nature it may also be found as dense cushions on drier, sunny cliffs. In cultivation this species loves to be tucked between stones on a raised bed and given full exposure. As with the next species, *A. lehmannii*, it requires lots of water during the growing season. In my experience, a week of drought results in a completely brown and deceased cushion with only the label for recognition. Winter protection is not so important on the east coast of Scotland but in damper areas may be essential.

A species I have found to be a little less demanding is *Androsace lehmannii*, found commonly in Nepal at altitudes ranging from 11,000 to 16,000 ft. (3360–4880 m). It prefers meadow slopes exposed to the summer rains and forms tight mats that may spread to several feet. I frequently worry, rather needlessly, at the state of the winter rosettes, which are a mass of tightly packed brown leaves. Yet the spring season produces fresh leaf rosettes of lime-green foliage, followed by masses of white, or occasionally pink, flowers on short stems with a lovely fragrance. Seed is the best means of increase.

My personal favourite is *Androsace delavayi*. It has variable flower col-

our, more typically white across Nepal and various shades of pink in .
north-western Yunnan. This species was first discovered by Delavay in
north-western Yunnan at the end of the 1800s; it was growing in open
moorland or rock outcrops at around 14,000 ft. (4270 m). In the central
Himalaya it is found much higher, between 15,000 and 17,500 ft.
(4580–5340 m), in consolidated screes, loose moraine and rock crevices.
I have not found the plants to be as long-lived as other related species,
but they do form the most perfect small cushions of woolly rosettes studded with flowers of a wonderful fragrance.

As with most of these species, *Androsace delavayi* is relatively easily
propagated by cuttings taken after flowering and rooted in pure, gritty

Androsace lehmannii, Langtang, central Nepal DIETER SCHACHT

sand or a mixture of sand and perlite, placed in a propagator, or a covered, heated box that can allow up to 50 percent shade in summer. Collecting seed of any species of *Androsace* can be time consuming, requiring a sharply-pointed pair of scissors to snip the seed capsules without losing the seed. Once the seed has been separated from the capsules, I recommend sowing it immediately as with the petiolarid primulas. A general, soil-based seed compost will prove satisfactory, and as long as the seed is not sown too thickly, the germinated seedlings may be left a full year before transplanting. This method reduces the danger of young seedlings drying out at their most susceptible stage. Where possible the seed pots should be plunged up to their rims in sand. Once the seed has germinated, feed with a very weak liquid fertiliser of a low nitrogen type.

Few genera found in the Himalaya have the potential for raising one's adrenaline to the degree that androsaces do. In the last few years suc-

Androsace delavayi, Khung Valley, central Nepal GEORGE SMITH

cessful expeditions have been made to south-eastern Tibet and to the rich hunting grounds of north-western Yunnan, where a number of exciting species grow that are sure to make a profound impact in horticulture as the years go by. I have seen slides of species, including *Androsace bisulca,* with cherry-red flowers, from Tibet, as well as its golden-yellow-flowered form, *A. bisulca* var. *aurata,* growing in an open, sun-baked slope by degraded pine forests in south-western Sichuan. Both of these form tight cushions with umbels of one to four flowers and will undoubtedly require all the cultivation skills of the grower to keep them true to character.

A final species is the taprooted *Androsace tapete,* seen at its stunning best as wide cushions in the Hidden Valley of central Nepal. Generally preferring dryer conditions in nature, the stemless flowers are most usually pure white, and undoubtedly, achieving a well-flowered cushion of this species, whether grown in the alpine house or out in a trough, would be a great achievement.

Primula

The primula family has proved to be one of the most popular Himalayan plant groups, represented by the genera *Androsace, Omphalogramma* and of course most notably *Primula* itself.

The alpine zone is host to a great selection of these exciting primula species, many of which are well established in gardens, but which certainly require skillful cultivation and regular propagation to maintain their vigour. Eventually, in many cases where a pollen-sterile clone has been introduced into cultivation as the sole representation, the plant will weaken and subsequently die. It is of great virtue when collectors obtain seed from the wild of as wide a variation of material as possible to widen the gene pool. When collecting vegetative material of primulas, collectors should secure several specimens of preferably both "pin-eyed" and "thrum-eyed" flowering forms, again to strengthen the breeding opportunities and thus maintain stocks of these plants in horticulture.

Over the decades, from the time of Ludlow and Sherriff to now, many efforts have been made to secure material of surely one of the most breathtaking of all primulas. It is *Primula calliantha,* a member of the section *Nivales* (*Crystallophlomis*), first discovered by Delavay in Yunnan. Although hardly coming into the alpine zone, growing typically at around 12,500 ft. (3810 m) in south-eastern Tibet, it warrants careful treatment in the garden. Ludlow's diary for 9 June 1938 reports their first acquaintance with this species in the field: "It was a breathtaking experience, and the sight of huge tracts of hillside aflame with its colour remain a picture of unparalleled beauty" (Fletcher 1975). They found it growing at high altitudes, on rock ledges and moss-covered boulder scree, always in damp situations. They noticed upon lifting a plant that it had become established over a large stone slab, the roots being splayed out over the surface. It forms large compact resting buds, rather akin to *P. sonchifolia* and *P. griffithii,* heavily coated with sulphury farina, requiring a period of reduced watering and protection from winter wet. At flowering, the foliage is narrowly strap shaped with yellow farina below, and the blooms, up to ten in a truss, are a glorious rich purple. Clearly, this is a very special plant requiring careful thought to choose the best position in the garden. Once established, the clumps are best left well alone, making seed the only viable means of propagation.

Closely related to *Primula calliantha* are the challenging primulas of the subsection *Agleniana.* These include *P. elizabethae* and *P. falcifolia,* stunningly beautiful plants found in south-eastern Tibet forming reddish, bulb-like resting buds and two to three beautifully fragrant, primrose-yellow flowers held on a scape. Growing conditions should apply as for *P. calliantha.* I hope that fresh seed will again be collected to reintroduce these exciting plants.

Two species belonging to the section *Amethystina* sometimes become available from seed collections. One is the widely distributed *Primula dickieana,* the only member of this fine section to reach Nepal. Its distribution extends along a 900-mile (14,400-km) belt from eastern Nepal, through Sikkim, Bhutan, south-eastern Tibet into north-western Yunnan. This lovely species was first introduced into cultivation by Ludlow and Sherriff in 1949 after they discovered it on many occasions while travelling in Bhutan and Tibet. On one occasion Ludlow and Taylor, when collecting on the Doshong La in south-eastern Tibet, observed specimens of the primula displaying white, yellow, mauve, violet and purple corollas, the variation sometimes occurring within the same mass of plants or other times a particular variation was more localised. The most typical habitat of this species ranges from steep, wet, scrubby meadows to boggy ground over a wide altitudinal range of 11,500 to 16,500 ft. (3510–5030 m).

Primula dickieana, Barun, eastern Nepal GEORGE SMITH

The whole plant is effarinose and grows from a small rootstock, the root system is shallow and rather weak. The scape varies from 3 to 9 in. (8–23 cm) in height and forms an umbel of from one to nine flowers. This primula is most desirable. Perhaps the best garden position for it involves growing a number of plants in close proximity amongst damp, moss-covered rocks next to a watercourse. While such a situation may prove to be a luxury, a cool spot on a raised bed that will never dry out fully, should also work. I have not found that the effarinose resting buds require winter cover, on the contrary serious losses may occur when they dry out during the dormant season.

Closely related and similar in habit is the more amenable *Primula amethystina* in its robust form, *P. amethystina* var. *brevifolia*. This plant is locally abundant on the Beima Shan, north-western Yunnan, at around 12,000 ft. (3660 m) in open, damp, turfy meadow where hundreds of plants grow in small areas. Similar to *P. dickieana*, this one makes a flat rosette of effarinose, glossy green leaves. The flower stem is typically up to 4 in. (10 cm) in height, producing an umbel of many violet to amethyst bells, nodding, beautifully fringed and similar to the European soldanellas. This attractive little plant grows well for me in eastern Scotland in a trough and has proved fairly resilient in a cool position.

Two species from this section *Amethystina* require that we patiently await their reintroduction: *Primula kingii* and *P. valentiniana*. They are similar in flower with velvety, rich wine-red flowers, which Ludlow and Sherriff found in vast numbers at various locations in south-eastern Tibet. What a rich Himalayan hunting ground this area has proved to be, and how we yearn to hunt there again!

A close link connects many sections of the genus *Primula*, and this is certainly evident with the sections *Rotundifolia* (*Cordifolia*) and *Nivales* (*Crystallophlomis*). The closest link shows in the species *P. obtusifolia* from the north-western Himalaya. The section *Rotundifolia* contains several important Himalayan species of which *P. rotundifolia*, the type species, has made a great impact in horticulture since about 1970. This species is confined to the south side of the central Himalayan range from Gosainkund, Nepal, eastward into Sikkim, being locally abundant in the Everest region. This is a markedly farinose plant found growing rather significantly beneath overhanging rocks, suggesting a position in the garden that will not be subject to excessive wet, requiring winter protection from overhead rain. The distinct foliage is rounded with yellow farina beneath. From it arise 9- to 12-in. (23- to 30-cm) stems carrying lax umbels of attractive pinkish purple flowers with a golden yellow eye. In its best forms this is a lovely species which I have been unable to take beyond mid-to-late summer, suggesting that I am not respecting its desire to have a marked dormancy at this stage. This has puzzled me as friends Mike and Polly Stone have grown it so well in what I call near-Himalayan conditions in north-western Scotland at Fort Augustus.

I have the same bitter experience with the very closely related *Primula barnardoana* (synonym *P. elongata*), similar in all respects to the foregoing *P. rotundifolia* except that it displays umbels of lemon-yellow flowers, often as two superposed umbels, such as amongst the candelabra primulas. This species is found on grassy banks or open rock ledges at elevations of 12,000 to 13,000 ft. (3660–3970 m) from eastern Nepal through to Tibet. In its best forms with rich golden yellow to orange flowers this is a plant worth giving pride of place, best tucked between rocks in a cool position. It may be worth experimenting and giving the plant protection from late summer as the resting buds form, making it ready to enter dormancy. This and the other members of the section *Amethystina* can be raised from seed. Other members are *P. gambeliana* and *P. caveana*. The latter grows at the highest altitude of all primulas, occurring in the Everest range at about 20,000 ft. (6100 m), growing in dry rock crevices.

Three members of the section *Petiolares* deserve special mention here despite the fact that much has already been written in earlier chapters about this important group of plants. The higher alpine reaches in the Himalaya no doubt have many secrets still to unfold, as more plant-hunting trips proceed into the side valleys in Tibet and Nepal. This expectation is supported by the history of probably the favourite petiolarid primula, one of the most desirable and beautiful of all Himalayan plants, *Primula aureata*. It is to be found in vertical crevices and earthy banks in central Nepal, most particularly in the Langtang and Gosainkund, both holy areas to the Nepalese. The species was hardly known by Western botanists until 1935, when Bailey brought seeds back to the Royal Botanic Garden in Edinburgh. Many reintroductions have been made subsequently and further seed or plant material has been introduced of both the type species and the subspecies, *P. aureata* subsp. *fimbriata*.

An ultimate reward for plant-oriented trekkers to this well-known area in April and May, before the onslaught of monsoon, must be the sight of steep rock bluffs stained yellow with silvery, farinose rosettes crammed into the vertical crevices and bursting into flower. The two forms seem to enjoy differing altitudinal range and habitats. The type plant *Primula aureata* has been collected at altitudes between 10,000 and 12,300 ft. (3050–3750 m) and always seeks shelter from the direct rain, whereas *P. aureata* subsp. *fimbriata* does not occur below 13,700 ft. (4180 m) and is frequently found in very wet conditions, sometimes under waterfalls. This observation benefits gardeners as we endeavour to grow the plants at home.

Primula aureata, Edrom Nurseries, Berwickshire JIM JERMYN

My experience of the type species has been to grow it in a trough, all on its own, wedged between pieces of rock and given overhead winter protection. The plants can be tucked tightly in a trough with a depth of at least 12 in. (30 cm) to allow the roots to penetrate into the soil. During the growing season I find that the plants require plenty of water and an occasional weak foliar feed. After the whole trough has been covered during the winter, beautiful silvery, farinose leaves begin to unfurl in March and April, revealing a perfectly formed posy of creamy yellow flowers with a broad orange eye, a truly spectacular sight for the successful cultivator. In this restricted, artificial habitat, the plants will need to be lifted every three years, split up after flowering when in full growth and replanted in a completely fresh mix.

Where several plants have been raised of both pin-eyed and thrum-eyed forms, then hand-pollination with a soft paint brush will encourage a good seed set. Alternatively an all-pin stock will often set seed producing all-pin progeny. During the early summer diligent search amongst the expanding foliage will reveal short, red stems carrying fat seed capsules. When they begin to reach maturity the seeds will be clearly visible beneath the transparent outer coat. As this outer coat begins to open, collect the capsule, put it in a paper bag and allow it to open in a cool, dry place, which should take a day or two. When the seed falls away naturally it should be sown immediately in a loam-based seed compost. Cover the seed with a little gritty sand and plunge the pot in sand to keep it cool.

Primula deuteronana, another genuinely alpine petiolarid species, is often to be found growing in close proximity to *P. aureata* subsp. *fimbriata.* It is found in central Nepal and Sikkim, often in fairly large populations, on open moorland and rock outcrops at an altitude between 14,000 and 15,000 ft. (4270–4580 m). First introduced by Lowndes in 1954, there is no reason why this species should not become widely grown in gardens. It requires a cool situation with plentiful moisture during the growing season. It forms congested rosettes, with the young leaves and overwintering buds often heavily farinose. The flowers are virtually stemless and form a neat posy of bright pink, lilac-purple or occasionally pure white. Several members of botanical trips to the Gosainkund region have reported finding hybrids between *P. aureata* and *P. deuteronana,* displaying exquisite flowers dark pink at the fringes, fading to cream with a bright orange-yellow eye. The feature distinguishing the true *P. deuteronana* are the hairs within the narrow tube at the internal base of the petals.

A final petiolarid species and one of the most outstanding of the Himalayan primulas introduced since 1980 is *Primula pulchra,* found by George Smith in north-eastern Nepal close to the Sikkim border at a site on the Singalila range in the shadow of Kanchenjunga (28,171 ft.; 8590 m). This is a high alpine species, looking for all the world like a tiny form of *P. tsariensis* or *P. calderiana.* I have found it to be amenable in a trough, tucked between rocks with a lime-free soil mixed with peat and gritty sand. Forming tight rosettes, it has proved to be stoloniferous and therefore easily propagated by detaching the young offshoots and replanting or potting them on. As yet I have not found this single clone to set seed, but in flower it is certainly a showstopper with its neat short-stemmed posy of purple-blue flowers with a yellow eye.

Two desirable species lying a little uneasily, from a taxonomist's point of view, in the section *Farinosae,* are *Primula sharmae* and *P. concinna.*

Primula pulchra, Edrom Nurseries, Berwickshire JIM JERMYN

Both occupy rocky areas, screes and open grassy slopes at altitudes up to 15,000 ft. (4580 m). *Primula sharmae* is rather local, distributed in western and central Nepal. It is an attractive primula, with purplish mauve flowers on short stems. The finely toothed foliage has distinctive white farina on the undersides. *Primula concinna*, a tiny plant, is found from western Nepal through to south-eastern Tibet, displaying pink flowers with a yellow eye. Both species would certainly grow satisfactorily in a trough, tucked between stones, as long as they never catch the full brunt of the summer heat. Seed is the means of propagation, and as with many members of this section, the plants may prove to be short-lived, necessitating rejuvenation from seed.

Probably *Primula caveana*, Langtang, central Nepal DIETER SCHACHT

Most of these higher alpines sadly become available only occasionally as a result of organised expeditions to the Himalaya. When the seed is distributed, it very often ends up in the hands of growers who are under the impression that the best place for a choice or rarely encountered Himalayan alpine is a pot in the alpine house. But in fact unless the plant is removed to the outdoors at the beginning of May, in the United Kingdom, and either plunged in sand in a cold frame or planted out in the open, it will likely succumb to overheating, not to drying out as may be suspected. Plants imprisoned in an alpine house often boil to death during the early summer, or fall under a fatal attack of aphid. Many readers will now understand my absolute discomfort at the thought of these specialised plants being given a home under glass for often their only chance in cultivation. A trough or raised bed is always preferable for all but a very few species which by nature of their woolly habit will prefer a well-ventilated glass house.

Two easy members of the same section *Farinosae* and subsection *Sibirica* (*Armerina*) are *Primula involucrata* and *P. tibetica*. *Primula involucrata* is widespread from Pakistan across to China, often found at high altitude in any damp or marshy pockets. In its best forms, this is a lovely primula, with white to pinkish-mauve flowers at the western end of its limit. Its popular form *P. involucrata* subsp. *yargongensis,* from the eastern Himalaya, displays deep pink or purple flowers. They are easily grown in any damp acid soil. Much the same can be said as to the cultivation of *P. tibetica,* which deserves a higher profile than it is generally given. This lovely species also enjoys a wide distribution across the Himalaya and is often seen at its best in bold drifts at altitudes up to 13,500 ft. (4120 m) wherever marshes form. Altogether, it is a smaller plant than *P. involucrata* with striking umbels of rose-pink, yellow-eyed flowers on stems varying from 2 to 6 in. (5–15 cm). Both these species may be raised from seed, which is best sown soon after harvesting.

I would like to recommend the use of live sphagnum moss, not sphagnum peat, which is formed after years of decomposition, in an open garden situation when growing many *Primula* species. In many parts of Europe and North America, though, sphagnum moss has become a rather rare commodity, and therefore I do not recommend the wholesale collecting of it from wild habitats. This type of acid moorland moss is unique in my experience for its moisture-retention and antiseptic properties, for the fact that it is simply wonderful to handle, for its good smell and for its added virtue of very often displaying an attractive pink colour. I find it very helpful to place a collar of live sphagnum around a plant, ensuring that part of the moss is exposed to the air to keep it active in growth. The roots of *Primula, Cremanthodium* or *Gentian* will find refuge in the moss, drawing from its reserve of moisture during periods of drought. Sphagnum moss may also be dried and sterilised in a microwave oven, to be utilised as a wonderful medium for raising seed of tricky species.

Primula involucrata, Schachen Garden, southern Germany DIETER SCHACHT

Few species of the section *Minutissimae* have become established in gardens. Two species have been established since the late 1940s. The first is *Primula primulina,* long known as *P. pusilla* and introduced as far back as 1886 when seed was sent to Kew. It is placed in the subsection *Bella* by Wright Smith and Fletcher, where it does fit in well with the closely related *P. bella* and *P. bella* subsp. *nanobella* together with *P. cyclostegia,* found in the 1990s in north-western Yunnan. *Primula primulina* is certainly a plant meriting the grower's careful consideration of position in the garden, as few have succeeded with it for many seasons. In nature *P. primulina* is often abundant at altitudes of 14,000 to 15,000 ft. (4270–4580 m) on rocky outcrops or open grassy slopes, and in this latter situation it may be seen in large numbers in the Langtang, growing with the lovely *Potentilla microphylla.* Ludlow and Sherriff frequently came across it in south-eastern Tibet and Bhutan, where at 15,500 ft. (4730 m) it covered the hillsides along with the cream-flowered *Primula sikkimensis* var. *hopeana;* what a superb and memorable experience it must have been. *Primula primulina* is a tiny plant with a farinose rosette of toothed leaves, producing an umbel of two to four purple to violet flowers easily distinguished by the tuft of white hairs in the throat. As to growing it in the garden, I recommend a trough positioned in a cool spot away from the full glare of summer heat, without being positioned in full shade. Tuck the little plantlets between stones and try to establish some moss to grow amongst the plants to protect them from both summer dryness and the winter ravages. Winter protection is beneficial too. Seed is the only practical means of propagation if the plants become established in this situation.

The classic member of this section *Minutissimae,* and a truly stoloniferous species, is *Primula reptans,* a plant I have grown since 1975 when I received a wee piece from Dieter Schacht upon leaving my apprenticeship under his tutelage at Munich Botanic Garden. Memories flood back of my first trip to the Schachen Garden, an alpine garden affiliated to the Munich Botanic Garden, situated in the Wetterstein Mountains in Bavaria, southern Germany. A friend and I set off eagerly from the railway station in Garmisch Partenkirchen very early in the morning one late June day. Gaining height quickly we clambered up through the forest out onto a stoney mountain road leading up to the garden. We passed by drifts of snow giving us concern that the garden would still be covered with snow. On arrival we found many areas of the botanical collection free of snow, and to my astonishment patches of the lovely *Primula reptans,* 1 ft. (30 cm) or more across and in fullest flower, were growing together with the stunning and equally floriferous *Aquilegia nivalis.* The flat mats of the primula were made up of tiny little incurved and toothed leaves covered with large, stemless flowers in a brilliant violet-purple. At that time, I had no idea that the plant was stoloniferous in habit and would one day enable me to fill 3-in. (8-cm) pots with tufts of rooted stolons and market them the length and breadth of Britain for £3 each. Maybe readers will understand how part of me feels uneasy at the thought of curtailing my retail nursery trade, with the fun of raising and disseminating such exciting plants.

Primula primulina, Langtang, central Nepal DIETER SCHACHT

I have greatly enjoyed reading articles written by Henry and Margaret Taylor documenting their trips to locations in the north-western Himalaya, including the Rohtang La at 13,100 ft. (3400 m) and the Nalgan Pass at 16,400 ft. (5000 m) in north-western India. On the Nalgan Pass on 29 August 1998 they report great masses of *Primula reptans* in full flower occupying steep wet slopes close to a snow bank. This setting is staggering, as the Taylors point out, considering that the first snows return in late September, allowing only a few weeks of growing season for these high alpines. During this short period the primula must emerge from the snow, produce flowers to be duly pollinated by insects and fertilised, and set seed ready for dispersal. The flower in nature is often a

Primula reptans, Schachen Garden, southern Germany DIETER SCHACHT

lilac colour, somewhat paler than the Ludlow and Sherriff collections many of us grow in our gardens.

I have grown this little primula in a trough satisfactorily. To produce a show-off, fill the trough with a richer medium of soil, grit and peat with a few handfuls of very well-rotted manure rubbed through a sieve. This mix should produce healthy plants covered with flowers in May or early June. At no time during the growing season should plants dry out or cook in the summer heat. As the autumn proceeds, the foliage will turn a lovely yellow and then brown as the deciduous clumps become dormant. During the winter I always sprinkle a little gritty sand amongst the mass of stems and exposed surface roots, as they are often drawn to the surface with the frost. Winter protection is not essential but is sensible. Propagation is simple, requiring only that after flowering the clump be lifted, teased apart then replanted in a fresh mixture. For gardens in hot, dry climates, do not incorporate too much grit into the soil, for promoting the drainage too much will lead to subsequent drying out. With just one clone in my possession I have never secured seed, but have received seed from the same pin-eyed clone grown in the Schachen Garden.

Trips of the 1990s to various parts of central Nepal located several other members of this fascinating section of *Primula*. No doubt it is just a matter of time until we will be able to welcome such species as *P. minutissima* and *P. tenuiloba*. The former displays lovely purplish-pink flowers, and *P. tenuiloba* generally has pure white flowers or bluish white with a white eye. These would be very desirable additions suitable for the same conditions in the garden as for *P. reptans*.

An alpine gem from the Sino-Himalayan province of Yunnan is *Primula dryadifolia,* belonging to a section all its own, *Dryadifolia*. This species is common on many mountains in Yunnan, growing in Sichuan and just into south-eastern Tibet. It frequents screes, rock crevices, also steep hillsides amongst dwarf rhododendrons at altitudes between 13,800 and 16,000 ft. (4210–4880 m). Significantly, plants are very often found growing in limestone scree, making this an excellent subject for a trough amongst dolomite limestone rocks. It forms wide mats of oval foliage with white farina beneath, on short stalks amongst a network of almost woody stems. The beautiful flowers are held tightly, one to five in number, beneath a purple, baggy calyx, and the best forms are a glorious deep reddish purple or ruby-red with a dark center. Pale pink forms are also found with a dark eye. The flowering stems rarely exceed 2–3 in. (5–8 cm).

Primula tenuiloba with *Potentilla microphylla*, Langtang, central Nepal
DIETER SCHACHT

Since its reintroduction from the successful Alpine Garden Society trip to Yunnan in 1994 I have grown this plant quite happily in a trough with a loamy soil including more than the usual gritty sand and a measure of peat. I have placed pieces of flattish dolomite stone vertically, almost down to the base of the trough, and planted the young primulas next to them. The roots clearly enjoy both the composition of the rock and the cool face it provides as a refuge in hot spells. *Primula dryadifolia* is a plant that needs a good measure of light all year round in order to flower well, and once happily established it should produce plenty of seed. I have noted to my cost that it is very susceptible to aphid, or greenfly, attack, and some form of control is crucial or plants will be overcome with it when they are in full growth. Winter protection is advisable, although this robust plant responds to plenty of air.

The pinnacle of my gardening experience thus far has come through the section *Soldanelloides,* perhaps the finest amongst all the primulas. The section embraces a number of species in the distinct class of high alpine plants, including some with the most heavenly fragrance. High alpine meadows in central Nepal are studded with the purplish blue *Primula wollastonii,* with masses of *P. wigramiana* in purest white and with hybrids between the two growing amongst other exciting plants. Growing these soldanelloid primulas in the garden will test the grower's skill to the full in all but the most amenable geographic locations where the growing season enjoys a naturally cool and humid atmosphere.

Should they become available I encourage readers to brace themselves for the following Himalayan species: *Primula wigramiana, P. wollastonii, P. buryana, P. buryana* var. *purpurea, P. klattii* (synonym *P. uniflora*), *P. soldanelloides, P. sandemaniana, P. sapphirina* and *P. cawdoriana.* This is rather a formidable group of plants in anyone's book, but they may make an entry into horticulture and when they do, will certainly deserve a Handelian fanfare. Having covered the widely available *P. reidii* and *P. reidii* var. *williamsii* in Chapter 3 as representatives of the section *Soldanelloides,* I will now describe the most likely species to appear from botanical expeditions, with the hope that in due time others will follow.

Primula wollastonii along with others encountered in central and eastern Nepal has been known to science for some time but has become fa-

Possible hybrid between *Primula wollastonii* and *P. wigramiana*, Langtang, central Nepal DIETER SCHACHT

miliar to gardeners only in the late twentieth century with the travels of George Smith giving us a glimpse of these superb plants. It was first discovered by Wollaston, a member of the 1921 Everest expedition in the

Primula cawdoriana, Schachen Garden, southern Germany DIETER SCHACHT

northern, Tibetan approaches to the mountain. The species is to be found in Nepal and the adjoining regions of southern Tibet, ranging from the Langtang valleys of central Nepal to the Lumbasamba Himal just east of the Everest massif. It occupies an altitudinal range from 14,800 to 18,000 ft. (4510–5490 m), while its western limits drop to 13,100 ft. (4000 m). The species is fairly abundant in the upper Barun Valley where the conditions are generally very damp. Mossy cliffs and gritty-earth banks also host dwarf rhododendrons.

Primula wollastonii has a very distinct appearance making it difficult to confuse with others except that it appears to hybridise with *P. wigramiana* in central Nepal. Typically it has most attractive thimble-like flowers of a sumptuous dark purple to violet blue, and the inside of the thimbles have dense, white farina. Each flower is tightly held in umbels of two to six, pointing downward with the bells not flaring out at all. The flowers give a subtle fragrance, not as intense as *P. reidii*. The baggy calyx varies in colour from green to purple and pure white in the albino-flowered form, *P. wollastonii* var. *alba*.

Primula buryana var. *purpurea*, Schachen Garden, southern Germany
DIETER SCHACHT

Primula wollastonii, Edrom Nurseries, Berwickshire JIM JERMYN

Cultivation is not too tricky when the plants are in a trough filled with an acid, freely drained mixture with added humus. Keep plants well watered when in growth, and they will send up little plantlets as a result of surface roots, forming leaf buds which eventually will grow to maturity. Placing a few deeply entrenched stones in the trough will keep the roots cool and plants will be more likely to survive a prolonged spell of heat. Propagate by division by severing the young plantlets while in full

Primula wollastonii var. *alba,* Langtang, central Nepal DIETER SCHACHT

growth but not under stress, or by seed which is by far the best means with all these soldanelloid species.

Primula wigramiana has not maintained as strong a hold in cultivation as *P. wollastonii*, mainly because although it requires the same conditions in the garden, it does not produce the adventitious root buds which subsequently form young plants around the main plant. This means the grower gets one chance with his plant and that is it. Flowering in June or July in Nepal at similar altitudes to *P. wollastonii*, it forms similar tight rosettes of pale green foliage with little evidence of a leaf petiole, which is so distinct with other soldanelloid primulas. The inflorescence held on 4- to 6-in. (10- to 15-cm) stems is made up of six or seven large, white, flared bells with a wonderful fragrance. Beauty is added as the flower-heads are topped with a cluster of purplish calyces. This is a gem amongst Himalayan high alpines, providing great excitement for those who have seen it dominating hillsides in central Nepal, generally in grass amongst *Potentilla arbuscula* and *Rhododendron lepidotum*.

Rhododendron lepidotum, Langtang, central Nepal DIETER SCHACHT

Primula wigramiana with *Corydalis cashmeriana,* Schachen Garden, southern Germany DIETER SCHACHT

A little more fragile in all respects is the distinguished *P. klattii* (synonym *P. uniflora*). This species was first collected by Hooker at the end of the nineteenth century but was introduced into cultivation in 1911–12. It did not persist, but was reintroduced by George Smith in 1977 when

Primula klatti, Barun, eastern Nepal GEORGE SMITH

he collected material in the Barun Valley in eastern Nepal. In its native habitat it thrives in steep meadows between 13,000 and 16,000 ft. (3970–4880 m) in a region which appears to have permanent humidity during the short growing season. Its distribution stretches from eastern Nepal through Sikkim to Bhutan and south-eastern Tibet. Finding this species for the first time while botanising in central Bhutan, Sherriff was moved to write in his notes on 24 July 1937, "This is a magnificent primula, now in full flower, on a very small patch of open grassy hillside. It opens more fully than any other primula in this section, being almost flat and looking straight out at one, not pendulous at all. The biggest flower was 1⅝ inches [4 cm] across" (Fletcher 1975).

In cultivation the resting bud takes the form of a tight cluster of tiny leaves, surrounded by persistent withered foliage. The summer rosette is lax, with long-petioled, hairy and toothed leaves, supporting the 3- to 6-in. (8- to 15-cm) stem carrying one or two glorious flowers, purplish blue or white with a wine-red or purplish calyx.

I have found this wonderful plant to be amenable in the open with winter protection. The challenge is to prevent the lax rosettes from rotting with so much decaying foliage attached, as well as anchoring them during the growing season. Surrounding the plants with a generous covering of grit has not proved to be satisfactory, possibly causing compaction which should be avoided at all cost. My goal is to locate a non-invasive type of moss that will grow around the plants and act as a protective layer at all times. Growing several plants hopefully will attract night-flying moths to act as pollinators and bring about a means of propagation from seed.

Along with many other growers of Himalayan primulas I also have had a measure of success with other members of this section, including *Primula buryana* and *P. cawdoriana,* but we eagerly await fresh seed of these species to augment the current material in horticulture.

Never should keen growers and lovers of these exquisite high alpine primulas be put off by anyone. They will respond to efforts to give them the correct conditions according to their natural geographic location. The golden rules for growing them are simply:

1. Try to grow mature plants out in the open.
2. Endeavour to keep the plants cool during the growing season.
3. Do not handle a plant when it is under stress.
4. When possible, grow several plants in close proximity.

Most important of all, even if the joy of growing and flowering a plant is fleeting, enjoy the experience, savour it and share it with others. These plants certainly were not created for the yaks to trample over—surely they were meant for our enjoyment.

Other Genera

While most lovers of the high Himalayan alpines will tend to favour the big genera, including *Primula, Androsace, Gentian, Saxifraga,* and *Meconopsis,* a great number of other genera demand our close consideration. One is *Corydalis* which was well monographed in 1997 by Magnus Liden and Henrik Zetterlund whose knowledge and hard work have been instrumental in helping horticulturists choose from such a wonderful and varied race of plants. Many newly introduced species have found their way into cultivation from the Sino-Himalaya since 1990, adding to the interest of this genus. The following plants are Nepalese species most likely to gain a foothold in cultivation. They are demanding of culture, as one may expect from this high alpine zone.

Three species belonging to the section *Latiflorae* of *Corydalis* may be found at high altitudes in the central Himalaya. *Corydalis latiflora* is a real gem of the alpine screes, often seen in central Nepal at locations well above 14,500 ft. (4420 m), including the Thorung La and the Toridwari Banyang in western Nepal. It produces racemes of beautifully fragrant, greyish blue or pink flowers above a loose cushion of greyish foliage. Equally exciting is the yellow-flowered *C. megacalyx,* a dwarf, scree plant producing a deep root stock and finely cut, glaucous foliage. Often found in central Nepal at altitudes up to 14,500 ft. (4420 m), the yellow flowers held in a dense cluster are striped dark brown. The third species is the more widespread *C. meifolia,* found from the Indian Himachal Pradesh to south-eastern Tibet. It is often seen amongst rocks in central

Nepal flowering between June and August. It is a floriferous species, producing striking racemes up to 2 in. (5 cm) long in yellow or sometimes orange with brown-purple or violet tips. In 1998 Henry and Margaret Taylor, while botanising in Kinnaur, north-western India, found on the Rupin Pass a superb form of this species, *C. meifolia* var. *violacea*, displaying the characteristic glaucous, feathery foliage but with pink, maroon-eyed flowers.

How, then, can we attempt to grow these choice alpine corydalises in our lowland gardens? The first hurdle to cross is to obtain the plants. Seed may be offered from time to time after trips to the Himalaya, but this is a genus with seed that is only viable for a short period of time, meaning that the sooner seed is sown after harvesting, the better the chances of germination. It can be sown in the usual way on a loam-based seed compost, with a thin covering of gritty sand and the pots plunged in

Corydalis meifolia, Langtang, central Nepal DIETER SCHACHT

sand. In my experience, it is better not to prick out newly germinated seedlings of this genus and other fragile subjects, but rather to wait another full season. Waiting gives the little rhizome a chance to form, which makes the transfer of the seedlings less hazardous. When the seed is sown fresh in the autumn, germination may take place prior to the turn of the year, with one single cotyledon present. The following season, the first true leaves will appear, to indicate that all is well. When the soil is moist and the year-old plants are several weeks into the new season's growth, prick them out into pots of a moisture-retentive but well-drained mix. The non-tuberous members of this section *Latiflorae* should grow well in a trough with an open mixture. Incorporate plenty of stones into the mix to invite the rhizomes to find a cool situation akin to their native conditions. Good light should encourage flowering. What a thrill it is to succeed with subjects such as these.

A number of isolated genera have just one or two species that are frequently found in this alpine zone. Amongst these species are some highly desirable garden plants, some rarely seen but nevertheless well worth seeking out and giving a chance in a trough or raised bed.

Arenaria glanduligera is a gem amongst the vast genus of sandworts belonging to the Caryophyllaceae, the pink family. Although by no means the only member of the genus worth growing, it is the one most would clamber for. I have not found it at all difficult, either to raise from seed or to cultivate. Though no doubt I overfed it one season when the result was a surfeit of rich growth at the expense of flowers. The challenge is to grow it according to its true character. It is widely distributed at high elevations, up to 18,000 ft. (5490 m), in scree from Kashmir across the Himalayan massif into Bhutan. It is a loosely tufted plant producing solitary deep pink, dark-eyed flowers on short stems. Tuck the plants between stones in a rather lean soil mix and they should be free flowering and willing to set seed, which is the best means of propagation.

The genus *Cremanthodium* has already been covered in Chapter 4, with a number of species recommended for the ravine garden or a dedicated spot that is naturally moist but freely drained with the extra presence of rocks. A few species occupy stable scree communities in the alpine zone, and one in particular is occasionally offered in horticulture and is certainly worth looking out for. It is *C. purpureifolium,* very easily distinguished from its close relatives by the reddish to purple undersides of the foliage. The flowers are sensational; the solitary, nodding, yellow, daisy-like blooms are more akin to miniature sunflowers just 4 in. (10 cm) high. Found at altitudes between 12,000 and 16,000 ft. (3660–4880 m) in western and central Nepal, this species could be grown in a raised bed dedicated to choice Himalayan alpines, made up of good mineral soil and a number of carefully placed stones, at least half their depth under soil. As long as these plants are not allowed to dry out in the summer they should become established and set good seed, which is the only recommended means of propagation for this species. These seedlings, too, resent root disturbance, therefore sowing in situ may be advisable. As with most of these high alpines, this species flowers in late spring to early summer.

Cremanthodium purpureifolium, central Nepal J. M. HIRST

Having just used "sensational," I am not sure which superlative would best describe *Cremanthodium palmatum* in all its forms. Found at altitudes in excess of 14,000 ft. (4270 m) in Sikkim and south-eastern Tibet and enjoying steep scree material, this species's combination of flower and foliage sets it on a pedestal. Attractive palmate, purple-coloured foliage provides the perfect base for short, 6-in. (15-cm) stems, each bearing a nodding, pink, daisy-like flower. In Sikkim the plant has been identified as *C. palmatum* subsp. *rhodocephalum*. Cultivation should follow the same course as with *C. purpureifolium*. Such pleasure is derived from flowering these alpine species.

In most alpine plant lovers' minds, the name *Diapensia* conjures up something rather exclusive and perhaps not growable. Exclusive yes, but the plants are certainly growable in a trough as I have recommended for the foregoing species. For all diapensias, a cooler spot on the leeside of a rock may be advisable to protect the cushions from direct sunlight at the hottest part of the day. Although closely related to the heathers of the Ericaceae, this genus belongs to its own family, Diapensiaceae, which also includes some other exclusive genera, such as the Japanese *Shortia*. *Diapensia himalaica* (synonym *D. purpurea*) is an exciting plant found from eastern Nepal, south-eastern Tibet and on into south-western China, notably in north-western Yunnan. In nature it colonises steep banks and gravelly slopes as well as cushioning rock ledges at altitudes from 12,000 to 14,500 ft. (3660–4420 m) with its glistening mats of minute, evergreen leaves. In May to June these mats are studded with large rose-pink flowers. To achieve a well-flowered plant in the garden is a pinnacle of success. The closely related species *D. lapponica* grows well in the garden of Mike and Polly Stone in Fort Augustus on the west coast of Scotland, but few of us have the high rainfall and summer humidity they do. They are able to give these plants full light as well, which is a considerable advantage for flowering. Most of us can only do our best to imitate these conditions and with the careful use of water create the cool position such plants demand.

I try to reassure myself that no one situation is ever absolutely ideal. What about all the rain that falls when the plants are dormant, necessitating careful winter cover? What about the moss and liverwort that threatens to overpower a neat cushion on a trough? What about the curse of midges which encircle the gardener early in the morning or in the evening, attempting to kill our joy in the ability to grow and flower the plants most people only dream about.

Seed of *Diapensia himalaica* is occasionally offered, and as with many high Himalayan alpines, great success has been achieved by starting such plants in dried and rehydrated sphagnum moss. My predecessor at Edrom Nurseries, Alex Duguid, successfully pioneered this method, taking into account the fact that when wet, sphagnum holds up to twenty times its own weight in water. The main reason that seed fails to germinate or does so inconsistently is due to drying out. The immediate benefit of this natural material is clear, and the technique is covered in more detail in Chapter 6. Once the seed has germinated, leave the seedlings to establish for another year in the seed pot, perhaps giving them a weak feed to hearten them. When pricking out subjects with extra fine roots such as this diapensia, soaking the seedlings in water to loosen the compost will make it easy to separate the seedlings. Place them in a cool shaded frame and at no time allow them to dry out or cook. The reward for this extra care is a well-grown plant of a challenging Himalayan subject soon to flower—few greater rewards could there be.

Closely related but generally assigned to Ericaceae is another Himalayan treasure, *Diplarche multiflora,* found in eastern Nepal and south-eastern Tibet at similar altitudes to the diapensia. Ludlow and Sherriff often encountered it on avalanche slopes. This species is often described as the nearest approach to a heath to be found in the Himalaya. It forms mats of densely leafy, wiry stems each terminating with a lovely, tight globose head of pink flowers. Though this treasure is not yet available in horticulture, should seed be offered it may be treated in the same way as for the diapensia.

From Nepal, which is the main state within the vast Himalayan range, come many local treasures, some of which will be photographed and looked upon with respect and the knowledge that their collection, by whatever means, is fraught with high risks and little prospect of cultivating them anywhere else in the world. Always, of course, someone will achieve the seemingly impossible, but how much better to concentrate efforts on plants that we have an honest chance of giving a good home.

Amongst the high alpine plants, an extreme challenge is to be met with the woolly *Chionocharis hookeri;* the Himalayan version of *Eritrichium nanum*; the intriguing *Oreosolen wattii,* a member of the Scrophulariaceae with tubular yellow flowers; and finally *Pycnoplinthopsis bhutanica.* This last species defies pronunciation and the botanist and taxonomist Jafri, who named it, must surely have had tongue in cheek while doing so. It is though, a choice member of the crucifer family, Cruciferae, producing a basal rosette of leaves and a mass of short-stalked white flowers. It occupies screes at high altitudes up to 14,500 ft. (4420 m) in central Nepal.

I have always felt that *Eriophyton wallichii,* a member of the Labiatae, could be grown successfully in a stoney mix on a raised bed. Growing in scree, flowering a little later in the season and appearing from western Nepal across to south-western China, it forms a dwarf, woolly plant with rounded over-lapping leaves and whorls of wine-red to pale purple flowers. As with other members of this family, seed will provide the best means of propagation. I have not yet grown this plant, however, and suspect that when grown and flowered it will bear little resemblance to the wonderful pictures often seen of it in its native haunts, dripping wet with monsoon droplets.

Another awkward name to cope with is *Gueldenstaedtia himalaica,* a classic Himalayan subject often seen growing on grassy slopes amongst soldanelloid primulas such as *Primula wigramiana.* A member of the pea family, Leguminosae, it is found throughout the Himalaya at high altitude forming mats of silky-haired leaves and producing showy mauve to red flowers, like those of a pea plant, on short stems. Since the deep roots are seemingly impossible to trace, gardeners hope that seed will be collected to assure this alpine treasure a good home in an open spot on the raised bed.

The composite or daisy family, Compositae, comprises many good alpine genera, several species of which feature amongst the very choicest found in the Himalaya. Besides those of *Cremanthodium,* which I have already covered, these species come from the genera *Aster, Leontopodium, Saussurea, Tanacetum* and *Waldheimia.*

Aster flaccidus is at its best at high altitudes in screes throughout the Himalaya where it produces typical clasping foliage above the basal leaves over which sits a huge mauve daisy on a short 1- to 3-in. (2.5- to 8-cm) stem. Maintaining this habit in the garden can be met by planting it between stones on the raised bed.

Eriophyton wallichii, Langtang, central Nepal DIETER SCHACHT

Edelweiss, *Leontopodium,* is one of the classic alpine plants of European fame, but much more spectacular and dainty are some of the species found in the high Himalaya. Of these, *L. monocephalum* must rank as one of the finest, a mat-forming, woolly plant of the high screes, found at 18,000 ft. (5490 m). Its form *L. monocephalum* var. *evax* from eastern Nepal has lower leaves of silvery colour and stunning yellow, woolly involucral leaves, those just below the flowers. Although I have raised and flowered it from seed, I have not brought out its true habit. In future I will grow it in a lean, stoney environment on a raised bed and hope that it will settle into its tighter character. When seed is set, harvest and sow it right away for the best means of propagation.

The genus *Saussurea* contains some of the most bizarre of all Himalayan alpines. The finest examples need much attention to detail if they are to grow successfully in the garden, let alone flower. Three notable spe-

Leontopodium monocephalum var. *evax,* Barun, eastern Nepal
GEORGE SMITH

cies are *S. gossypiphora*, *S. simpsoniana* and *S. tridactyla*. They are often found on screes up to 18,000 ft. (5490 m), flowering from July to September in nature. When seed is collected and made available, sow it individually in deep, cellular trays of a loam-based seed compost. The seeds should be covered with the customary gritty sand and kept cool until germination. Once the seedlings have grown into small plants, preferably early in the second year, they can be planted out in the raised bed or rock garden designed with a good depth of lime-free mineral soil and gravel mixed with small and medium-sized stones. Initially the plants will resemble any other composite genus, with dandelion-like leaves.

Saussurea gossypiphora, Langtang, central Nepal DIETER SCHACHT

The next stage, awaiting the flowers, takes patience and care. The plants will send down deep taproots, so a deep, cool root-run is essential. The flower-heads are usually purple, but in the case of these high alpine species, they are densely embedded with white woolly hairs. The ripe seeds can be removed by opening up the protective woolly covering, which will allow the seed to disperse naturally. Although highly desirable, these species remain a serious challenge.

The more amenable *Saussurea obvallata* is found in eastern Nepal and Sikkim on rocky slopes. It may prove a little large for a raised bed but would accompany the larger cremanthodiums and *Rheum nobile* in the ravine garden. This one, rather than having wool-covered flowers, utilises large boat-shaped bracts, translucent and conspicuously veined. The flowering stem may attain some 12–18 in. (30–46 cm).

The two final Himalayan genera within the daisy family are *Tanacetum* and *Waldheimia*. Amongst the tansies, one choice species is well worth growing. It is *T. gossypinum,* a typical scree-loving species found from central Nepal to Bhutan. It forms white, woolly cushions of dense rosettes from which arise yellow flower-heads on short stems. The challenge is to maintain this tight woolly habit in the garden. The raised bed should suit this species along with the several members of *Waldheimia* also frequenting screes throughout the Himalaya. Three very desirable species may be offered from seed-collecting trips: *W. glabra, W. tomentosa* and *W. stolitzkae.* Each of the species is spreading, mat-forming and made up of small, woolly rosettes which produce a mass of solitary, short-stemmed daisy-like flowers, rose-pink or white in colour. As with all these scree plants the raised-bed conditions should suit admirably for these waldheimias, with seed a viable means of propagation, sown as soon as it is harvested.

The genus *Potentilla* plays an important role in the garden, whether as free-flowering shrubs or herbaceous plants. A few alpine species merit our consideration, two of which are rarely seen in gardens and deserve pride of place on a trough or raised bed. Both *P. microphylla* and *P. coriandrifolia* may be found in central Nepal at high altitude amongst rocks and on open grassy slopes. Their range is widespread in the Himalaya, reaching heights of 13,500 ft. (4120 m). *Potentilla microphylla* is a choice dwarf, tufted cushion or mat-forming plant with dark green, pinnate leaves with numerous leaflets. The flowers are generally large, solitary and yellow on short stems. A well-flowered mat of this species is a sight to behold on a raised bed with full light. Closely related and equally ex-quisite is *Potentilla biflora,* another species widespread across the Hima-laya yet rarely seen in gardens. This one also forms lush cushions of tiny palmate leaves and huge yellow flowers. *Potentilla coriandrifolia* is of a similar, mat-forming habit but in this case displays very showy, pure white flowers with reddish centers. All these potentillas can be propa-gated from seed, but sadly they are rarely offered. Hopefully the seed col-lectors in Nepal will not overlook them in the future.

The true *Potentilla eriocarpa* is a choice species found over a wide area from Pakistan across the Himalaya into south-western China inhabiting rocks and stony slopes at heights up to 15,000 ft. (4580 m). In horticul-ture it is often confused with *P. cuneata,* the spreading species, while *P. eriocarpa* has woody stems emanating from a central root stock and in na-ture has a tendency to hang down over rocks. Plants are best positioned to trail over the edge of the raised bed. Bright yellow flowers are plenti-ful at a useful time in the summer when other colour is less forthcoming.

Alpine willows of the genus *Salix* are always a great asset in the rock garden or, when dwarf enough, also in the raised bed. An outstanding species encountered on alpine slopes throughout the Himalaya, notably in Nepal, is *S. calyculata,* found at altitudes up to 14,000 ft. (4270 m) where it forms a low, creeping shrublet with shiny, hairless leaves and reddish stems. As is customary with willows, the flowers are unisexual. This species, one of the finest of all alpine willows, has catkins bright red in colour. It is easily grown and, again, is best situated where it can hang over the corner of the raised bed.

A plant of immense beauty and sadly all too rarely seen in gardens is *Trigonotis rotundifolia,* a member of the borage family, Boraginaceae, and closely related to *Myosotis.* This species is found on rock ledges and screes at around 12,000 to 15,000 ft. (3660–4580 m). In 1998 the Taylors of Invergowrie came across this attractive subject growing as large patches of blue amongst tumbled boulders under the north-eastern ridge of the Rhotang Pass in north-western India. Wide mats of rounded foliage are an attractive base for the terminal clusters of bright blue, yellow-eyed flowers held on short stems. Choose a cool position between rocks on the raised bed with maximum light to encourage flowering during the summer months.

Salix calyculata, Langtang, central Nepal DIETER SCHACHT

Saxifraga

Saxifraga is amongst the most important of all the alpine genera to be found in the Himalaya. Only since the late 1990s has more become known of them. With more than eighty species found in the true Himalaya, excluding China, I have had to make a balanced choice to highlight the best known as well as the most garden worthy and attractive flowering plants.

Undoubtedly the plants of section *Kabschia* (*Porophyllum*), characterised by plants with lime-encrusted foliage, are the most popular of the alpine saxifrages. It is important though, not to overlook from other sections the many green cushion-forming subjects as well as ones with taller flower stems, all valuable garden plants. The following four species have attractive flowers over green cushions or basal rosettes of foliage.

Saxifraga caveana would be anyone's first choice and is occasionally offered from seed expeditions. Occupying screes and stony slopes between 13,500 and 16,000 ft. (4120–4880 m) across the Himalaya, it forms dwarf, tufted cushions with small, leathery leaves in which the large yellow flowers nestle. A cool position should be chosen avoiding the full heat of the sun.

Saxifraga jacquemontiana is equally widespread but enjoys stony slopes in drier areas. It forms a hard mat made up of crowded rosettes. The yellow flowers protrude just beyond the foliage making this a wonderful sight in the summer.

Two unusual species which would be exciting introductions worth looking out for are *Saxifraga lychnitis* and *S. nutans*. The first species is rather rare and would be a wonderful plant for a cool spot on the raised bed. More often seen in the western Himalaya, it occupies gravelly areas and produces a basal rosette of leaves in a deep green with red edges. The nodding, golden yellow flowers with hairy maroon calyces are most attractive. Similar is *S. nutans*, found farther east from central Nepal into south-western China. This species is densely glandular, making it distinct, producing 6-in. (15-cm) stems carrying up to nine nodding yellow flowers in a cluster with dark red calyces. These high Himalayan saxifrages require cool conditions and cannot dry out while in growth. They may be propagated by seed and should not be overlooked in favour of the more famous kabschia types.

More than twenty-five species of the section *Kabschia* of *Saxifraga* are relevant to this title. I would like to extol the virtues of just ten in the hope that these will more than whet the appetites of keen alpine gardeners. At shows of both the Alpine Garden Society and the Scottish Rock Garden Club in the spring months across the length and breadth of Britain, very often the large pans of Himalayan saxifrages steal the show. Such pans can be grown successfully for exhibiting either in a cool frame or the alpine house but must be given close attention to detail. This would include turning the pan to ensure even flowering and removing dead or decaying rosettes, aborted flowers and any parts of the plant even

Saxifraga caveana, central Nepal J. M. HIRST

just possibly affected by pests or diseases. While always marvelling at the plants that win the Farrer and Forrest medals, the best-in-show awards, I wonder what joy these plants would give if they were grown on a raised bed or trough in the garden rather than the somewhat more artificial scene under glass. One fact to be sure of is that much is to be learnt by observing these wonderfully grown plants at the shows, and we owe much to the keen exhibitors who give us a glimpse of their work. Their measure of success must be balanced against the worry that such plants may succumb more easily to overheat or ravages of pests and diseases that are more commonly found under glass than in the open garden.

When these saxifrages are grown out in the open they are best positioned in a trough or raised bed and given winter cover, not because of dubious hardiness but to protect them from excessive wet and to enhance

Saxifraga jacquemontiana, Langtang, central Nepal DIETER SCHACHT

the lime-encrusted cushions. The soil must be well-drained yet typically moisture retentive, and in most cases the cushions respond well to being wedged between stones. Most Himalayan species are lime-hating and a few will not tolerate full sun, at least not on the east coast of Scotland, most notably those akin to the European species *Saxifraga oppositifolia*, including *S. lowndesii* and *S. poluniniana*. *Saxifraga lowndesii* is a species local to central Nepal found amongst wet rocks on steep hillsides at elevations of around 13,000 ft. (3970 m). Lowndes found it in 1950 on only one site, the Sabsche Khola. It bears a superficial likeness to a compact-growing *S. oppositifolia*, forming a lax cushion producing large rose-lilac-coloured flowers. This is a fine plant for a trough situated in a slightly shaded situation. The same spot will suit the more easily cultivated *S. poluniniana*, found in western and central Nepal occupying crevices of vertical rock, often beside running water in dappled shade at elevations between 11,000 and 11,500 ft. (3360–3510 m). It forms a lax mat with pale green foliage and short-stalked, white, pink-flushed flowers in the spring. A well-flowered cushion tucked between rocks on a trough

Saxifraga lowndesii, Schachen Garden, southern Germany DIETER SCHACHT

is a memorable sight, but I have found the plant to be intolerant of summer heat and direct sunlight. Both these species should set seed, providing a means of propagation until cushions are large enough to give cutting material. Cuttings taken after flowering easily may be rooted in a mixture of sand and perlite.

Two splendid species which meet at high altitudes in central Nepal, particularly in the Hidden Valley and the Kali Gandaki, are *Saxifraga andersonii* and *S. hypostoma*. These plants are found at altitudes of around 16,500 ft. (5030 m). *Saxifraga andersonii* grows in profusion in the flat beds of glacial streams, preferring flat ground amongst stones in a gritty, sandy loam, growing cheek by jowl with species of *Saussurea* and *Androsace*. This is a dense-cushion-forming plant made up of many lime-encrusted rosettes and short, compact, terminal clusters of up to five white flowers. It is a fine, uncomplicated plant now well established in cultiva-

Saxifraga andersonii, Schachen Garden, southern Germany DIETER SCHACHT

tion. The species *S. hypostoma* may be less known but is no more demanding when planted in a trough amongst stones in gritty loam and given plenty of water in summer. It is often found in vertical, north-facing crevices where it forms both large and small cushions. Very fine examples are reported in the upper Marsyandi Valley where it forms iron-hard buns hidden by the stemless white flowers.

Two of my favourite species which must rank amongst the best of all late-twentieth-century introductions from Nepal are *Saxifraga stolitzkae* and *S. rhodopetala*. *Saxifraga stolitzkae* was introduced by George Smith from a batch of wild-collected seed from the Kali Gandaki region in 1970. While similar to *S. andersonii*, it may be distinguished by its relatively short flower scape, its large white flowers and its tight cushion habit. On the other hand, the two species are so alike that if it were possible for a comprehensive botanical field study to be carried out in central Nepal in this area rich with *Saxifraga* species, one variable species may well result.

Saxifraga rhodopetala, as the name suggests, is a wonderful break from the majority of white-flowered kabschia species found in the Himalaya. This one produces two to six deep-pink, maroon-centred flowers borne on a short-stalked, flat-topped cluster. Again the habit is similar to *S. andersonii,* forming a steeply domed, hard cushion. Seed was introduced from a side valley off the Marsyandi in central Nepal at around 13,000 ft. (3970 m). It flowers in the garden over a long period in April to early May.

Further evidence of the as yet undetermined distribution of many of these saxifrages is the material grown today under the name *Saxifraga clivorum*. I suspect it is a variant of another species growing in a different geographical area. This species was found by Ludlow and Sherriff in Bhutan in 1937. It is a very desirable species now grown from material collected by both Smith and McBeath in Nepal. It is a slower-growing plant producing a fine cushion and a dense cyme of eight to ten white flowers, pink in bud and with attractive red anthers.

Three further species of *Saxifraga* are gradually becoming better known. *Saxifraga alpigena*, *S. cinerea* and *S. pulvinaria* may all be grown quite satisfactorily in the garden, given a little shade during the summer months. *Saxifraga alpigena* was introduced by George Smith in the 1970s from the Barun Khola in eastern Nepal. It may be found at altitudes up to 13,700 ft. (4180 m) in river shingle or on rock outcrops on steep hillsides where it forms flat cushions and short stems bearing solitary white flowers up to ½ in. (1 cm) across with attractive anthers of purple to deep pink. The plants must not, on any account, be exposed to scorch from the summer heat. *Saxifraga cinerea* is different from its allies in that it resembles the European encrusted species, producing neat cushions made up of large rosettes and short flowering stems carrying cymes of three to six flowers purest white in colour. This is one of the lesser-known Nepalese species and is certainly worth searching for. And *Saxifraga pulvinaria* (synonym *S. imbricata*) may be located amongst rocks and stony slopes from Kashmir across into eastern Nepal at elevations around 16,000 ft. (4880 m). In nature it may form wide cushions up to 18 in. (46 cm) across made up of many tiny rosettes. The stemless, solitary flowers are white with yellow bases and violet anthers.

No doubt the coming years will bring several exciting new saxifrages to our gardens. Surely our reading of species existing in the wild and as yet not in commerce behooves us to support legitimate expeditions into the Himalaya to search them out.

Meconopsis

The genus *Meconopsis* has very few species represented at this high alpine level. Most species have a greater presence in the subalpine zone and have been discussed in Chapter 4. The four species highlighted in the alpine zone are *M. horridula*, *M. discigera*, *M. delavayi* and *M. bella*.

I hope above all that dividing the plant coverage into distinct altitudinal and ecological zones has clarified where particular species should be planted in the garden. Of course sometimes the zones seem to overlap, and I admit to describing one plant or another in a particular chapter under one zone when it could well have fitted elsewhere. The importance of understanding these altitudinal guidelines, though, is apparent when we look at these *Meconopsis* species. In each case an examination of the root system will identify the substrate the species has been used to growing in and will indicate what it requires for growth in the lowland garden. Not observing these requirements will lead to inevitable failure. For example, I would generally recommend planting *Meconopsis* species in a bed rich in humus with plenty of summer moisture, or others I would give a position in the peat bed. The danger is that we lump all *Meconopsis* species together and unwittingly place them all in the peat bed. Such generalising would prove disastrous for these high alpine species.

For years I have looked on in awe at slides and pictures of *Meconopsis horridula* tucked between boulders on scree at high altitudes in Nepal. It is found throughout the Himalaya at elevations up to 18,000 ft. (5490 m). The flowers seem to be borne on short spikes or sometimes on leafless stems arising from the rootstock, no more than a few inches in height. The electric blue of the flowers is often so stunning, though they also take pale blue to turquoise colours. I have grown this species successfully, but one thing I can consistently report is that the flower colour has not been as I have seen in the pictures. What am I doing wrong? I have never planted them in a scree, which I must try soon. Of course, many forms in nature are typified by taller spikes up to several feet high with purple-coloured flowers. The leaves and stems are covered with sharp, bristly spines (hence the species name) which may be brightly coloured yellow or purple. I have not found this species to be 100 percent monocarpic, or dying after it has flowered. It is sometimes biennial and at other times even lives a further year after flowering. We can certainly treat it as a biennial, flowering for a second year and then dying. It forms a deep taproot, and if it is allowed to penetrate into cool quarters between stones it may persist and flower again. Even if simply monocarpic, it will set plenty of seed to enable a means of propagation.

Requiring similar treatment as *Meconopsis horridula* but significantly more tricky to grow is *M. discigera*. As yet, it is not fully understood due to the paucity of field notes. Its distribution appears to extend from western Nepal across to Sikkim and south-eastern Tibet. Its flower colour is generally a lemon-yellow, although Taylor states that it may also be blue, purple or red. A monocarpic species, requiring up to four years to flower, it dies back to a fairly large resting bud, nestling amongst the decayed foliage until reaching flowering size. At flowering, the rosette may assume

7–8 in. (18–20 cm) across, developing a flowering spike up to 18 in. (46 cm) in height with up to twenty flowers which open from the top, each held on short pedicels. One of the main identifying features is the flat disc-like extension at the base of the style, covering the top of the ovary or fruit. A well-grown specimen is certainly something to look forward to as seed of this species becomes more readily available. For each of these

Meconopsis horridula, Schachen Garden, southern Germany DIETER SCHACHT

four species, the deep taproot determines the need for a freely drained mixture on the raised bed.

The next species is the highly acclaimed *Meconopsis delavayi*, introduced by George Forrest from Lichiang at the beginning of the twentieth century. Although this part of China does not fall into the designated area appointed to the Himalaya, it does fall within the extended Sino-Hima-

Meconopsis horridula, Khumbu, eastern Nepal GEORGE SMITH

Meconopis discigera, eastern Nepal J. M. HIRST

laya and certainly warrants mention, so great an impact has it made in horticulture since its reintroduction.

The Lichiang Range forms a chain of craggy limestone peaks, some rising to 18,000 ft. (5490 m), with many glaciers and deep gorges. The tree line here lies at about 14,000 ft. (4270 m), and many exciting plants are found within the woodland zone. This far east the zones may be assessed very differently from those of the high altitudes in Nepal. The

Meconopsis delavayi, Inshriach Alpine Nursery, Aviemore JIM JERMYN

woodland and meadow zones here in Yunnan almost merge into a band between 10,000 and 14,000 ft. (3050–4270 m), for rich meadows flow out amongst *Abies, Larix* and mixed shrubberies. Without an accurate measurement of the soil pH in this area, we can assume that the soil is influenced by the limestone mountains above the meadows. Within this open terrain the lovely *Meconopsis delavayi* is found. Perfectly perennial, the meconopsis forms deciduous clumps of glaucous foliage above a stout rootstock made of a branching and swollen storage organ with a main taproot that may extend a good 9–12 in. (23–30 cm) into the soil. The nodding flowers, borne on leafless scapes, are a glorious deep violet-blue and sometimes up to eight in total. Within the petals is a lovely boss of yellow stamens completing this perfect work of creation. Those privileged to have visited this part of Yunnan in June and July report the richness of the alpine meadows at about 13,000 ft. (3970 m), full of both *Anemone demissa* and *A. trullifolia*, the bright yellow *Trollius acaulis* with flowers over 2 in. (5 cm) across and, yes, hundreds of blooms of *Meconopsis delavayi* from pale to violet-blue. No wonder Forrest could refer to this area as the Eldorado for plant hunters.

Growing this species in the garden presents few difficulties as long as it can have a cool, open site with a deep, mineral soil freely drained but not subject to drying out. A little alkalinity is not a liability but a dry chalky soil will not work. After flowering, the plants produce long, narrow pods of seed which, when ripe, should be sown right away. I have found that with these deciduous species it is wise to leave the seedlings a second year in the seed pan before pricking them out, to enable the little fleshy rootstock to develop. Once plants have settled down in the garden, either in a specially prepared bed or a deep raised bed amongst rocks, the side shoots will begin to throw up little plantlets which in time can be lifted for other locations. This species can also be propagated by root cuttings, but goodness knows what sort of person would risk such a thing. I would prefer to put money on England's cricket team winning a test match than lifting an established plant of the *Meconopsis,* applying major surgery to its roots and expecting it to survive.

The fourth species from the Himalayan alpine zone is *Meconopsis bella,* most aptly named by the botanist Prain. It is found from central Nepal to south-eastern Tibet at altitudes from 11,500 to 16,500 ft. (3510–5030 m) in rock crevices and grassy cliff ledges. Ludlow and Sherriff often encountered this exquisite species in Bhutan and Tibet and one day experimented by removing a growing plant from a 1-in.-wide (2.5-cm) crack in a rock face, to reveal a taproot exactly 56 in. (142 cm) in length.

This deciduous perennial species dies back in the autumn and winter to a resting bud from which emerges in the spring a tuft of basal leaves which may be entire or pinnately lobed. The flowers are borne singly,

Meconopsis bella, central Nepal J. M. HIRST

often with several flowers produced from the same rosette in succession. They are nodding with large petals of superb pale-blue to violet, purple and pink. The flowers may be disproportionately large, up to 2 in. (5 cm) across resting on a short 4-in. (10-cm) stem.

A horrible dilemma threatens to ravage all such precious plants including *Meconopsis delavayi* and *M. bella*. It is the ubiquitous and wretched little slug. I say "little" because in my experience the big ones tend to lurk around big game, leaving the little ones, which can easily be missed, to devour the delicacies of such treasures as meconopses. I am afraid I resort to the employment of slug pellets which can be administered so as to prevent harmless creatures from obtaining them.

If we are lucky enough to obtain plants or seed of *Meconopsis bella,* the ideal position for plants is a cool, half-shaded raised bed between deeply anchored rocks. As with the majority of *Meconopsis* species, this one can be propagated from seed but is difficult. As far as this operation is concerned, particularly in raising this species, follow the instructions covered under "seed-raising" in Chapter 6 and good luck.

Gentiana

A genus making a major impact within this alpine zone is *Gentiana*. The gentians found at these high altitudes are quite varied, and placing them in their various botanical sections, as listed for the meadow species in Chapter 4, makes identifying them easier and clarifies their needs.

From the species in the section *Kudoa* we may expect the best results, as some of them prove easier to cultivate. As a general rule we may safely assume that these plants prefer to be grown in the open garden in a dedicated bed, a raised bed proving ideal for most of them.

Gentiana ornata is a classic Himalayan alpine plant, sadly rarely seen in gardens today despite its relative ease of culture and common occurrence in central Nepal. Early October is the best time to enjoy this particular gentian in nature, when trekking is made all the more enjoyable without the monsoon rains. The plants grow on open grassy slopes between 11,800 and 18,000 ft. (3400–5490 m), ranging from central Nepal to Sikkim, Bhutan and southern Tibet. They often grow in abundance showing a considerable amount of variation in form, size and flower colour. Above Gosainkund Lake, this species grows together with the lovely *G. depressa*.

Typically *Gentiana ornata* forms a low, matted plant with short, spreading stems up to 4 in. (10 cm) long, each terminating with solitary, widely bell-shaped, sky-blue flowers, including a full range of blue and white colours in some areas. When given full light and a moisture-retentive, acid soil this species has proved an easy gentian to grow, with most of the stock emanating from material collected by George Smith in Nepal. At no time during the growing season will this gentian or the other Himalayan species tolerate drying out.

A species encountered at high levels from the Indian Uttar Pradesh across to central Nepal is *Gentiana stipitata*. This is a fairly distinct subject, producing a tufted rosette with a few short spreading stems. The flowers are tubular in shape generally pale blue to mauve in colour with

Gentiana ornata, Barun, eastern Nepal GEORGE SMITH

darker lines inside the tube. It prefers stony slopes at elevations between 11,800 and 14,700 ft. (3400–4480 m). Henry and Margaret Taylor spotted the western form, *G. stipitata* subsp. *tizuensis,* growing in large numbers on dry, turfy ridges on the Nalgan Pass in the Kinnaur region of north-western India. In its dwarfer stature the blue-purple flowers rest on short stems so that the whole plant is only a few inches tall. Both forms of this species should be happy on a raised bed.

One of the most prized species belonging to this section is *Gentiana georgei* commemorating collector George Forrest who first discovered the species in 1906. He found it in the Lichiang range at around 11,000 to 12,000 ft. (3360–3660 m) in open meadows and on stony calcareous slopes. It was collected and successfully introduced by Kingdon Ward in the early 1930s. This plant is reminiscent of the well-known European *G. acaulis,* forming basal rosettes with sharply pointed foliage up to 3 in. (8 cm) in length. The flowers are terminal and solitary, varying considerably in colour from dark purple through lavender-blue and often heavily spotted dark purple within. Since it was first discovered, those who have encountered it in nature and have been fortunate enough to raise it in cultivation all say *G. georgei* is the finest gentian ever to be introduced. Indeed, therefore, how important it is to secure further seed collections. Sadly, it tends to flower very late in the season, which makes collecting viable seed before the winter snows return very difficult. It remains, though, a good perennial producing a short taproot. Having a native habitat in stable screes at altitudes as high as 15,000 ft. (4580 m), it requires a dedicated position in the garden on a raised bed in full sun. Dolomite stones with a rich mineral soil should suit it well, along with plentiful summer moisture at the root.

Two species found in commerce from time to time following successful seed-collecting trips to the Himalaya are *Gentiana obconica* and *G. meiantha*. Both of these species are distinct yet may prove to be subspecies of already well-recognised taxa. *Gentiana obconica* was supposedly collected in the early 1990s on a trip to north-western Yunnan and is generally found in alpine meadows in south-eastern Tibet, Bhutan, Sikkim and eastern Nepal. The material in cultivation seems to be somewhat intermediate between *G. obconica* and *G. caelestis,* a lovely little gentian with neat rosettes and small flowers of variable colour but generally deep blue. *Gentiana meiantha* may be found as a local species in eastern Nepal and Sikkim, forming a distinct overwintering cluster of young shoots and flowers more tubular in shape than *G. ornata.*

The section *Frigida* contains two species both widely distributed in nature yet sadly not frequently encountered in horticulture. *Gentiana nubigena* and *G. himalayaensis* are closely allied to *G. algida,* a well-known species with a very wide distribution including North America, Japan and Siberia. Both *G. nubigena* and *G. himalayaensis* form short rhizomes with basal leaves in the form of several erect rosettes. The sessile, or stalkless, flowers are dark blue to purple with a creamy-coloured base and dark blue streaks. *Gentiana nubigena* is frequently seen in Nepal at high altitudes between 16,000 and 18,000 ft. (4880–5490 m) in alpine meadows, while *G. himalayaensis* is found at elevations between 13,000 and 13,700 ft. (3970–4180 m) in south-eastern Tibet, Bhutan, Sikkim and eastern Nepal. Both species should be easy to raise from seed and may be cultivated in a raised bed amongst stones in an acid substrate.

One important Himalayan species belonging to the section *Pneumonanthe* is *Gentiana cachemirica* (synonym *G. loderi*). This attractive plant is found from Pakistan across into Kashmir at altitudes up to 13,000 ft. (3970 m) always amongst rocks. I have had no difficulty growing this species but have failed to experience a seed set. It forms a rosette from which spread several stems up to 6 in. (15 cm) in length bearing up to three pale blue, funnel-shaped flowers with toothed plicae. This is a very desirable plant which I have found grows best when tucked between rocks in a trough in full sun.

One of the most exciting species to be found in Nepal is *Gentiana phyllocalyx,* the single member of the section *Phyllocalyx.* It may be found on open, grassy slopes sometimes amongst rhododendrons at elevations up to 18,000 ft. (5490 m). This plant reminds me of the European *G. alpina* with more ovate or rounded leaves. It forms a rosette of basal leaves and three to five pairs of stem leaves surrounding the sessile and solitary flower held erect, a striking deep blue tubular trumpet, a little inflated in the centre. I grew this plant successfully for a while until I neglected its needs for water during a critical spell and lost it. It should grow well in a cool position in a deep trough or raised bed and may be raised from seed collected after it flowers in midsummer.

The section *Isomeria* is the largest and most exciting in many respects, yet its species are rather exacting in their requirements. These species typically occur at high altitudes in scree and produce creeping stolons with sessile flowers. I cannot overemphasise that these species require a special position in the garden that is open yet cool with a good depth of freely drained soil. The bed should include stones in varying sizes where the creeping roots may find refuge and anchorage. At no time during the summer months should these gentian species be allowed to dry out; therefore, it would be wise to install an irrigation system to ensure a good soaking last thing at night.

The most frequently encountered species of the section *Isomeria* is *Gentiana tubiflora,* found from the Himachal Pradesh through Nepal to south-eastern Tibet on screes and open grassy slopes from 13,000 to 16,000 ft. (3970–4880 m). When gentian lovers travel to the mountains, whether the Himalaya, the Rockies or the European Alps, they encounter nothing more frustrating than finding their favourite flowers with petals tightly closed due to the lack of sunlight or warmth. They know that if only the cloud would lift to reveal the sun the sights to behold would be breathtaking. This frustration is well known to us who have exhibited gentians at flower shows, particularly the autumn varieties, only to see the beautiful blooms closed tightly during the time of judging. Many who have seen *G. tubiflora* in nature have found it similarly reluctant to open its narrow tubular flowers. When it does it is rather akin to *G. prolata,* solitary deep blue and unspotted. It is an attractive tufted, cushion-forming plant with rosettes up to ½ in. (1 cm) across, deserving its popularity and growing well in a sunny bed with an acid soil. It may be propagated by seed.

Several species have been relocated since the late 1990s but need great skill to be collected. *Gentiana amplicrater* and *G. gilvostriata* are two beautiful species seen in the Tsari district of south-eastern Tibet. Both grow in unique plant communities formed on grassy hummocks of rich mineral soil.

Gentiana amplicrater produces a rosette with stolons and short, leafy flower stems carrying up to four flowers of a lovely blue-purple with a pale green base and dark blue stripes. As it becomes better known and hopefully gets a hold in cultivation, this species surely will prove a spectacular introduction. It first was introduced by Ludlow and Sherriff with the number L.S. 9077 from south-eastern Tibet during the years of WWII but persisted only fleetingly. Andrew Harley of Devonhall in Perthshire obtained some of the original material and was able to grow it well, however, describing it as a "magnificent plant."

Certainly very special is *Gentiana gilvostriata*. Jack Drake once told me the story of an occasion when he was being shown around a large garden by a prominent horticulturist who was extolling the virtues of a fine stand of *G. sino-ornata*. While all others present were in awe of this gentian, Drake was completely distracted by a small plant of another species, quite the most beautiful he had ever seen. It was *G. gilvostriata*. This species was found by Kingdon Ward in Upper Burma near the Tibetan border and by Ludlow and Sherriff in south-eastern Tibet where it grew in abundance at the edge of a coniferous forest at 12,500 ft. (3810 m). It is a tufted species with short prostrate branches ending in a small rosette and short flowering stems each bearing a solitary flower. The large, sky-blue trumpets are paler within with brownish-purple bands on the outside. For a decade at least after its introduction, this plant was grown successfully with few difficulties, but it has since died out of horticulture. Maybe it produced little in the way of seed, which is so often the cause of a species's gradual dwindling and subsequent loss to cultivation. This one was relocated in south-eastern Tibet on a 1999 expedition to Tsari, and we may soon have another chance to cultivate this wonderful plant.

A distinctive plant sometimes found in eastern Nepal is the lovely *Gentiana elwesii* growing in open, grassy or scrubby slopes. It produces stems up to 3 to 9 in. (8–23 cm) in length from elliptic basal leaves. The flowers are held on a terminal head, a stunning deep violet-blue above and white below. If seed could be obtained of this rarely grown subject it would prove an exciting addition to the raised bed.

The greater knowledge of Sino-Himalayan plants gained as a result of late-twentieth-century expeditions to north-western Yunnan has led to heightened expectations of finding further *Gentian* species to be brought into cultivation. These expeditions have also heightened our awareness of their garden requirements relative to the habitat in which they have been found growing. One species we are looking forward to is *Gentiana wardii,* distributed from south-eastern Tibet into south-western Sichuan

Gentiana elwesii, Barun, eastern Nepal GEORGE SMITH

and north-western Yunnan. Its flowers look rather similar to G. *phylloca-lyx*, upright and more or less stemless, emerging from a congested rosette of lime-green foliage. This would prove to be a wonderful addition for the trough or raised bed.

One of the most sought after of all truly Himalayan alpine species is *Gentiana depressa,* and it is fortunately widely available in horticulture. While demanding great care, this is the choicest species that most readers could succeed with in a variety of locations, particularly as it has no intolerance of sunshine. In the changing climate on the east coast of Scotland, when the sun does shine it combines a greater intensity with an extreme heat, burning human skin more easily and scorching plants to death. Some high alpines, as long as their roots are well down in a cool protective area of stones, seem to enjoy this exposure, finding it like their native habitat, and flower more profusely. *Gentiana depressa* fits into this category yet is intolerant of hard frosts, expecting the Himalaya's protective covering of snow. It may be found from central Nepal to south-

Gentiana depressa, Schachen Garden, southern Germany DIETER SCHACHT

eastern Tibet enjoying high altitudes between 11,000 and 14,000 ft. (3360–4270 m). In the Gosainkund area of central Nepal it may be seen in large colonies growing on short-grass banks and rocky outcrops forming low tufted rosettes with spreading stems that pop up at least 6 in. (15 cm) from the parent plant. The flowers are a most lovely, broadly bell-shaped structure in a sumptuous pale-blue to greenish blue and occasionally pure white, sitting upright amongst the somewhat glaucous rosettes. Some patches will have at least eleven flowers, while in the garden at home in a rich mineral soil large mats will be covered with flowers, but significantly weakening the plant as a result. Keep the plant strong by lifting it, teasing it apart, and replanting.

On a trip to the Langtang and Gosainkund areas in the month of October 1995, Ian Christie reported fine flowering colonies of both *Gentiana depressa* and *G. ornata* with positive sightings of hybrids between the two species. He noted immense activity of large bumble bees passing from one species to another, making hybridisation not surprising. Offspring of these two species does represent an intra-sectional cross. It shows the very close relationship these plants share in their ancestry as within other large, varied genera like *Primula* which also has a history of intra-sectional hybrids. Most keen alpine growers favour growing *G. depressa* in pans, and no doubt the ability to exhibit by growing plants in this way is a clear advantage, but no finer sight is there than a well-grown mat of *G. depressa*, growing on a raised bed amongst rocks and slates with other associated plants.

My final choice to conclude this section on *Gentiana*, this chapter on the alpine zone and the part of this book on recommended plants is fittingly one of the most distinguished of all Himalayan plants. It is *G. urnula*, which I mentioned at the start of this chapter in reference to George Smith's exploration and photography in Nepal. Until he began his travels there, few Britons had explored Nepal or collected plant material. Smith added immeasureably to our knowledge with his vast photographic records which he so willingly shared with others. It may well be the photographic record of *G. urnula* in particular that has so inspired lovers of high Himalayan alpines to travel there. It is to be found at altitudes between 14,500 and 20,000 ft. (4420–6100 m), nestling down between rocks in stable scree where little else survives. It displays an austere beauty at an altitude that we as relatively fit humans can safely enjoy without employing supplementary oxygen. I find the clumps of tightly overlapping foliage satisfying even without a flower, but added to these are the solitary, broadly urn-shaped flowers in varying shades of blue with a slate-grey base to the outside of the petals. Sherriff reported a fine stand of this gentian growing in loose shale on the Tulung La in south-eastern Tibet where the flowers were white and streaked with slate-purple.

As to growing the plant, important first of all is to secure strong plant material either as seed-raised plants or from collected vegetative material. I have had the pleasure of seeing young plant material thriving in the open garden on the west side of northern England in a rock garden where the roots have been set into a mineral soil with added shale. This garden uses an artificial irrigation system to ensure that the plants will at no time dry out. I am confident that the plant will thrive there, although time will tell. I am also confident that should this glorious treasure choose not only to survive but to thrive and flower, the telephone will ring and I will pay more than a casual trip to share my friends' experience. After all, is this not what gardening is all about, accepting challenges and then sharing our successes with others?

In conclusion I can only say that whatever extra efforts are employed to research the requirements for a plant we may choose to grow, then the time spent creating the right home for it will be richly rewarded. Plants growing on the very roof of the world in such varying conditions according to their situation relative to exposure to monsoon or rain shadow demand attention to detail in horticulture. I hope these chapters will help gardeners find and create the right home for their favourite plants.

CHAPTER SIX

Propagation

THIS CHAPTER on propagation is intended to be an aid for gardeners who would like to maintain stocks of their favourite plants, to guide them through the methods of raising newly acquired seed. The successful propagator must pay very careful attention to good hygiene, the provision of healthy mother plants and obtaining the best possible materials for the job.

I have in the preceeding chapters already suggested particular types of propagation suitable for individual types of plants, so I will not give detailed accounts in this chapter. This is very much a general treatment which I break down into three sections: division, cuttings and seed-raising.

Division

Division will certainly rank as the simplest method of all, with the newly formed plants being ready for transplanting immediately. It is the ideal means of propagation when a gardener requires only a few extra plants. Often plants need to be rejuvenated for their own well-being. For example, *Primula whitei*, if not lifted periodically and divided, will eventually lose its vigour and die. This is added reason for the keen gardener to be aware of this means of regeneration.

Subjects to consider for division are generally those which produce underground lateral roots, notably plants which can produce new growth from dormant buds, such as some species of *Meconopsis*. Herbaceous plants with this kind of root system such as *Bergenia, Iris, Meconopsis* and the various species of *Primula* can be divided very simply.

Division can be carried out in two main periods, either when the plants are in full growth but flowering has ceased, or during the early part of the growing season when the roots are just beginning to stir sufficiently to allow the young divisions to take hold in their fresh soil. Generally for most climates in the northern hemisphere March and early September are the principle months for division.

Perennial meconopses deserve particular mention here because they have a number of forms. *Meconopsis grandis, M. betonicifolia* and the hybrid between the two *M. ×sheldonii* should be regularly divided, especially when planted in drifts in the woodland garden. I have always found early spring, March or April, the best time to manage this project as the new vegetative growth is just becoming apparent. Pull away the old decaying leaves and stems if this was not already done during the winter. Young greenish brown, hairy buds are beginning to form just above the surface of the soil. Feel carefully to insert the garden fork without damaging any shoots, then lift the whole clump. The previous year's flowering crowns have a hollow stem which can be removed carefully. With the perennial forms of *Meconopsis* mentioned above, the flowering shoots die after flowering to be replaced by several side shoots. The whole clump now can be loosened and teased apart revealing half a dozen or more strong plants from a three-year-old clump. These will have roots attached and should be set aside for replanting in fresh soil or in the same bed enriched with rotted compost or leaf mould. Should a few smaller side shoots come away, without roots, set these in a wooden box of soil to develop roots and be planted out later.

After a plant is divided, the new plantlets require plenty of water. Ignoring this need will result in disappointment. Also, solid firming of the soil when planting is important to reduce the risk of drying out.

Some of the more vigorous forms of *Meconopsis grandis,* such as *M.* George Sherriff Group, produce a number of finger-like lateral shoots around the base of the clump. These may be severed and again laid out vertically in a box of soil. They can be planted in their final position once rooted. Each one will mature, to flower in one or two year's time.

This early-season division is really quite straightforward, but dividing a plant when in full growth is a little more demanding. I will use as an example this time the petiolarid primulas which may be divided after flowering in May or later when they make a further set of adventitious roots in September. The optimum time to divide a congested clump of *Primula whitei* is in late spring, April or May. The key to success is en-suring that the plant is not under stress or undergoing a period of drought during division. If the plant's strength is in doubt, dig up the clumps and soak them a few days before dividing. When lifting this prim-ula do look out, both in the soil and within the roots, for the most awful pest ravaging plants at present, the vine weevil. Good hygiene is vital for growing a healthy batch of these primulas. Old, tired, or virused stock

Meconopsis George Sherriff Group, Schachen Garden, southern Germany
DIETER SCHACHT

should be lifted and burned and replaced with fresh material, if available. The divisions should be replanted with extra leaf mould, well firmed into the soil, and watered in to complete the job. A little shading material placed over newly planted divisions may be wise during the hottest part of the day.

Another group of plants suitable for division are those which produce mats or clumps with side rosettes, such as the species of *Androsace, Saxifraga* and *Potentilla,* and *Diapensia himalaica.* After flowering, these plants form side rosettes which produce adventitious roots. Gently lift the mat or prise up the rosettes and sever them from the parent plant with a sharply pointed pair of scissors. These little divisions, or "Irishman's cuttings," may now be potted up or replanted into an appropriate soil mix, and take care to ensure they do not dry out. A mature mat of *Saxifraga stolitzkae* may produce a number of rooted rosettes around the perimeter, and this is the best means of propagation. Experience will indicate the best time for tackling this very rewarding operation, but soon after flowering is generally the best time, allowing a season's growth to re-establish the divisions.

Cuttings

The two types of cuttings for the Himalayan plants we are endeavouring to propagate are stem and leaf cuttings. The most important is the stem cutting, which may be taken from either soft or semi-ripened material. Softwood cuttings are taken from the new season's growth that has not yet ripened, and semi-ripened cuttings are taken from the new season's growth that has ripened by mid- to late summer, July or August. In the case of softwood cuttings it is crucial that the mother plant is both healthy and free from stress. The cutting material must be turgid, or full of sap, before the cuttings are taken.

The next point to consider is where to place the cuttings to give them the best chance of rooting. Since most readers will neither be running a nursery nor have a dedicated propagation house for rooting cuttings, more modest measures will be appropriate. All that is required is a small cold frame about 4 ft. (1.2 m) square, in this case a cutting frame, constructed of timber. Situate it in a squarely north-south position if possible, and slope the "lights," or glass sheets covering the cutting frame, to have a slight fall to ensure rapid run-off for both rain and internal condensation. I strongly recommend ordinary clear glass to give maximum light. The south side of the cutting frame could be utilised for all sun-loving and alpine cuttings while the north side can be used for ericaceous subjects. The design shown in the figure demonstrates the importance of making the cutting frame air tight. Any ventilation required can be facilitated by propping open the lights. High humidity, as much as 80 to 95 percent, is necessary for cuttings to root successfully. Artificial heat, usually in the form of soil-warming cables, will not be required as we generally will not need to root cuttings in the winter months, although if a source of power can be provided safely, a heating system may be a bonus.

The soil base beneath the rooting material must be freely draining, as a cutting frame requires more water than the average cold frame. A generous 6 in. (15 cm) of coarse rubble should be the base for the frame—the frame itself should sit on this drainage layer. Above this drainage layer

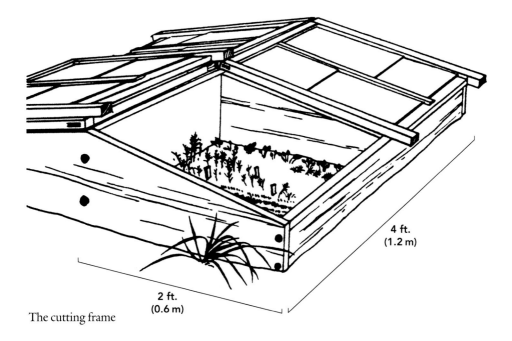

The cutting frame

4 ft.
(1.2 m)

2 ft.
(0.6 m)

and inside the walls of the frame place a sheet of fine mesh polypropylene netting to prevent the rooting medium from washing into the drainage material. On top of this mesh, spread a layer about 3 in. (8 cm) thick of rooting material, allowing a further 3 in. (8 cm) of headroom for the cuttings at the lowest part of the frame. The content of the rooting medium, then, will be one of the main factors as to whether the cutting frame is a success or failure. The main part of the medium should be a clean, sharp sand, although a whole host of substitutes are on the market that will work equally well, such as perlite, vermiculite, or pumice. Ian Christie, who runs a nursery near Kirriemuir in east-central Scotland, enjoys the huge benefit of a nearby quarry which supplies a sand that I would say is gold dust in horticultural terms. Completely free from any clay particles which deem a sand useless for growing plants, this sand may even be used on its own for rooting all alpine subjects, with the exception of woody or ericaceous plants. The most difficult subjects will root well in a fine pumice instead of sand, while I have also found the addition of perlite, a heat-expanded volcanic rock material of neutral pH with fine water-retention properties, to give better and stronger root systems.

If the full bed of sand or similar rooting material will provide too much space for the planned number of cuttings, clean, sterilised pots may be used. Fill them with the same rooting material and then plunge them up to their rims into the sand inside the frame. Using pots or shallow pans in in this way certainly may be advantageous for rooting small cuttings such as the saxifrages of the section *Kabschia*.

When using the whole frame, pack the sand into the corners and firm it well throughout. This job is best done with a block of wood. Then water the bed well, and it is ready for the cuttings to be inserted. After inserting the cuttings, water them in well with a fine rose so that none are missed. Close the frame completely, and the following morning damp down the sand with the rose to supply only a little water in the upper layer of sand. This will be sufficient for a dull day. Further damping down is required whenever the surface of the sand takes on a pale colour. Shading the cutting frame may be necessary on sunny days to prevent scorching, particularly if no one will be at home during the day, as is often the case. Too little light, though, will tend to "draw" the cuttings, or encourage them to stretch toward the light, and rooting will be impaired.

Construct the frame the same way for ericaceous plants, but it is important to give it more shade. The rooting mix also should be more acid and more moisture retentive—ideal would be a 4:1 ratio of sand to sieved peat or a 1:1:2 mixture of sand, peat and perlite. Each gardener, though, will surely experiment and find a personal preference.

This more acid and moisture-retentive mix also would be suitable for the autumn-flowering gentians and *Cyananthus* species, but the latter will root well in a sunny aspect. A shaded frame needs less watering, perhaps half as much as a sunny frame. But also, more shade will ecourage more moss and liverwort to form. Modern chemicals can be used to combat this problem, but take care to avoid scorching the cuttings. A few crystals of potassium permanganate sprinkled into every 2-gallon (8-litre) can of water used on the cuttings will help combat the problem of moss and liverwort. Again, each individual will find a preferred remedy.

Ventilation should be given only when the outside temperatures rise to over 70–80°F (21–27°C), and then raise the glass lights only 1 in. (2.5 cm) or so. Once the cuttings have rooted more ventilation may be given during the day and less shading. The cuttings should be well rooted before potting up, as they will suffer a severe check if only a few roots have formed. If left for a while in a pot or a pan the rooted cuttings may be given a weak, balanced foliar feed at frequent intervals to hold them over until potting.

A serious pest of the cutting frame, however it has been constructed, is the fungus gnat or sciarid fly. The tiny, black, two-winged flies may be seen hopping and flying just above the surface of the rooting medium and immediately under the glass. The transparent-looking larvae possess a conspicuous black head and can devastate the roots of plants. While running my nursery I was able to obtain a chemical which I applied as a drench to the compost, but once again individuals will have to choose whatever means possible to control this pest. Just available is a drench containing the active ingredient imidacloprid.

Let me now highlight a few genera ideally propagated from cuttings. Bear in mind that many plants covered in this book can be propagated by this means, and experimenting is a good way to discover the best timing and methods.

In the discussion in Chapter 4 on subalpine meadow plants I highlighted the genus *Cyananthus* and suggested taking cuttings early in the spring. These cuttings may be placed in a cutting frame as I have described, or a small propagator such as could fit on a wide windowsill, too, would work perfectly satisfactorily.

The autumn-flowering gentians may also be propagated successfully from stem cuttings. This method is often utilised to bulk up a particular clone which is loath to division. The best time to take the cuttings is at the end of April or early May before the new growth has extended beyond 1 in. (2.5 cm) or so and prior to any bud formation. The current owners of Edrom Nurseries, Terry Hunt and Cath Davis, have made good use of rooting hormones when propagating by this method and have employed the proprietary chemical named Synergol to very good effect. For the gentian cuttings they have diluted the hormone to one-fourth strength in water, and for woodier subjects one-third strength.

Other genera to propagate by cuttings are *Cassiope, Rhododendron, Daphne, Salix, Saxifraga* and *Androsace*. The woody, ericaceous subjects such as *Cassiope* and *Rhododendron* certainly prefer more peat and perlite than sand, but perlite, while holding moisture, tends to dry out faster in my experience than peat and sand. Cuttings of these genera are best taken in mid- to late summer from semi-ripened, young growth. As with other subjects it will be necessary to remove the bottom leaves to make a clean cut just below a node or leaf joint. In the case of daphnes and rhododendrons I recommend carefully keeping the bottom leaves from touching the surface of the rooting medium to reduce the risk of fungal attack. These subjects will root more quickly with a dip in a rooting hormone such as Synergol.

Leaf cuttings present a different approach, with fewer subjects lending themselves to this means of propagation. Many of the petiolarid primulas can be propagated by this means. Those that root well are *Primula boothii* and *P. irregularis,* although other closely related species may also root. In the late summer, around August or September in Scotland, I have found that healthy clumps of these primulas may be lifted in order to get at the base of the leaf petiole, and the leaves when ready will practically fall away when given a little pressure. The leaves have a long petiole, or stem, with a tiny axillary bud that needs to be evident to effect successful rooting and regeneration. The best rooting medium is a mixture of sand, peat and perlite in whichever ratio the grower feels is best. I choose a mix with mainly perlite and peat with just a little sand. The leaf cuttings should be inserted in the damp rooting medium at an angle and up to the base of the leaf. Water the cuttings in well, and if using pots or trays place them in the cutting frame. After several weeks the little axillary bud will produce a plantlet which itself will root. Once established, the rooted cuttings may be potted up or held in the cutting frame bed or trays over winter with an occasional liquid feed.

Seed-Raising

I believe raising plants from seed to be the most rewarding and useful of all means open to gardeners for propagating plants. It is of course the most natural of processes and has been built into the plants' ingenious blue print for survival. That we humans can tap into this natural means of regeneration is surely a great privilege that we should never take for granted. In this modern world, where greed appears to dominate many peoples' thinking, plants, whether endangered in nature or not, still are exploited by being dug up in wholesale numbers to meet the demands of craving gardeners. This seems extraordinary to me, because with few exceptions plants can be propagated by seed at specialised nurseries or laboratories and then disseminated to keen plantsfolk without ever damaging the plant stocks in nature.

To save seed for personal use or for passing it on to others, begin by collecting the seed pods or capsules when ripe. Dry them inside paper bags hung on a line with clothes pegs in a dry, airy shed. It is important to mark clearly on the bag the name of the plant. When collecting moist or juicy fruits, as for species of *Paris, Gaultheria* and *Vaccinium,* place them on a layer of dry paper or smooth towel and gently prise them open as they dry.

Once the seed capsules are fully dry and ripe they should be cleaned as thoroughly as possible, removing the chaff from the seed. I find that a

Primula waltonii with *P. sikkimensis,* Schachen Garden, southern Germany
DIETER SCHACHT

variety of sieves (liberated from my wife's kitchen) and a strong card serve this purpose admirably. If the seeds are to be sown soon after collection, as for aquilegias and androsaces, then they can be put aside for immediate sowing. In the main text I mentioned special cases such as *Anemone, Adonis* and the petiolarid primulas in which the seeds should be collected earlier in the season and sown at once. This section refers to seed collected later in the season.

Meconopsis horridula with *Primula sikkimensis,* Schachen Garden, southern Germany
DIETER SCHACHT

For subjects that will be sown at the turn of the year or in early spring, the cleaned seed should be placed in a special seed envelope and marked again with the name of the plant. Store the seed packets in an airtight plastic container with a sachet of silica gel to absorb any moisture, and place them in the refrigerator but not the freezer. Dry refrigeration will preserve the seed in the best condition to be ready for sowing in the early spring, or from January onwards for alpine subjects.

Some genera require a period of cold over winter, called stratification, before the seeds will germinate. This can best be achieved by sowing at the turn of the year in Scotland to allow a few months where the air temperature drops to freezing from time to time, thus breaking dormancy. In warmer climes stratify seeds by lowering the refrigerator temperature to about 36°F (2°C) for up to eight weeks prior to sowing.

When seeds are received from an organised seed-collecting expedition, sow them immediately. Some genera, such as *Iris,* produce hard-coated seeds, and these should be soaked in water for forty-eight hours prior to sowing.

Usually I recommend a John Innes seed compost, a U.K. brand, for seed-sowing. This is basically a loam-based compost designed to hold plants, be they seedlings or cuttings, for a longer period of time than loamless compost. Loamless composts are ideal for seeds that germinate quickly, and a whole host of loamless, peat-based composts will suit the Himalayan plants covered here. I have not yet experienced a good substitute for peat, but this does not mean one is not available. The choice of compost is wide and depends on the grower's preference.

The use of sphagnum moss as a medium for seed-sowing is a system devised by my predecessor at Edrom Nurseries, Alex Duguid, for raising a number of Himalayan species from seed, notably members of Ericaceae, Diapensiaceae, Liliaceae and Primulaceae. Its immediate advantage over other soil or soil-less mixtures is its ability to retain moisture, thus avoiding the drying out which is so disastrous for seed germination.

The most suitable of the several species of sphagnum is the one seen frequently on the high moor in Britain, usually pink in colour. Leave the moss in the sun to dry out thoroughly, or bake it in the oven. The sphagnum must be dead prior to its use as a growing medium. Once it is completely dry, rub it through a ¼-in. (0.6-cm) sieve. Soak the moss in water, then drain and squeeze it to remove the surplus moisture. Pack it into sterile pots or pans to within ½ in. (1 cm) of the surface of the pot. Sow the seed thinly and label. Do not cover fine seed such as those of the Ericaceae or the finer primulas. Larger seeds, such as those of lilies, may be covered with a thin layer of gritty sand to prevent drying out. Now plunge the seed pots in sand in a covered frame or greenhouse. The pricking out, or transplanting, of seedlings is as with other methods of seed sowing, but as with all bulbous species, the liliaceous seedlings are best retained in their pots without disturbance for a full year's growth and given a weak liquid feed until well established.

After choosing a good, sterile seed compost, preferably acid in nature for Himalayan subjects, be sure it is not dry but also not too moist. Then choose a container. I use square plastic pots, as they are easy to fit with a little board for pressing down the compost. The pots should be either brand new or sterilised. Any coarse roughage can be placed in the base of the pot as supplementary drainage material to prevent water-logging. Fill the pot or seed tray to the top and level the compost. I then settle the compost by gently knocking the bottom of the pot flat down onto the table top to make room to add a little sieved compost, which will aid an even germination. Gently press down the surface with a board and it is now ready for sowing. Larger seeds can be placed singly on the surface with the fingers. For finer seed, scatter it evenly but never thickly on the compost. Extra-fine seed either may be mixed with some fine sand particles to spread more evenly or may be sown on top of a thin covering of chick-grit or vermiculite and the pot gently tapped to help the seed down between the particles of the topping.

In conventional seed-sowing the seed is now ready for a covering of at least twice the depth of the seed's diameter. This covering may be a layer of fine vermiculite, chick grit or a fine washed grit.

I recommend sitting the pots in a tray of water, once they have been labelled clearly with the name of the plant and the date of sowing. When they have taken up water to the point where the surface material is also wet, then plunge the pots up to their rims in sand to aid moisture retention, especially if they are clay pots. Cover them with a fine mesh, either wire or soft plastic will do, to protect the seeds from mice or bird damage. I cannot think of anything more frustrating than to arrive in the morning to examine the seeds and find them ravaged by mice.

Before germination, the seeds may benefit from a watering with copper oxychloride, such as Murphy Traditional Copper Fungicide in the United Kingdom. An alternative chemical is the Cheshunt compound. These will prevent the "damping off" of seedlings, the fungal infection of *Botrytis*. And keep careful watch for weed seedlings and remove them. Some gardeners recommend covering seeds with sheets of newspaper to retain moisture, but I have found no benefit from it.

For species not requiring stratification, the best germination will be effected with a minimum temperature of 50°F (10°C) which is easy to achieve in a cold frame or cool glasshouse. Some ericaceous plants will germinate better when sown in an ericaceous compost, an acid mix made of predominantly peat, with a very thin covering and then given some warmth up to 60°F (16°C).

Once the seeds have germinated, the decision has to be made when to prick out the seedlings into trays or individual pots. I prefer to wait until true leaves have formed and then choose a cool day or part of the day to transplant, so that the seedlings are not placed under extreme stress. The choice of compost depends very much on the plant in question. In most cases a peat-based or loamless compost will prove satisfactory for easier subjects that grow quickly. For plants requiring a longer spell in the transition stage I would choose a John Innes mix or other proprietary loam-based mix. Fill a tray with compost and gently firm it, do not compact it, around the edges. A standard seed tray should hold forty seedlings in eight-by-five rows, which could be marked out with a dibber or pencil. Then make the proper holes and place the seedlings in them, one per hole, with the roots carefully towards the bottom. Fill and firm the holes so that no air pockets surround the roots. Label the tray and water thoroughly. The seedlings can be placed in a cold frame and protected from scorching sun by shading during the day. Be sure to remove the shading on cloudy days, and as the seedlings develop into young plants plenty of ventilation and water should be given. Once fully established into young plants, they may be exposed to full light without glass or polythene cover, to be shaded only from excessive sunlight. The plants are now ready for their final position in the garden, and in most cases the planting is best carried out in the spring to give plants a full season to develop prior to their first winter.

A luxury that any amateur gardener may wish to have is a small propagator. A propagator is usually an enclosed frame about 2 by 1 ft. (60 by 30 cm) with a soil-warming cable and the optional extra of a misting unit. A heated propagator may well broaden the scope of items that can be propagated, while speeding up the germination process and lengthening the transitional season under glass.

This chapter on propagation is designed to help the keen grower with the basic principles of the subject. There can be no doubt that much pleasure comes from raising one's own plants and being able to give away favourite species as gifts or swaps to friends.

CHAPTER SEVEN

Pests and Diseases

G ARDENING IN every part of the world is barely possible without expecting plants to be subject to some kind of malady. All gardeners are therefore constantly on the lookout for ways of reducing the incidence of attack. The first and foremost means of deterrent is good hygiene, particularly important when growing a collection of plants in containers. This involves keeping the surroundings clean and free from debris. A glasshouse or cold frame needs to be cleaned every year, every three years with a disinfectant, such as Jeyes Fluid in the United Kingdom. The majority of harmful pests find lodgings in detritus that has formed between panes of glass or along and underneath benching. If old leaves and herbage are thrown under a bench or left between pots, this is the perfect home for vine weevil which can completely destroy a collection of plants in a few years. Rather than bombard the plants and ourselves with organophosphate chemicals, so much better it is to pay attention to good hygiene.

A word of caution must be said to alert growers who plan to concentrate on one genus of plants and build up a collection of, let us say, primulas, gentians or saxifrages. In each of these cases particular pests or diseases will attack these plants, but such attacks are more prevalent with monoculture, a fundamental abuse of agricultural laws. A well-managed garden has a balanced collection of plants. And, according to the law of rotation, try to move plants around if possible. While I was running my nursery, a young man began to take a great interest in primulas and purchased a goodly number of them, to which he added as many Asiatic species and hybrids that I had available. One part of me was delighted with the business, while another had to warn him of the dangers involved. Soon he had built up a great collection of plants, but after a few years experienced many problems with, first of all, vine weevil, then root aphids and finally virus. There was no easy antidote. His only natural safeguard would have been to try to exercise some self-control and limit his collection, or spread it around in a series of gardens.

Gentians are no less of a worry when under monoculture. I never experienced any serious worries with pests and diseases while growing hundreds of them each year, yet wholesale growers who deal in tens of thousands find that gentians suddenly begin to experience a nasty fungal disease. It is unlikely that the amateur gardener will approach such numbers of plants, but I sound a warning nevertheless.

For the saxifrages, the formation of several specialist societies has naturally moved devotees to concentrate on this one group of plants. A pest that can ruin these lovely cushion plants is the nematode, which attacks in two forms. The result of a serious attack is that plants fail to make fresh growth while the existing rosettes, stems and flowers become distorted. A highly toxic chemical is available to the commercial grower to kill nematodes, but it requires extremely careful use. Biological controls continue to be developed, and I hope they will diminish the problem caused by the harmful parasitic nematode, which can be seen effectively only under a microscope.

A modest collection of any of these particular genera planted out in the open garden is unlikely to be affected by a fatal attack of this nature. In a garden with a number of trees, perhaps broadleaf and coniferous, birds will be attracted both to nest and to remain for the summer, and others such as blackbirds and thrushes will become permanent residents. Creating a balanced ecology with effective food chains, including these birds for example, will help to keep down any build-up of harmful pests such as vine weevil, slugs, snails and the larvae of leather jacket moths (*Fipula*).

Gardeners must decide for themselves whether or not to employ chemicals in the garden to combat harmful pests and diseases. Advantages in not using them are obvious, but their limited use may prove a sensible compromise, resorting to them only when it is absolutely necessary, and then taking care to apply the chemical only at the recommended dose and only in the area where the pest or disease is concentrated. I have found that slug pellets have to be used to combat this destructive pest, but the active chemical ingredient seems to make a considerable difference. The chemical methiocarb is very effective. To ensure that other harmless molluscs and annelids, or worms, are not affected, I place these pellets inside a small section of tube close to the prized plant under attack. Sadly and unnecessarily, birds sometimes are killed by this chemical when they consume a partially affected snail.

One of the most common diseases in the garden is mildew, and *Meconopsis* may be attacked by it from time to time. I have noticed that these poppies are particularly prone to this disease when they are under stress, notably during a prolonged dry spell. The normal remedy is to apply fortnightly doses of fungicide, either a systemic or a non-systemic, contact type. "Systemic" describes a chemical which may be applied as a drench and will be taken up by the roots to help protect the whole plant from attack. I strongly recommend watering infected plants at night for several days and removing and destroying all the foliage badly affected with the silvery-coloured mildew.

Some older hybrid cultivars of our favourite plants can be attacked by virus, reducing vigour and causing discolouration of the foliage. In primulas, virus is most prevalent in hybrids with infertile pollen, meaning no seed is set. Through constant vegetative propagation such as division or cuttings, the plants lose vigour and become susceptible to attack by virus. The most common ones to affect primulas are cucumber mosaic and arabis mosaic viruses. These viruses are usually spread by aphids, or greenfly, which in turn need to be controlled, particularly in protected areas under polythene or glass. When plant material becomes infected with virus, destroy it, as virus is easily spread by division and transmitted to clean stock. Both species and hybrid petiolarid primulas seem to be especially susceptible.

Another serious disease which can affect many plants, more particularly during the production cycle, is *Botrytis,* or greymould. Generally associated with stagnant air, it is less prevalent in the open garden and more often encountered in conditions under polythene or glass. This disease may also cause basal rot to plants in hot weather. The rotten parts of the plants should be removed and the infected parts drenched with a systemic fungicide.

By far the most serious pest in gardens across Europe and the United States is vine weevil. Without intending to be sexist, I sadly must say that all adult vine weevil are female, and each has the capacity to lay 200 eggs. This is particularly alarming considering that many of those eggs will form small larvae or grubs—comma shaped, off-white and with an orange-brown head—that will live amongst the root systems of most plants, most notably primulas and woodland species. They will eat through all the roots until reducing them to mere stubs, causing the plant to wilt and eventually die. The first tell-tale sign during the growing season is the wilting of healthy foliage. Lifting the plant will reveal a number of grubs in the soil around the base of the plant. They should of course be destroyed. Other plants close by should also be checked for similar attacks.

The adult weevil may be spotted at night, after dusk with a torch. It is a grey-brown-coloured insect resembling a beetle with a protruding snout. It may be seen clinging to a leaf, leaving the usual rounded, notching effect on the foliage to alert us to its presence. Unfortunately the dazzle of light will cause it to scuttle for cover. The most common host plants for the adult are *Rhododendron, Pieris, Epimedium* and many liliaceous subjects. It is always worth every effort during a warm spell to locate the adults and destroy them. I use a dim torch and a pair of pliers.

Again, I hope that a biological control for vine weevil will be developed that will be effective in the open at any temperature. Trials already have given encouraging results. A simple tip that has certainly worked for me is occasionally to mix a few drops of Jeyes Fluid into every 2½ gallons (10 litres) of water when giving plants their routine watering. This will act as a deterrent, presumably by its strong odour, causing the adults to go elsewhere.

For growers of *Lilium* and *Fritillaria* the scourge of lily beetle is of great concern. The adult beetle is a bright red colour and eats the leaves and buds of lilies. The larvae—particularly horrid as they are covered in their own excrement—can easily strip a lily of its leaves. Persistent watchfulness is the best means of control as the adult is reasonably easy to detect.

A problem that is increasing, in my experience, is caterpillar damage on a variety of Himalayan subjects, notably during dry conditions. The particular pests are the cut-worms, green or brown caterpillars of various noctuid moths, including the yellow underwing (*Noctua pronuba*), and the turnip moths (*Agrotis* spp.). They may be found at night feeding on the foliage of *Meconopsis*, *Primula* and other subjects while by day hiding several inches below the soil. The best control is to collect them by torchlight and deal with each one.

A number of less common pests and diseases may show up in isolated areas or on rare occasions. A number of horticultural societies or local clubs may help with specialised advice to deal with a particular problem. I cannot overemphasise the need, though, to pay attention to the details of good hygiene, whether it be in the open or under cover. Out in the garden, diseased wood or foliage should be removed and burned. Reduce the risk of an attack by minimising the occasions when susceptible plants are allowed to experience stress. Plant stress is generally caused by under-watering in the open or over-watering in containers. Be alert and observant, remembering that many pests can be effectively controlled at night for the sake of a few minutes vigilance with a torch.

Finally, I will relate an embarrassing personal experience which hopefully will bring the point of good hygiene home to all of us. A knowledgeable friend was visiting me at the nursery one day during the height of the growing season. I was showing him around the garden and stopped for a moment beside an old and very sick plant of the South African composite *Euryops acraeus*. I realised that it had been attacked by a form of rust and was not responding to my treatment. My learned friend consoled me saying, "It's a pity you have not controlled the host plants, groundsel." Groundsel (*Senecio vulgaris*), a common garden weed very prone to this disease and very easily pulled up at any time, had passed on the rust. To add insult to injury, my friend looked up at a row of Scots pine trees and said, "That's your secondary host." What a fool I had made of myself, simply because I had not removed the groundsel from the mixed border. Yes, the rust had passed from the Scots pine to the groundsel to the euryops, killing the last and teaching me a simple lesson in good plant husbandry and hygiene.

Sources of Choice Himalayan Plants and Newly Introduced Seed

SEED EXCHANGE

The Alpine Garden Society
AGS Centre
Avon Bank
Pershore
WorcestershireWR10 3JP
England

Chadwell Plant Seed (available by
    shares)
81 Parlaunt Road
Slough
Berkshire SL3 8BE
England

The North American Rock Garden
    Club
P.O. Box 67
Millwood, New York 10546
U.S.A.

The Scottish Rock Garden Club
SRGC
P.O. Box 14063
Edinburgh EH10 4YE
Scotland

NURSERIES–EUROPE

Aberconwy Nursery
Graig
Glan Conwy LL28 5TL
Wales

Ardfearn Nursery
Bunchrew
Inverness-shire IV3 6RH
Scotland

Christie's Nursery
Downfield
Main Road
Westmuir
Kirriemuir
Angus DD8 5LP
Scotland

Edrom Nurseries
Coldingham
Eyemouth
Berwickshire TD14 5TZ
Scotland

Ger. van den Beuken
Zegersstraat 7
5961 XR Horst (L)
Netherlands

Hartside Nursery
Alston
Cumbria CA9 3BL
England

Inshriach Alpine Nursery
Aviemore
Inverness-shire PH22 1QS
Scotland

Lamberton Nursery
No. 3 Lamberton
Berwickshire TD15 1XB
Scotland

NURSERIES–NORTH AMERICA

Arrowhead Alpines
P.O. Box 857
Fowlerville, Michigan 48836
U.S.A.

Forestfarm Nursery
990 Tetherow Road
Williams, Oregon 97544
U.S.A.

Heronswood Nursery
7530 NE 288th Street
Kingston, Washington 98346
U.S.A.

Mt. Tahoma Nursery
28111 112th Avenue
E. Graham, Washington 98338
U.S.A.

Porterhowse Farms
41371 SE Thomas Road
Sandy, Oregon 97055
U.S.A.

The Primrose Path
R.D. 2, Box 110
Scottsdale, Pennsylvania 15683
U.S.A.

Siskiyou Rare Plant Nursery
2825 Cummings Road
Medford, Oregon 97501
U.S.A.

We-Du Nurseries
Route 5, Box 724
Marion, North Carolina 28752
U.S.A.

Glossary

achene—a one-seeded fruit, usually one of many in a fruiting head

anther—the part of the stamen containing the pollen grains

Arunachal Pradesh—formerly Assam Himalaya in India

axil—the point of connection between the leaf and stem, hence axillary flower or bud

basal—usually leaves, arising from the base of the stem

biennial—living two years from seedling to death, usually flowering in the second year

blade—the expanded, flattened part of a leaf

bract—a modified leaf immediately below a flower

bulbil—a small bulb which can be detached from the larger bulb on which it grows, to form an independent plant

calyx—the sepals collectively, forming the outer whorl of the perianth

clone—a plant always vegetatively propagated, resulting in genetically identical offspring

corolla—the petals collectively, forming the inner whorl of the perianth

cyme—an inflorescence formed of axillary branches terminating in a flower, the central flowers maturing first

effarinose—describes plant parts lacking farina

entire—without lobes, usually describing leaves

epiphytic—growing on other plants but not parasitic on them

farina—a mealy or powdery covering of a plant part, as in *Primula*

farinose—describes plant parts covered with farina

filament—the slender stalk of the stamen which bears the anthers

genus—a nomenclatural group containing closely related species

glabrous—smooth, not hairy

glaucous—having a grey or bluish fine coating

herbaceous—without woody stems, dying down each year or season

hermaphrodite—a plant with both fertile stamens and ovaries present in the same flower

Himachal Pradesh—A new state in India incorporating Lahul, Kulu, Kinnaur and Simla; formerly Punjab Himalaya

hybrid—result of cross-breeding between two different species of plants, the offspring possessing some of the characters of each parent

hybrid swarm—groups of plants of varying shapes and colour derived from a number of different species

indumentum—the hairy covering of a plant part, as in *Rhododendron*

inflorescence—the part of the plant on which the flowers are borne

involucral—describes bracts which lie together to form a cup-like structure

lanceolate—shaped like a lance, with the broadest part nearest the base

lobed—rounded, deep divisions at the edge of a leaf, not completely dividing it

monocarpic—taking a number of years to reach flowering, and dying afterwards, as in *Meconopsis*

node—a point on the stem from which one or more leaves or buds arise

ovary—part of the female reproductive organ of the flower containing the ovules which develop into the seeds

panicle—a branched flowering stem

parasitic—living and feeding on another organism

pedicel—the stalk of a single flower

perennial—living for more than two years, or theoretically living indefinitely

perianth—collectively the calyx and corolla of a flower

petiole—the stalk of a leaf

pin-eyed—primula flower in which the style is long, so that the stigma appears at the mouth of the corolla, and the anthers are inserted in the corolla tube; compare to thrum-eyed

pinnate—the regular arrangement of leaflets in two rows to either side of the leaf stalk

plicae—the inner membrane or lobe joining the corolla lobes

polycarpic—living for many seasons, not dying after flowering

polymorphic—occurring as more than one form of individual in a single species within an interbreeding population

pseudobulb—a thickened bulb-like stem borne above ground which stores water and nutrients, as in *Pleione*

raceme—a simple inflorescence with flowers on short, nearly equal stalks

rhizome—an underground modified stem, often swollen and fleshy

rosette—an arrangement of leaves radiating from a crown or centre, often spreading over the ground

scape—a flowering stem without leaves

sepal—a segment of the calyx, the outer set of perianth segments

sessile—stalkless

species—the basic unit of nomenclatural classification; a group of plants with similar characteristics in which the individuals breed freely with each other

spike—a slender, elongated cluster of numerous flowers

stamen—one of the male reproductive organs of the flower, bearing the pollen

stigma—the part of the female reproductive organ which receives the pollen

style—the more or less elongated part of the female organ which bears the stigma

subspecies (subsp.)—a nomenclatural group within a species showing certain minor differences

symbiotic—describing an association of two dissimilar organisms, usually to their mutual advantage

taproot—the main descending root

tepal—the subdivision of a perianth that is not clearly differentiated into calyx and corolla

thrum-eyed—primula flower in which the style is short, so that the stigma is included in the corolla tube, and the anthers are positioned at the mouth of the flower; compare to pin-eyed

tuber—a swollen portion of a stem or root, usually below ground

umbel—a flat-topped inflorescence in which all the flower stalks arise from a single point

Uttar Pradesh—Indian state which formerly also comprised Kumaon and Garhwal

variety (var.)—a nomenclatural group of plants subordinate to species and sub-species

whorl—more than two parts of the same kind, such as leaves or sepals, arising from the same level around the stem

Xizang—new geographical name for Tibet

Bibliography

Baker, W. J. 1994a. Three men and an orchid, part 1. *Bulletin of the Alpine Garden Society* 255: 99–114.

——. 1994b. Three men and an orchid, part 2. *Bulletin of the Alpine Garden Society* 256: 181–199.

Christie, I. 1996. Autumn gentians in Nepal. *Journal of the Scottish Rock Garden Club* 98: 61–64.

Cobb, J. S. 1989. *Meconopsis.* Portland, Oregon: Timber Press.

Cowley, E.J. 1982. A revision of *Roscoea. Kew Bulletin* 36(4): 747–776.

Cox, P. A. 1985. *The Smaller Rhododendrons.* Portland, Oregon: Timber Press.

Cribb, P., and I. Butterfield. 1999. *The Genus Pleione: A Botanical Magazine Monograph.* 2d ed. Borneo: Natural History Publication in association with the Royal Botanic Garden Kew.

Evans, A. 1974. *The Peat Garden.* London: Dent.

Farrer, R. 1919. *The English Rock Garden,* vol. 1. London: Jack.

Fletcher, H. R. 1975. *A Quest of Flowers.* Edinburgh: Edinburgh University Press.

Grey-Wilson, C. 1989. Behind Annapurna, part 1. *Bulletin of the Alpine Garden Society* 237: 242–266.

——. 1998. A new look at *Incarvillea. The New Plantsman* 5: 76–98.

Halda, J. J. 1996. *The Genus Gentiana.* Dobré, Czech Republic: SEN.

Hills, L. D. 1950. *The Propagation of Alpines.* London: Faber and Faber.

Horny, R., K. M. Webr and J. Byam-Grounds. 1986. *Porophyllum Saxifrages.* Stamford: Byam-Grounds Publications.

Hunt, P. F., and I. Butterfield. 1979. The genus *Pleione*. *The Plantsman* 1: 112–123.

Ingwersen, W. 1978. *Manual of Alpine Plants*. Eastbourne: Will Ingwersen and Dunnsprint.

Kretz, R. 1987. Destination Rupina La. *Bulletin of the Alpine Garden Society* 230: 297–304.

Liden, M., and H. Zetterlund. 1997. *Corydalis*. Worcestershire, U.K.: AGS Publications.

McBeath, R. J. D. 1985. The Marsyandi Valley. *Journal of the Scottish Rock Garden Club* 75: 185–193.

McNaughton, I. H. 1996. Autumn gentians. *Journal of the Scottish Rock Garden Club* 98: 84–94.

Polunin, O., and A. Stainton. 1984. *Flowers of the Himalaya*. Oxford: Oxford University Press.

Richards, J. 1993. *Primula*. London: Batsford.

Science Press (Beijing). 1995. *Flora of China*, vol. 16. St. Louis: Missouri Botanical Garden.

Smith, G. F., and D. B. Lowe. 1977. *Androsaces*. Woking: The Alpine Garden Society.

———. 1998. *The Genus Androsace*. Worcestershire, U.K.: AGS Publications.

Smith, W. W., and H. R. Fletcher. 1941–1948. The genus *Primula*. Transcript. Edinburgh: Botanical Society Edinburgh.

Stainton, A. 1988. *Flowers of the Himalaya*, supplement. Oxford: Oxford University Press.

Taylor, G. 1934. An account of the genus *Meconopsis*. London: New Flora and Silva.

———. 1947. In *Journal of the Royal Horticultural Society* 72: 139–142.

Taylor, M., and H. Taylor. 1994. A taste of India. *Journal of the Scottish Rock Garden Club* 93: 395–408.

———. 1998. New Flowers in the north-west Himalaya. *Journal of the Scottish Rock Garden Club* 101: 375–385.

———. 1999. Flowers of the Baspa Valley. *Journal of the Scottish Rock Garden Club* 104: 199–208.

Wendelbo, P. 1961. *Primula* classification. *Aca Universitatis Bergensis* 11: 33–49.

Wilkie, D. 1936. *Gentians*. London: Country Life.

Index

Boldfaced page numbers indicate color photos.